Learning PowerShe

Second Edition

Automate deployment and configuration of your servers

James Pogran

BIRMINGHAM - MUMBAI

Learning PowerShell DSC

Second Edition

First published: October 2015

Second edition: September 2017

Production reference: 1060917

Published by Packt Publishing Ltd.
Livery Place
35 Livery Street
Birmingham
B3 2PB, UK.

ISBN 978-1-78728-724-2

www.packtpub.com

Credits

Author
James Pogran

Reviewers
Mark Andrews
Steve Parankewich

Commissioning Editor
Vijin Boricha

Acquisition Editor
Prateek Bharadwaj

Content Development Editor
Sharon Raj

Technical Editor
Vishal Kamal Mewada

Copy Editor
Stuti Shrivastava

Project Coordinator
Virginia Dias

Proofreader
Safis Editing

Indexer
Aishwarya Gangawane

Graphics
Kirk D'Penha

Production Coordinator
Aparna Bhagat

About the Author

James Pogran has been working with computers in one way or another for over 15 years. His first job involved systems administration for a large military installation. He then moved on to develop monitoring software and automating large-scale Windows environments for a major managed services provider. He is currently a senior software engineer at Puppet, Inc, where he helps make Windows automation even better with Puppet.

I would like to express my gratitude to the many people, more than I can name here, who saw this book through with me.

To my wife, Jessica, without whose support and confidence in me, I would not have attempted so many things in my life. For now, for always, and forever.

To my children: Ethan, Charlotte, and Amelia, who are my constant inspiration and my constant joy.

To my dad, who has seen me through many things in life and will see me through much more.

In memory of my mother, who taught me so many things in life; may I continue to learn from her example.

About the Reviewers

Mark Andrews's career in technology has been a varied one; over the last 20 years, he has held several different positions, ranging from customer service to quality assurance. Throughout all of these positions, the responsibility of configuration management and build management has always fallen either on Mark personally or on one of the groups that he managed; because of his "keeping a hand in" management style, he has been closely involved with the scripting and automation framework for this area. Creating scripted frameworks that intercommunicate across machine/operating system/domain boundaries is a passion for him.

- *PowerShell 3.0 Advanced Administration Handbook*
- *Windows PowerShell 4.0 for .NET Developers*
- *PowerShell for SQL Server Essentials*
- *Microsoft Exchange Server PowerShell Essentials*
- *Microsoft Exchange Server PowerShell Cookbook (Third Edition)*
- *AWS Tools for PowerShell 6*

Steve Parankewich is a professional systems analyst, architect, and engineer. With over 20 years of experience, Steve has always had a passion for automation. He is currently a PowerShell evangelist and leads the Boston PowerShell user group, organizing monthly meetups with fellow IT professionals. Steve currently focuses on implementation and migration to both Office 365 and Azure. You can reach him or read additional PowerShell based articles that he has written at powershellblogger.com.

www.PacktPub.com

For support files and downloads related to your book, please visit www.PacktPub.com.

Did you know that Packt offers eBook versions of every book published, with PDF and ePub files available? You can upgrade to the eBook version at www.PacktPub.com, and as a print book customer, you are entitled to a discount on the eBook copy. Get in touch with us at service@packtpub.com for more details.

At www.PacktPub.com, you can also read a collection of free technical articles, sign up for a range of free newsletters and receive exclusive discounts and offers on Packt books and eBooks.

https://www.packtpub.com/mapt

Get the most in-demand software skills with Mapt. Mapt gives you full access to all Packt books and video courses, as well as industry-leading tools to help you plan your personal development and advance your career.

Why subscribe?

- Fully searchable across every book published by Packt
- Copy and paste, print, and bookmark content
- On demand and accessible via a web browser

Customer Feedback

Thanks for purchasing this Packt book. At Packt, quality is at the heart of our editorial process. To help us improve, please leave us an honest review on this book's Amazon page at `https://www.amazon.com/dp/1787287246`.

If you'd like to join our team of regular reviewers, you can email us at `customerreviews@packtpub.com`. We award our regular reviewers with free eBooks and videos in exchange for their valuable feedback. Help us be relentless in improving our products!

Table of Contents

Preface

Windows PowerShell, a scripting language specially designed for system administration, lets you manage computers from the command line. PowerShell DSC enables you to deploy and manage configuration data for software services and also manages the environment in which these services run.

What this book covers

Chapter 1, *Introducing PowerShell DSC*, helps you identify PowerShell DSC and configuration management concepts, covers the features included in DSC, and provides an overview the different DSC versions.

Chapter 2, *DSC Architecture*, offers in-depth explanations of the three phases of DSC, the two different DSC deployment models, and the considerations when deploying a pull server or using push deployment.

Chapter 3, *DSC Configuration Files*, covers authoring DSC configuration scripts and configuration data files and explains how to use them together effectively.

Chapter 4, *DSC Resources*, covers the DSC resource syntax and file structure in both PowerShell V4 and V5. It shows how to find DSC resources both on the local system as well as using community and Microsoft-provided online resources.

Chapter 5, *Pushing DSC Configurations*, offers step-by-step instructions on how to push DSC configurations to remote target nodes. It covers the extra steps the user must take in order to make push deployments work as well as the pros and cons of using push deployments.

Chapter 6, *Pulling DSC Configurations*, offers step-by-step instructions on how to set up both a DSC pull server and your environment to best utilize a pull-based deployment. It covers the pros and cons of using pull deployments in comparison to push deployments.

Chapter 7, *DSC Cross Platform Support*, instructs you on setting up DSC on Linux platforms, including software installation and configuration. It explores the future of PowerShell by showing how to install PowerShell Core.

Chapter 8, *Example Scenarios*, covers how to use DSC in the real world and how to integrate DSC into not only new environments but also with legacy deployments. It walks you through the processes of handling the changing requests and the requirements of different software deployments using DSC.

What you need for this book

Any of the following operating systems required for this book:

- Windows 10
- Windows 2012 R2
- Windows 2016

Software: PowerShell V4, V5, V5.1

Who this book is for

This book is intended for system administrators, developers, and DevOps engineers who are responsible for configuration management and automation and wish to learn PowerShell DSC for the efficient management, configuration, and deployment of systems and applications.

You must have some basic knowledge of Windows PowerShell and should have experience of installing and configuring operating systems and Windows servers. You must also understand the basics and principles of configuration management and know how to apply them to deploying and managing systems and applications using PowerShell DSC.

Conventions

In this book, you will find a number of text styles that distinguish between different kinds of information. Here are some examples of these styles and an explanation of their meaning. Code words in text, database table names, folder names, filenames, file extensions, pathnames, dummy URLs, user input, and Twitter handles are shown as follows: "What this DSC configuration does is ensure that a file is created in the `D:FooProduct` folder called `foo.txt`, with the contents `this is example text`."

A block of code is set as follows:

```
configuration BaseServerConfiguration
    {
        File ExampleTextFile
        {
            Ensure = 'Present'
            Type = 'File'
            DestinationPath = 'D:FooProductfoo.txt'
            Contents = "this is example text"
        }
```

```
WindowsFeature DotNet
{
    Ensure = 'Present'
    Name = 'NET-Framework-45-Core'
}
}
```

When we wish to draw your attention to a particular part of a code block, the relevant lines or items are set in bold:

```
configuration BaseServerConfiguration
{
    File ExampleTextFile
    {
        Ensure = 'Present'
        Type = 'File'
        DestinationPath = 'D:FooProductfoo.txt'
        Contents = "this is example text"
    }
    WindowsFeature DotNet
    {
        Ensure = 'Present'
        Name = 'NET-Framework-45-Core'
    }
}
```

Any command-line input or output is written as follows:

```
[PS]> Get-HotFix -Id KB2883200
Source Description HotFixID InstalledBy InstalledOn
------ ----------- -------- ----------- -----------
HOSTNAME Update KB2883200 HOSTNAMEAdmini... 9/30/2013 12:00:00 AM
```

New terms and **important words** are shown in bold.

Warnings or important notes appear like this.

Tips and tricks appear like this.

Reader feedback

Feedback from our readers is always welcome. Let us know what you think about this book-what you liked or disliked. Reader feedback is important for us as it helps us develop titles that you will really get the most out of. To send us general feedback, simply email feedback@packtpub.com, and mention the book's title in the subject of your message. If there is a topic that you have expertise in and you are interested in either writing or contributing to a book, see our author guide at www.packtpub.com/authors.

Customer support

Now that you are the proud owner of a Packt book, we have a number of things to help you to get the most from your purchase.

Downloading the example code

You can download the example code files for this book from your account at http://www.packtpub.com. If you purchased this book elsewhere, you can visit http://www.packtpub.com/support and register to have the files emailed directly to you. You can download the code files by following these steps:

1. Log in or register to our website using your email address and password.
2. Hover the mouse pointer on the **SUPPORT tab at the top.**
3. Click on **Code Downloads & Errata.**
4. Enter the name of the book in the **Search box.**
5. Select the book for which you're looking to download the code files.
6. Choose from the drop-down menu where you purchased this book from.
7. Click on **Code Download.**

Once the file is downloaded, please make sure that you unzip or extract the folder using the latest version of:

- WinRAR / 7-Zip for Windows
- Zipeg / iZip / UnRarX for Mac
- 7-Zip / PeaZip for Linux

The code bundle for the book is also hosted on GitHub at
`https://github.com/PacktPublishing/Learning-PowerShell-DSC-Second-Edition`. We
also have other code bundles from our rich catalog of books and videos available at
`https://github.com/PacktPublishing/`. Check them out!

Errata

Although we have taken every care to ensure the accuracy of our content, mistakes do
happen. If you find a mistake in one of our books-maybe a mistake in the text or the code-
we would be grateful if you could report this to us. By doing so, you can save other readers
from frustration and help us improve subsequent versions of this book. If you find any
errata, please report them by visiting `http://www.packtpub.com/submit-errata`, selecting
your book, clicking on the Errata Submission Form link, and entering the details of your
errata. Once your errata are verified, your submission will be accepted and the errata will
be uploaded to our website or added to any list of existing errata under the Errata section of
that title. To view the previously submitted errata, go to
`https://www.packtpub.com/books/content/support` and enter the name of the book in the
search field. The required information will appear under the Errata section.

Piracy

Piracy of copyrighted material on the internet is an ongoing problem across all media. At
Packt, we take the protection of our copyright and licenses very seriously. If you come
across any illegal copies of our works in any form on the internet, please provide us with
the location address or website name immediately so that we can pursue a remedy. Please
contact us at `copyright@packtpub.com` with a link to the suspected pirated material. We
appreciate your help in protecting our authors and our ability to bring you valuable
content.

Questions

If you have a problem with any aspect of this book, you can contact us at
`questions@packtpub.com`, and we will do our best to address the problem.

1
Introducing PowerShell DSC

"Begin at the beginning," the King said, very gravely, "and go on till you come to the end: then stop."
- Lewis Carroll, Alice in Wonderland

"Don't Panic."
- Douglas Adams, The Hitchhiker's Guide to the Galaxy

Welcome to PowerShell **Desired State Configuration (DSC)**, the new configuration management platform from Microsoft. We begin with a quote from *Alice in Wonderland*. Besides pertinent advice from the author, it is apropos of what DSC is at its very core. DSC, by the very simplest definition, allows you to write down the beginning, the middle, and the end of your deployment story. The second quote we see is from *The Hitchhiker's Guide to the Galaxy*, and it is something to remember throughout this book. We will cover a lot of new concepts, some old concepts with new importance, and a lot of PowerShell. Don't panic; we'll get through fine.

This book will begin with the basics of PowerShell DSC, covering its architecture and many components. It will familiarize you with the set of Windows PowerShell language extensions and new Windows PowerShell commands that comprise DSC. Then, it will help you create custom DSC resources and work with DSC configurations with the help of practical examples. Finally, it will describe how to deploy a configuration data set using PowerShell DSC.

By the end of this book, you will be able to deploy a real-world application end to end.

In this chapter, we will cover the following topics:

- What is PowerShell DSC?
- Why do we need configuration management and what is DevOps?
- How does DSC help?
- A high-level overview of DSC
- DSC requirements
- DSC versions

What is PowerShell DSC?

Do you have some software that needs to be installed in a certain order? Software with special configuration steps? Software along with some security policies that must be applied to every server? How about ensuring that a set of services are never enabled to start? Have you ever written scripts to handle this kind of work but found them brittle because of changes in software from release to release? Needed to make these changes on dozens or hundreds of servers repeatedly on schedule? Ever had someone change something and have your script break because the state is not what you expected? These and many more scenarios are handled by DSC.

PowerShell DSC is a new management platform in Windows PowerShell that enables the deployment and management of configuration data for systems and software services and the management of the environment in which these services run. DSC allows you to define the current state of a machine and ensure that the machine is always in that state.

What we mean by state here is everything that is on that machine, including the operating system and software installed, all the configuration settings for the OS and software, and any files or process that need to be present or set with specific content; the list goes on. Whether you considered this earlier or not, all this makes up the configuration of your system. DSC is designed to help you deal with all this configuration data and execute it consistently and repeatedly.

What is PowerShell?

While we assume in this book that you have a basic understanding of PowerShell command-line use and scripting, before we go too much into DSC, it is helpful to describe what PowerShell is compared to PowerShell DSC.

First released in 2006, PowerShell is a scripting language and command-line shell built on the .NET framework. PowerShell provides complete access to COM, WMI, and .NET and also provides a large set of commands called **cmdlets** to perform administrative tasks on both local and remote systems.

PowerShell can execute PowerShell scripts, PowerShell cmdlets, and standalone executable programs or other language files. PowerShell also provides a hosting API that allows programs to run PowerShell natively inside their program, enabling scripting or automation scenarios. Being both a shell language and a scripting language allows it to be quick as well as terse on the command line, along with being verbose and consistent in scripts.

Over the years, PowerShell has become the de facto way to administer and automate Windows OS and software. As computing environments grow larger and engineering teams become smaller, it is paramount in automating processes and procedures that used to be done by hand. PowerShell provides a consistent command-line language to automate the administration of a large number of scenarios, which are growing every day and were previously not available on Windows. Because of PowerShell's hosting API, applications such as Microsoft Exchange have enabled a command line, first, GUI—second, mode of development, which enables quick deployment and management using automated tools.

PowerShell not only enables the automation at the single system level, but it also scales out to the multi-node environment. Being able to automate your system from the command line or script is fine, but if you have to manually run that script on every system in your environment by hand, then we still have a bottleneck on efficiency. Using an industry standard protocol, PowerShell provides PowerShell remoting as a way of running commands or scripts on any number of remote hosts in parallel. Thousands of computers can be managed at the same time, consistently, in a repeatable and automated manner.

Consistent repeatable automation is important, but PowerShell is also extensible, which is not only essential, but it also leads us into DSC. PowerShell is a both a typed and dynamic scripting language, which means that it supports both static typed objects (`System.IO.FileInfo`) and objects with methods and properties that are defined at runtime (`PSCustomObject` and `Add-Member`). This enables PowerShell to be extended to suit the needs of the user. You do this every day to an extent, by creating functions and scripts to wrap common operations into reusable components or modules. Taking this a step further, PowerShell can be extended to support specific scenarios that were not envisioned when the product was made. DSC is such an extension, as it builds on the existing PowerShell language and infrastructure to enable new uses of the program.

On to PowerShell DSC

PowerShell DSC is released as a feature of PowerShell, so it comes bundled with specific versions of PowerShell that are part of the **Windows Management Framework** (**WMF**). The PowerShell DSC version section goes into greater detail about the versions of PowerShell and PowerShell DSC and the available features in each, so we won't get into too much detail here.

The WMF release notes describe DSC in this way:

> *"Windows PowerShell DSC helps ensure that the resources in your data center are correctly configured. DSC is a set of Windows PowerShell language extensions and providers that enable declarative, autonomous, and idempotent (repeatable) deployment, configuration, and conformity of data center resources. DSC enables an IT Pro, developer, or fabric administrator to define the configuration of target nodes (computers or devices) and prevent configuration inconsistencies or drift."*

PowerShell DSC provides a set of Windows PowerShell language extensions, new Windows PowerShell cmdlets, and resources that you can use to declaratively specify how you want your operating system and software environment to be configured. It also provides a means to maintain and manage existing configurations. It supports both an interactive push model, where configurations are executed on target nodes on demand, and a pull model, where a central server manages and distributes configurations.

We won't delve into too much architecture talk here. (The next chapter discusses the architecture and inner workings of DSC in detail.) For now, it is sufficient to say DSC is comprised of both a data file and configuration file that are translated into a text file following the **Managed Object Format** (**MOF**). This file is then parsed and executed on the target server, using DSC features that know how to configure the system.

That was a lot of information in a short space, so don't worry if it is a lot to take in at once. We will go over each part as we move on. You don't have to know right away what MOF is or how DSC executes the configuration to use DSC. DSC abstracts all the details away for you. When you get to the point that you need to know these details, DSC still exposes them so you can tweak them under the hood or find out what is really going on.

At a high level, DSC work isn't programming work; it lists how you want a server to look in a special format. The execution of this list is abstracted from the listing, allowing the how to work separately from the why. This is an important concept and really the key to understanding the importance of DSC. Jeffrey Snover, the architect and inventor of PowerShell, explained it best using *Star Trek*. Captain Picard often used the line "Make it so," and Commander Riker had to figure out how to actually make what the Captain wanted to happen, happen. Captain Picard knew what needed to be done but didn't particularly care how it got done. Commander Riker knew how to get things done but did not concern himself (most of the time) with deciding when and what to do. This separation allowed both officers to be good at their jobs without interfering with each other.

It may be useful to see the following short, complete example of an entire DSC configuration:

```
configuration BaseServerConfiguration
    {
        File ExampleTextFile
        {
            Ensure = 'Present'
            Type = 'File'
            DestinationPath = 'D:FooProductfoo.txt'
            Contents = "this is example text"
        }
        WindowsFeature DotNet
        {
            Ensure = 'Present'
            Name = 'NET-Framework-45-Core'
        }
    }
```

That's it! Sure, there is more to understand and cover, but as we can see here, this is plain PowerShell code that is as readable as any script you've written before, and all it does is list what should be on a system. What this DSC configuration does is ensure that a file is created in the `D:FooProduct` folder called `foo.txt`, with the contents `this is example text`. It then ensures that the .NET framework V4.5 is installed. Yes, .NET 4.5 is most likely already there, but the point of DSC is to describe the state of the target node regardless of what you think *might* be there. This way, if someone removes .NET 4.5, DSC will ensure that it is installed, thereby maintaining the known good state of the target node.

We will get into this further later, but now you may be asking why it is important to manage the configuration of your systems this way. Read on.

Why do we need configuration management?

Whether you manage a few servers or several thousands, the traditional methods of server and software installation and deployment are failing to address your current needs. These methods treat servers as special singular entities that have to be protected and taken care of, with special configurations that may or may not be documented, and if they go down, they take the business with them.

For a long while, this worked out. But as the number of servers and applications and configuration points grows, it becomes untenable to keep it all in your head or consistently documented by a set of people. New patches that are released, feature sets change, employee turnover, poorly documented software—all these reasons introduce variance and change into the system. If not accounted for and handled, these *special* servers become ticking time bombs that will explode the moment a detail is missed.

Written installation or configuration specifications that have to be performed by humans and be error-free time and time again on numerous servers are increasingly self-evident as brittle and error-prone affairs. To further complicate things, despite the obvious interdependence of software development and other IT-related departments, the software developers are often isolated from the realities faced by IT professionals during the deployment and maintenance of the software.

The answer to this is **automation**: defining a repeatable process that configures servers the right way every time. Servers move from being special snowflakes to being disposable numbers on a list that can be created and destroyed without requiring someone to remember the specific incantation to make it work. Instead of a golden image that has to be kept up to date with all the complexities of image storage and distribution, there is instead a set of steps to bring all servers to compliance regardless of whether they are a fresh installation or a number of years old.

What is being described is **Configuration Management (CM)**. CM ensures that the current design and build state of a system is a known good state. It ensures trust by not relying on the knowledge of one person or a team of people; it's an objective truth that can be verified at any time. It provides a historical record of what was changed as well, which is useful not only for reporting purposes (such as for management), but also for troubleshooting purposes (this file used to be there, now it's not). CM detects variance between builds, so changes to the environment are both easily apparent and well known to all who work on the system.

This allows anyone to see what the given state of the system is at any time, at any granularity, whether on one system or over the span of thousands. If a target system fails, it's a matter of re-running the CM build on a fresh installation to bring the system back to a steady state.

CM is part of a set of ideas called **Infrastructure as Code**. It requires that every step in provisioning an environment be automated and written down in files that can be run any time to bring the environment to a known good state. While CM is infrastructure automation (replicating steps multiple times on any amount of target nodes), Infrastructure as Code takes things one step further and codifies every step required to get an entire environment running. It encompasses the knowledge of server provisioning, server configuration, and server deployment into a format that is readable by sysadmins, developers, and other technical staff. Like CM, Infrastructure as Code uses existing best practices from software development, such as source control, automated code testing, and continuous integration, to ensure a redundant and repeatable process.

The approaches being described are not that new and are part of a larger movement that has been slowly accepted among companies as the optimal way of managing servers and software, called **DevOps**.

What is DevOps?

The set of concepts we have been describing is collectively termed DevOps and is a part of a larger process called **continuous delivery**. DevOps is a shortened form of **development operations** and describes a close working relationship between the development of software and the deployment and operation use of that software. Continuous delivery is a set of practices that enables software to be developed and continuously deployed to production systems on a frequent basis, usually in an automatic fashion that happens multiple times a week or day.

Each year, a company called Puppet Labs surveys over 4,000 IT operations professionals and developers about their operations procedures. Of those surveyed, companies that have implemented DevOps practices have reported improved software deployment quality and more frequent software releases. Their report states that these companies shipped code 30 times faster and completed those deployments 8,000 times faster than their peers. They had 50% fewer failures and restored service 12 times faster than their peers.

Results such as the ones shown in the Puppet Labs survey show that organizations adopting DevOps are up to five times more likely to be high performing than those who have not. It's a cumulative effect; the longer you practice, the greater the results from adoption and the easier it is to continue doing that. How DevOps enables high performance is something that centers around deployment frequency.

To define and explain the entirety of DevOps and, since continuous delivery is out of the scope of this book, for the purposes here the goals can be summarized as follows: to improve the deployment frequency, lower the failure rate of new releases, and shorten the recovery time if a new release is faulty. Even though the term implies strict developer and operations roles as the only ones involved, the concept really applies to any person or department involved in the developing, deployment, and maintenance of the product and the servers it runs on.

These goals work toward one end: minimizing the risk of software deployment by making changes safe through automation. The root cause of poor quality is variation, whether that is in the system, software settings, or in the processes performing actions on the system or software. The solution to variation is repeatability. By figuring out how to perform an action repeatedly, you have removed the variation from the process and can continually make small changes to the process without causing unforeseen problems.

DSC quick wins

While there are many aspects to DSC that are beneficial, it is useful to pause here and list some **quick wins** that DSC brings us to inspire us to keep reading:

- DSC configuration and supporting files are all written in the PowerShell syntax. Investments in knowledge about PowerShell are improved upon and expanded in using DSC.
- DSC is designed to support continuous deployment, so it will react and adjust as your environment changes.
- When DSC applies a configuration to a target node, DSC resources only change that which does not match the expected state (we will cover the terminology for this and how important this is in `Chapter 2`, *DSC Architecture*), ensuring a quick deployment.
- DSC separates configuration logic from configuration data, reducing the rate of change in your configuration scripts and the variation in your deployments.

- DSC operates on more platforms than just Windows. DSC has a set of DSC resources that know how to install, configure, and manage Linux target nodes and some network switches. In a heterogeneous environment, having one tool that can address many different platforms is a huge time and cost saver.

DSC high-level overview

We will look into the DSC architecture in much greater detail in the next chapter, but it is useful to show a quick overview of how all the concepts we just covered fit together. DSC has several steps that can be bucketed together into three large phases.

The authoring phase

You begin with DSC by writing a configuration script in PowerShell. The script itself doesn't actually do anything. You can run the script interactively all you want; it won't change a thing. Since the configuration script is the DSL we were talking about earlier, it's only a list of things to do, not the things that actually execute the list. Because there can only be one MOF per target host and each configuration script is translated to an MOF, this means there is usually only one configuration script you write, which handles all the variances in your environment. This sounds like it will get complicated and difficult to manage quickly, but there are DSC patterns to follow in order to manage this. We will cover these in Chapter 3, *DSC Configuration Files*.

The next step is to translate the configuration script to an MOF file. The translation, or compiling, happens only once—when you deploy the MOF file to the target node or to the DSC pull server. The configuration script is often kept in a version control system and only compiles and deploys the MOF file when the configuration script changes.

The staging phase

The next step is to get it over to the target computer. The deployment of the MOF happens in two ways: push and pull. A push method is when you execute the Start-DSCConfiguration cmdlet, which compiles the MOF and copies over to the target system. The pull method involves putting the MOF file on the DSC pull server, which handles distributing it to all the target hosts.

The execution phase

Whether an MOF file was pushed (using `Start-DSCConfiguration`) or pulled (using a DSC pull server), the next step is the actual execution of the MOF file. If pushed, the execution happens interactively or in a PowerShell job depending on how you called the cmdlet. If pulled, the **Local Configuration Manager** (**LCM**) schedules and executes the MOF file without user input or oversight.

LCM is part of the DSC system installed on the target node and is responsible for receiving, coordinating, and executing configurations on target nodes. LCM itself is configurable using DSC and is flexible enough to allow multiple types of deployments.

The phases described earlier will be covered in much more detail in the upcoming chapters, so do not worry if some of it does not make sense.

Why all the abstraction?

It seems like we are writing scripts just to have them turned into another format altogether, which in turn is converted into something else. Why all the indirection and abstraction? Why don't we write the final result ourselves the first time? The primary reasons are readability and flexibility.

DSC configuration files are written in the PowerShell syntax, which we already established as being consistent and readable. When the configuration is human-readable, it's understandable to the whole team and not just the implementer. It's written down in textual format, so it can be controlled in a source control system such as **Git**, **Subversion** (**SVN**), or **Team Foundation Server**. Deployment processes (sets of instructions on how to complete a task) are automatically saved and backed up by the source control system and made available to the entire team instead of one person's desktop.

Readability serves more than just the implementer and the team. Written configuration files codify the deployment process in a historical record. In that record, we can see the progression of the system by comparing the text files between releases, thereby monitoring drift and variation.

This increases flexibility by enabling a variety of tools to produce the output DSC can execute. You may have noticed that we keep referring to the compiling to MOF, that the DSC engine reads MOF, and that there is only one MOF per target host. There's a good reason why the end format is MOF and not something else, such as a PowerShell Script.

The MOF was defined by the **Distributed Management Task Force (DMTF)**, which is a vendor-neutral organization that works toward standardized interoperation between platforms. You may not be aware of it, but you have been using their work for quite some time if you have been using **Windows Management Instrumentation (WMI)**. WMI is an implementation of **Common Information Model (CIM)**, which is a DMTF standard that defines a structured way to describe a system and its properties. The **Microsoft Developer Network (MSDN)** site, `https://msdn.microsoft.com/en-us/library/aa389234.aspx`, explains that WMI can use CIM on target nodes. The Wikipedia site, `https://en.wikipedia.org/wiki/Common_Information_Model_(computing)`, goes into more information about the history and open standards of CIM.

The DMTF defined the MOF syntax and format so that any vendor or system could implement it. Microsoft happens to be the largest implementer so far, but other tooling companies use it as well. Since any vendor can implement the standard, it means that several important things can happen.

If all DSC needs to function is the MOF file, you don't necessarily need PowerShell to produce the MOF file. Any third-party tool can implement the specification and provide their own (possibly improved) way of compiling MOF files. An open market for tooling gives options to the user. For example, there are many different text editors to write your scripts in; each has its benefits and compromises that you can evaluate and choose between. This enables third-party vendors to compete and provide solutions that suit a given user's needs. Companies such as Puppet and Chef can implement their own or extend what Microsoft has already done.

The most exciting thing is that since the MOF standard is platform independent, the configuration scripts you write can run on multiple operating systems. So whether you run Windows or Linux or both, you can manage the configuration of your systems with PowerShell DSC using a single standard and consistent syntax.

How does DSC help?

PowerShell DSC enables a DevOps structure by providing a consistent, standardized configuration of operating systems and software as part of a continuous deployment pipeline. It increases the rate at which you can deploy by reducing the variation and drift from your existing configurations.

In simpler terms, DSC separates the who from the what and how. This separation of what and how is the core of DSC. Because they are separated, you can continually change the data points of your systems without touching the parts that actually set the system to the desired state.

The who

Band name jokes aside, the who DSC refers to is any target node. Why the separation and distinction? Well, as explained in the MOF earlier, we aren't dealing with just Windows servers. We could possibly be dealing with network switches, Linux servers, storage devices, and so on; the list potentially includes any device in your environment. By setting target node definitions in a structured way, we can describe the nodes in ways that make sense to anyone reading the configurations, as well as the computer's processing the configurations.

The what

The DSC **Domain Specific Language** (**DSL**) defines a standardized way of describing the expected configuration of a target system, whether that is one system or several thousand systems. It describes the what of the target node.

A DSL is a specialized set of language extensions and grammar that makes it easier to codify a specific set of problems. On the other hand, a product such as PowerShell is a general-purpose language, DSLs are specifically built to address a specific set of problems.

You may wonder why we are bothering to define and discuss DSL here. You may think it's an advanced topic or something only developers need to know, but you would be incorrect to discount it. DSLs are all around you, and you use them every day. For example, HTML is a human-readable DSL for web browsers to display content. The actual content is binary, but the HTML specification allows humans to write in a language they understand yet also have the computer understand it.

In the case of DSC, the DSL is oriented at expressing all the different ways in which you can describe the expected state of a system in an easy-to-read manner. If you can read PowerShell code, then the DSC DSL is no different than reading a function declaration with a set of parameters. Most importantly, this easy-to-read structure for you is also easy for the DSC parser to read and turn into an MOF file. This abstraction of an abstraction allows you to write configurations in a language you understand and for that to be translated into a language the system understands.

For example, the target system should have a list of software installed, several settings modified, some services that should be enabled and started, some users to be created and then added to a local group, and several files to be created and have content added to them. It reads like a grocery list to you, but the computer can understand and execute it the same way every time it runs.

The how

The DSC language extensions, cmdlets, and resources provide a standardized way of testing whether the expected state is present on a target system.

This allows the different aspects of the actual execution of configuring a system to be codified away from the information, deciding what settings to change or software to install. While the **what** dealt with writing down the expected state, the **how** is concerned with how to make it happen that way. Or, as Captain Picard would say, how to **make it so**.

This separation is important because it is expected that the list of things to do on a target computer will change, but it is not expected that how to execute that setting will change frequently. For example, there will be many types of files that you will create on many filesystems, but there are only a few ways to create these files. By separating the listing of the **what**, it allows the **how** to reduce variation by employing the idempotent DSC resources, an important part of a DevOps workflow.

To summarize the preceding content, we can say:

- The DSC DSL defines a standardized way of describing the expected configuration of a target system, whether that is one system or several thousand systems
- The DSC set of language extensions, cmdlets, and resources provide a standardized way of testing whether the expected state is present on the target system(s)
- The DSC engine provides a structured way of executing this expected state in an idempotent manner

We have seen the word *idempotent* in several places in this chapter so far, yet we haven't really defined it or covered why it is important. Let's clarify what exactly idempotence means now.

Idempotence

Idempotence is an important concept, sometimes confusing, that we will touch on many times throughout this book. Idempotence is defined as an operation that has no additional effect if it is called more than once with the same input. Put another way, it is an operation that can be executed as many times as desired, and it will only change the system state if, and only if, it is not what the desired state is. For example, a PowerShell function looks for the x state and guarantees that it will only change the state of the system if it is not x.

It may seem silly to state something as obvious as this. If you feel this way, think of an MSI installer that installs version 1.1.1.0 of an imaginary software product. When you run the MSI, it only ever installs the software if it isn't already present on the system or if the version present is older than the current version. No matter how many times you execute the MSI, it will only change the system if version 1.1.1.0 is not on the system. This is idempotency. The MSI will only ever change the system state if it is not the desired state, no matter how many times you run it.

Idempotent operations are often used in network protocols or API design between dependent systems and are used in DSC by DSC resources. DSC resources are required to be idempotent in that they do not change the system if the system is in the state that the resource expects it to be in. For example, a DSC resource that operates on Windows Services will only try to start a given service if it is stopped, not if it is started. Another example is the DSC file resource, as that will change a file only if the contents do not match the expected string. By requiring idempotency, DSC resources can be run as many times as you want without ever performing an unexpected change.

When you install a piece of software on a machine that already has that software installed on it, you don't want there to be two copies of the software after you're done. You want the installer to be smart enough to detect the version of the currently installed software and then examine the version that you're attempting to install and ultimately decide that the versions match and no installation needs to be done. That is idempotency in a nutshell.

Isn't this Group Policy or SCCM?

At this point, you may be wondering whether DSC isn't a re-implementation of **Group Policy** (**GPO**) or **System Center Configuration Manager** (**SCCM**). It's a valid question, as there are some overlaps in these technologies.

Group Policy is similar in that it is also a system of configuring operating systems, applications, and user settings in an environment. However, Group Policy is tied to **Active Directory** (**AD**) and has a lot of configuration overhead, a complex and sometimes confusing deployment methodology, and is very inflexible. This is not to say that GPO is bad; some of these apparent limitations are by design. GPO has been around since Windows 2000 days and has had to deal with several decades of different approaches to software and server management.

In comparison, DSC is not tied to AD or a specific operating system platform. It is, by design, very flexible. As we have covered, it is designed to be responsive to the frequently changing technology and dynamic business environments we have today. Instead of obtuse schedules, DSC deployments are declarative and upfront about what exactly will happen and when it will happen. GPO has rudimentary tooling that writes binary files for its configuration that can't be read by a human and can't be version controlled. DSC has human-readable configuration files that are version controllable.

SCCM is also a configuration management system and is a huge piece of software that requires several servers and many hours to set up and maintain. It is not a small expense to purchase and continue to run, and it is clearly designed for a large enterprise that not only manages servers, but also manages user devices such as desktops and laptops. It is definitely an all-purpose tool that tries to encompass any need. Managing servers comes free with PowerShell and requires little setup time. While clearly designed for server management, some desktop management scenarios are supported. It is definitely a fine-honed tool for specific purposes.

DSC features

At this point, we have covered what PowerShell DSC is and how it relates to DevOps and configuration management, and lightly stepped through how it is structured and how it compares to other solutions out there.

We will now cover the requirements and available versions of PowerShell DSC.

DSC requirements

To use DSC, both the computer you author the configuration files on (more on this later) and the target computers *must* have PowerShell 4 or higher installed. This means that at least WMF 4 is installed on all target hosts and the computer in which you are making your configuration files.

PowerShell DSC comes as part of PowerShell starting in version 4. PowerShell 4 will already be present on the following operating systems and no further action is needed to enable PowerShell V4:

- Windows Server 2012 R2
- Windows 8.1

PowerShell 4 will have to be installed on the following operating systems:

- Windows Server 2012
- Windows 7 SP1
- Windows Server 2008 R2 SP1

PowerShell 5 and 6 support the installation on all the preceding operating systems.

 Windows 8.1 and Windows Server 2012 R2, DSC require an update to function correctly. The Windows update KB2883200 (also known as the **GA Update Rollup**) is required.

While it may already be installed depending on your patching process, you can check whether it is installed or not by running the following command:

```
[PS]> Get-HotFix -Id KB2883200
    Source          Description       HotFixID        InstalledBy
InstalledOn
    ------          -----------       --------        -----------          -----
------
    HOSTNAME        Update            KB2883200       HOSTNAMEAdmini...
9/30/2013 12:00:00 AM
```

The only dependency PowerShell has is on the .NET framework. PowerShell V4 and V5 require .NET framework V4.5. If you have Windows 2008 R2, read the release notes at https://www.microsoft.com/en-US/download/details.aspx?id=40855, carefully because the WMF 4 installer will not alert you that .NET 4.5 is not already installed.

Some functions of DSC do not work on the client operating systems as either the features needed aren't present on the client OS, or due to various other reasons, such as licensing or software availability. Where applicable, we'll call out these differences as we come across them. Something to note is that some DSC resources, the ones provided by the community or the xDSCResourceDesigner project (more on that later in Chapter 4, *DSC Resources*), do not work on Windows 2008. You will have to check the release notes for each DSC resource to determine what operating systems it is compatible with.

DSC versions

In the next chapter, we will delve into the details and inner workings of the DSC architecture. Before we do that, it will help to have an overview of the cmdlets and tools at your disposal when working with DSC. Some terms and concepts may be fuzzy here but will be explained in much more detail in further chapters. We can also use this section as a reference while authoring our own DSC configurations and resources.

PowerShell DSC is released as a feature of PowerShell, so its versioning scheme follows that of PowerShell. PowerShell is distributed as part of the WMF. When referring to the installed version of DSC, we use the version of PowerShell that is installed to denote which version of DSC it is currently running.

PowerShell V6, at the time of writing this, has not been released yet and is still in the alpha status, but we will still cover V4, V5, and V6 in this book. This will make things somewhat more complex to explain, as we will have to list, compare, contrast, and cover all the similarities and differences between the two versions as we move along. However, it is important to cover these because we fully expect you to have to deal with both PowerShell V4 and V5 deployed in your environments at the same time while looking at the future with V6. The final version of PowerShell V6 does not have a release date published yet, so realistically, you will have PowerShell V4 and V5 on your production systems for quite a while before moving to V6.

PowerShell V4 DSC

PowerShell V4 was released as part of WMF 4 on October 24, 2013, and contained the first released version of DSC. Even though this was the first release of DSC, it is still referred to as being version 4 of DSC. While confusing at first, this is largely something you can ignore, as versioning of DSC resources is a more frequent point of variance.

As the first release, this version of DSC largely focuses on bringing a minimally viable product to the market for Microsoft. Microsoft is a little late to the DevOps game with DSC, as there are several toolsets out there that have been in use for many years. Puppet and Chef are the most notable, but there are many others. What sets DSC apart here is that it is not an add-on or separate product; it's a core part of the Windows OS and can be used by other tools as much as it can be used by itself.

The first version contains most features needed out of the gate to start automating your deployment process, but only the built-in DSC resources were available and were lacking in addressing commonly used products such as IIS, SQL, or Exchange. In the early days, Microsoft relied heavily on the community to expand its DSC resource list, which resulted in mixed success. Microsoft released a set of DSC resources it authored to the community in batches to address the gap. The combination of community and Microsoft contributions has greatly expanded the reach of DSC, and it has been expanding it ever since.

V4 DSC language extensions

DSC adds three new functions as language extensions to support declaring the expected state of a machine:

- **Configuration**: The configuration keyword is a DSC function that declares a set of operations to perform on a target system.
- **Node**: The node configuration keyword is a DSC function that declares the target host to perform operations on.
- **Import-DscResource**: This looks like a PowerShell cmdlet but really is a keyword. It locates the DSC resources needed to parse and compile the DSC configuration script.

V4 DSC base resources

The following table lists the DSC base resources of V4:

Base resource	Description
Service	The Service DSC resource performs operations against Windows services. It can start or stop a service or configure the account it runs under and the startup type of the service. This resource cannot install services; it operates only on services that are already present. Look at the xService resource for additional functionality.
Script	The Script resource is a versatile generic resource. It allows you to specify an arbitrary block of code to be executed on the target host. There are some restrictions such as variable expansion and access to some system resources. Generally, this should be used for short term or one-off situations that are not handled by an existing DSC resource, as error handling and proper idempotency is difficult to achieve in the limited space you have.

User	The User DSC resource performs operations on local users on the target system. It allows the creation or deletion of users and setting passwords and password policies as well as basic attributes of the user.
WindowsProcess	The WindowsProcess DSC resource performs operations on processes on the target system. This is commonly used to execute arbitrary executables with specific parameters that are not handled by an existing DSC resource.
WindowsFeature	The WindowsFeature DSC resource adds or removes features of the Windows operating system. This uses the built-in **Deployment Image Servicing and Management (DISM)** infrastructure of the Windows Server platform; some features are not operable using this resource on a client OS.
Registry	The Registry DSC resource adds, removes, or modifies registry entries in the target system. Support for the full range of registry keys and values is present.
Environment	The Environment DSC resource adds, removes, or modifies environment variables on the target system.
Archive	The Archive DSC resource performs operations on compressed files.
Group	The Group DSC resource performs operations on local groups on the target system. It can add, remove, or modify membership on local groups.
Package	The Package DSC resource installs software bundled in MSI or EXE formats. In the case of MSI, it can also remove software if all the necessary options are provided to the MSI command line. Refer to the MSI documentation for more information on this.
Log	The Log DSC resource writes messages to the DSC operational log. This is useful for troubleshooting or diagnostic purposes.

V4 DSC cmdlets

Cmdlet	Description
Get-DSCConfiguration	This cmdlet returns the current DSC configuration status of the node if the configuration exists. If it does not, this will throw an error. This can also be run on remote systems.
Get-DSCLocalConfigurationManager	This returns the current settings, or meta-configuration, of the LCM on the system if the settings exist. This can be run on remote systems and is useful for troubleshooting DSC deployments that use DSC pull servers.
Get-DSCResoure	This cmdlet returns a list of all DSC resources on the system. This is vital in troubleshooting and authoring DSC resources, as it helps show what resources are present on the system. If the resource you are authoring is not present, then DSC cannot read the resource.
New-DSCCheckSum	This cmdlet returns a hash from the DSC configuration MOF file. This is used to deploy MOF files to pull servers.
Remove-DSCConfigurationDocument	This cmdlet removes the compiled MOF from the target node, along with additional cleanup tasks. This cmdlet is available only as part of the November 2014 update rollup for Windows RT 8.1, Windows 8.1, and Windows Server 2012 R2: http://support.microsoft.com/en-us/kb/3000850, from the Microsoft support library. Before you use this cmdlet, review the information in *What's New* in Windows PowerShell: http://technet.microsoft.com/library/hh857339.aspx in the TechNet library.
Restore-DSCConfiguration	This cmdlet restores the previous configuration for the target node if a previous successful configuration exists on the target node.

`Stop-DSCConfiguration`	This cmdlet stops a currently running configuration on a target node. This is useful in aborting interactive configuration runs initiated using `Start-DSCConfiguration`. This cmdlet is available only as part of the November 2014 update rollup for Windows RT 8.1, Windows 8.1, and Windows Server 2012 R2: `http://support.microsoft.com/en-us/kb/3000850` from the Microsoft Support library. Before you use this cmdlet, review the information in **What's New With PowerShell**: `https://docs.microsoft.com/en-us/powershell/scripting/What-s-New-With-PowerShell?view=powershell-6` in the TechNet library.
`Test-DSCConfiguration`	This cmdlet runs the specified configuration against a target node but does not execute it. It compares the current state of the system to the expected configuration and reports back if they match. No changes are made to the system using this cmdlet.
`Set-DSCLocalConfigurationManager`	This cmdlet is used to change the settings, or meta-configuration, on the LCM on the target computer. This is most often used in pull server scenarios.
`Start-DSCConfiguration`	This cmdlet executes the specified MOF file against the target computer. This is by far the cmdlet you will use the most, as it's helpful in both authoring and troubleshooting DSC configurations and DSC resources.
`Import-DSCResource`	This cmdlet is really a dynamic function that is only available at runtime. It specifies which DSC resources need to be loaded to parse and compile the DSC configuration script.

V4 DSC pull server

The DSC pull server is the management server that the DSC agents on target nodes pull DSC configurations and DSC resources from. This will be explained in greater detail in `Chapter 6`, *Pulling DSC Configurations*.

PowerShell V5 DSC

PowerShell V5 was released on February 24, 2016, and contains the next version of DSC.

New DSC-specific features focus on improving upon the existing functionality provided by DSC in PowerShell 4, while introducing new ways to organize and execute configurations on target hosts.

V5 DSC language extensions

DSC V5 brings several new language extensions that are explained in the *V5 Improvements* section. It would be redundant to list them in both places, so we will only cover them later.

V5 DSC base resources

The built-in DSC resource list has not expanded, but the existing Microsoft-released community DSC resource project has provided over a hundred new DSC resources and is now available on GitHub with an open issue page and source.

V5 DSC cmdlets

Several new cmdlets have been added or improved upon in the DSC V5 release. Listed here are the most interesting ones for the purpose of our book:

Cmdlet	Description
Get-DSCConfigurationStatus	This cmdlet reports the high-level status of the configuration on the target node. You can obtain the last status or all statuses of all configurations that have been run.
Compare-DSCConfiguration	This cmdlet compares a specified configuration against the actual state of a target node. This is useful to determine configuration drift interactively and compare differences between actual and expected states of your systems.

Publish-DSCConfiguration	This cmdlet copies the configuration to the target node but does not perform initial execution of the configuration on the target node. The configuration will be applied to the next consistency pass or when you run Update-DSCConfiguration.
Update-DSCConfiguration	This cmdlet forces the configuration to be processed when the cmdlet is executed. If the target node is attached to a DSC pull server, the agent will pull the configuration from the pull server before applying it.

V5 improvements

The V5 improvements are meant to call out certain aspects of the new release. It would be both futile and redundant to just list the release notes here, not to mention a waste of time. Instead, certain features are called out and explained in short detail to help you evaluate what is to come.

The PowerShell ISE

The PowerShell **Integrated Scripting Environment** (**ISE**) has been improved for authoring DSC configuration files. IntelliSense and inline help on demand increase the usability and discoverability of DSC resources.

PowerShell ISE IntelliSense allows the dynamic discovery of all the DSC resources inside a DSC configuration block by entering *Ctrl* + spacebar. Automatic completion of DSC resource names, property name and type, and enum is now supported. Automatically completing the value for DependsOn is a huge time saver when completing long dependency graphs.

Partial configurations and dependencies

DSC partial configurations allow you to deliver configurations in fragments to nodes. This is potentially a great feature to break up the large configuration documents you may have or help stagger the deployment of some distributed applications.

Support for cross-computer dependencies has also been added. This provides node-to-node synchronization without external input using CIM session connections between nodes. This means one configuration can wait for another to finish executing before executing itself. For example, a member server can wait to execute until the configuration on a domain controller has finished creating the domain the member server has to join.

Additional support for the DSC RefreshModes has been added to partial configurations. This allows you to specify whether a configuration is supposed to be pulled or pushed on an individual configuration level.

This feature is still in an experimental status at the time of writing this, so we are unable to accurately cover the feature in this book.

Class-based DSC resources

Instead of PowerShell module folders and supporting module files, DSC resources have been simplified to one file using class-based code.

 We will cover how to make DSC resources in Chapter 4, *DSC Resources*, for both PowerShell V4 and V5, but we will briefly mention the improvements V5 brings. If this is confusing at this point, don't worry; we will get into more detail in Chapter 5, *Pushing DSC Configurations*.

Each file has the get, set, and test functions declared as methods to a single class, which DSC knows how to parse and execute. This is a huge feature in and of itself and leads to several exciting possibilities, not the least of which is class inheritance, which reduces some of the duplication required in DSC V4.

The concept of software classes, functions, and methods may sound more like programming than what you want to know, but it is not as scary as it sounds, and it will be further explained in the PowerShell class-base DSC resource section in this book.

DSC built-in support for help

DSC configuration blocks now support the addition of PowerShell standard comment-based help text. This is a real improvement regarding documenting your configuration scripts, as the help text added here will show up in the PS ISE help text added here will show up in the PS ISE IntelliSense or using the Get-Help cmdlet.

DSC run as credential support

In DSC V5, you can now specify a credential that DSC will use to execute the DSC resource under.

In DSC V4, all configurations were run under the LocalSystem account. This means care must be taken when executing commands or DSC resources and expecting them to be able to do things like network access or other normal user actions.

DSC resource side-by-side installation

In DSC V4, you can only have one version of a DSC resource installed. DSC V5 detects versions of DSC resources now, which allows you to have more than one version present on the filesystem. Different DSC configurations can now rely on different versions of DSC resources and not affect each other.

Currently, class-based DSC resources do not allow more than one version of a DSC resource on a target node. This will most likely be fixed by the time of release, as what is currently available is only in preview. We mention it here as a warning while using the preview releases and expect it not to matter when the final version is released.

DSC resource script debugging

With DSC V5, you can debug DSC resources as they run on target nodes. This uses the remote debugging enhancements introduced by PowerShell V5 that allow you to attach to remote PowerShell runspaces and interact with the running code. This is hugely helpful, as often, the remote system is different from the system you are authoring the DSC resources on.

Separation of node and configuration IDs

In DSC V4, the ID of the specific DSC configuration applied to a given node uniquely represented the actual configuration and node that it was run on. In DSC V5, this has been separated into a configuration name and agent ID. The configuration name identifies the configuration on a target node, and the agent ID uniquely identifies a node.

This allows you to track both the configuration and node status independently and in relation to the other, giving a holistic picture of the coverage deployment of the whole environment.

DSC LCM MetaConfig updates

Since configuration names have friendly names instead of unique IDs, anyone can set them. This is mitigated by adding a registration step for the target node before the node can start requesting configurations to apply. This registration uses a shared secret that both the DSC pull server and the target node know already, as well as the name of the configuration it will request.

DSC LCM rich state information

The amount of detail about the LCM state has been improved to include the status of the DSC configuration on the machine. It will report whether the LCM is Idle, Busy, PendingReboot, or PendingConfiguration.

This is very useful in determining the status of your target nodes as time moves on when using DSC.

DSC LCM RefreshMode values

DSC V5 introduces a new RefreshMode value, Disabled. The LCM will not manage the configuration documents on the system and any third-party can invoke DSC resources directly using the Invoke-DSCResource cmdlet. This is yet another addition to allow outside vendors to take advantage of the consistent common tooling provided by DSC.

DSC status from a central location

This is very much an experimental feature, but it is an important one in viewing DSC as an entire replacement of existing products in this space, such as Puppet or Chef. As of DSC v4, there is no way to report the status of configurations centrally or at a granular level. Terse information describes the current state, with very little information on what went wrong or right. Information is available on a per-pull server basis.

In DSC V5, this information is improved with more detail and can be forwarded to a central DSC pull server. High-level status can be sent to a central server running the DSC service, which is then stored in a database. A new OData endpoint is created when the DSC service is installed, which exposes the information stored and can be queried by any tool able to make HTTP calls.

PowerShell V6 DSC

The PowerShell V6 release has been focused on several non-DSC specific features, but DSC benefits from their inclusion indirectly. No new built-in resources or cmdlets have been added.

While there hasn't been much new core to DSC, there has been a huge focus on making DSC cross-platform. Early support for Linux that was released around the first edition of this book has been fleshed out into fully featured support. Not only can DSC run on Linux, but it also has a complete set of built-in DSC resources. Underpinning this is a version of PowerShell that can run on Linux.

Summary

PowerShell DSC is a configuration management platform that enables a DevOps deployment of systems and services. In this chapter, we covered the different DSC versions, the available features in each version, and the concepts of configuration management and continuous delivery.

In the next chapter, we will cover DSC architecture and how DSC manages both systems and software in detail.

2

DSC Architecture

"As an architect you design for the present, with an awareness of the past for a future which is essentially unknown."
– Herman Foster

In the last chapter, we covered what PowerShell DSC is and how it fits into a continuous delivery and DevOps process. DSC uses PowerShell language extensions to define configuration files that express the expected state of a target node. We know that DSC uses DSC resources to determine whether the current state of the target node matches the expected state and that these resources know how to change the current state to the expected state.

In this chapter, we will cover the following topics:

- Push and pull management
- General workflow
- Local configuration manager
- DSC pull server
- Deployment considerations

Overview

We are in a precarious position in writing about DSC. In order to explain any one concept, we tend to have to explain a couple more before we get to it. We are going to start out here with some terms and examples of configuration files, DSC settings, and workflow models, but for the most part, the words and actions used will not be clear at first. They are explained in the chapters ahead in greater detail. Remember the previous chapter? Don't panic! If you find yourself getting confused as to why something is important, it may become clear as we move from the explanation to putting it into practice. So for now, look at them and get a feel for the flow of operations and then come back to them as we touch each step in the operations process in later chapters.

DSC enables you to ensure that the components of your server environment have the correct state and configuration. It enables declarative, autonomous, and idempotent deployment, as well as the configuration and conformance of standard-based managed elements.

By its simplest definition, DSC is a Windows service, a set of configuration files, and a set of PowerShell modules and scripts. Of course, there is more to this; there's push and pull modes, MOF compilation, and module packaging, but this is really all you need to describe the DSC architecture at a high level.

At a lower level, DSC is much more complex. It has to be complex in order to handle all the different variations of operations you can throw at it. Something this flexible has to have some complicated inner workings. The beauty of DSC is that these complex inner workings are abstracted away from you most of the time, so you can focus on getting the job done. And if you need to, you can access the complex inner workings and tune them to your needs.

To ensure that we are all on the same page about the concepts we are going to cover, let's cover some terms that we have seen over the course of the last chapter, since we will be seeing them in this chapter. This won't be an exhaustive list, but it will be enough to get us started:

Term	Description
Idempotent	An operation that can be performed multiple times with the same result.
DSC configuration file	A PowerShell script file that contains the DSC DSL syntax and list of DSC resources to execute.
DSC configuration data	A PowerShell data file or separate code block that defines data that can change on target nodes.

DSC resource	A PowerShell module that contains idempotent functions that brings a target node to a desired state.
DSC cmdlets	PowerShell cmdlets specially made for DSC operations.
MOF file	Contains the machine-readable version of a DSC configuration file.
LCM	The DSC engine that controls the entire execution of DSC configurations.
CM	The process of managing configuration on the servers in your environment.
Drift	A bucket term to indicate the difference between the desired state of a machine and the current state.
Compilation	Generally a programming term, in this case, it refers to the process of turning a DSC configuration file into an MOF file.
Metadata	Data that describes other data. Summarizes basic information about other data in a machine-readable format.

Push and pull modes

First and foremost, you must understand how DSC gets the information required to configure a target node from the place it's currently stored to the target node. This may sound counter-intuitive; you may be thinking we should be covering syntax or the different file formats in use first. Before we get to where we're going, we have to know how we are getting there.

The more established CM products available on the market have coalesced into two approaches: **push** and **pull**. Push and pull refer to the directions and methods used to move information from the place where it is stored to the target nodes. It also describes the direction commands being sent to or received by the target nodes.

Most CM products primarily use the pull method, which means they rely on agents to schedule, distribute, and rectify configurations on target nodes but have a central server that holds configuration information and data. The server maintains the current state of all the target nodes, while the agent periodically executes configuration runs on the target nodes. This is a simplistic but effective approach, as it enables several highly important features. Because the server has the state of every machine, a query-able record of all servers exists that a user can utilize.

At any one point in time, you can see the state of your entire infrastructure at a glance or in granular detail. Configuration runs can be executed on demand against a set of nodes or all nodes. Other popular management products that use this model are Puppet and Chef.

Other CM products primarily use the push method, where a single workstation or user calls the agent directly. The user is solely responsible for scheduling executions and resolving all dependencies that the agent needs. It's a loose but flexible network as it allows the agents to operate even if there isn't a central server to report the status to. This is called a **master-less deployment**, in that there isn't anything keeping track of things. An example of management products that use this model is Ansible.

The benefit of this model largely depends on your specific use cases. Some environments need granularity in scheduling and a high level of control over how and when agents perform actions, so they benefit highly from the push model. They choose when to check for drift and when to correct drift on a server-to-server basis or an entire environment. Common uses for this approach are test and QA environments, where software configurations change frequently and there is a high expectation of customization.

Other environments are less concerned with low-level customization and control and are more focused on ensuring a common state for a large environment (thousands and thousands of servers). Scheduling and controlling each individual server among thousands is less important than knowing that eventually, all servers will be in the same state no matter how new or old they are. These environments want a new server quickly that conforms to an exacting specification without human intervention, so new servers are automatically pointed to a pull server for a configuration assignment.

Both DSC and other management products, such as Puppet and Chef, can operate with and without a central server. Products such as Ansible support are only a push method of agent management. Choosing which product to use is more a choice of which approach fits your environment best rather than which product is best.

The push management model

DSC offers a push-based approach that is controlled by a user workstation initiating an execution on agents on target nodes, but there isn't a central server orchestrating things. Push management is very much an interactive process, where the user directly initiates and executes a specified configuration.

The following diagram shows the **Push Deployment** model:

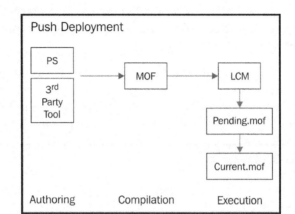

This diagram shows the steps to perform a **Push Deployment**. The next section discusses the DSC workflow, where these steps will be covered, but for now, we see that a push deployment is comprised of three steps:

- Authoring a configuration file
- Compiling the file to an MOF file
- Executing the MOF on the target node

DSC operates in a push scenario when configurations are manually pushed to target nodes using the `Start-DscConfiguration` cmdlet. It can be executed interactively, where the configuration is executed and the status is reported back to the user as it is running. It can also be initiated in a fire and forget manner as a job on the target node, where the configuration will be executed without reporting the status back to the user directly, but is logged to the DSC event log instead.

Pushing configurations allows a great deal of flexibility. It's the primary way you will test your configurations. Run interactively with the `Verbose` and `Wait` parameter; the `Start-DscConfiguration` cmdlet shows you a log of every step taken by the LCM, the DSC resources it executes, and the entire DSC configuration run. A push-based approach also gives you an absolute time when the target node will have a configuration applied instead of waiting on a schedule. This is useful in server environments when servers are set up once and stay around for a long time.

This is the easiest to set up and the most flexible of the two DSC methods but is the hardest to maintain in large quantities and over the long term.

The pull management model

DSC offers a pull-based approach that is controlled by agents on target nodes, but there is a central server providing configuration files. This is a marked difference from the push models offered by other CM products.

The following diagram shows the **Pull Deployment** model. The diagram shows the steps in a **Pull Deployment** and also shows how the status is reported for the compliance server. Refer to the following diagram; we will cover pull servers later on in this chapter:

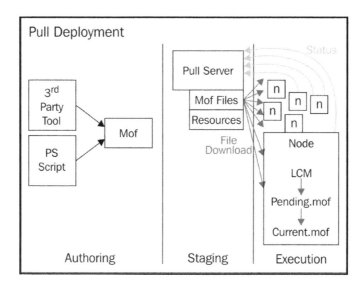

DSC operates in a pull scenario when configurations are stored on a DSC pull server and pulled by LCM on each target node. The **pull server** is the harder of the two DSC methods to set up, but the easiest to maintain in large node quantities and in the long term.

Pull management works great in server environments that have a lot of transient machines, such as cloud or data center environments. These kinds of servers are created and destroyed frequently, and DSC will apply on a triggered basis. Pull servers are also more scalable, as they can work against thousands of hosts in parallel. This seems counterintuitive, as with most pull servers, we have a central point of drift detection, scheduling, and so on. This isn't the case with a DSC pull server; however, it does not detect drift, compile MOFs, or other high-cost actions. Compilation and the like happen on the author workstation or **Converged Infrastructure** (**CI**), and the drift detection and scheduling happen on the agent, so the load is distributed across agents and not on the pull server. We will cover more benefits of pull servers at the end of this chapter and at the end of this book in Chapter 6, *Pulling DSC Configurations*.

The general workflow

In Chapter 1, *Introducing PowerShell DSC*, we covered a high-level overview of DSC and introduced the three phases of DSC use. We also covered the MOF file and its importance in the grand scheme of DSC usage. Since we have already established the "why" of these concepts, we will now dive into the details of each phase.

What follows won't be a step-by-step process; this will be handled in Chapter 3, *DSC Configuration Files*. Instead, what we discuss here will be more explanatory and might make you move around a bit. Concepts that are introduced may not be fully explained until later, when supporting concepts are fleshed out. DSC is a very modular product, each module a separate entity that is also interdependent with other entities. This makes explaining some concepts a *chicken and egg* scenario, so we will try our best to reference other sections as they apply.

The following diagram shows the **Authoring, Staging,** and **Execution** phases of the DSC workflow. You will notice that it does not look much different than the push or pull model diagrams. This similarity is on purpose, as the architecture of DSC allows its usage in either a push or pull deployment to be the same until the execution phase. This reduces the complexity of your configuration files and allows them to be used in either deployment mode without modification. Let's take a look at the entire DSC workflow:

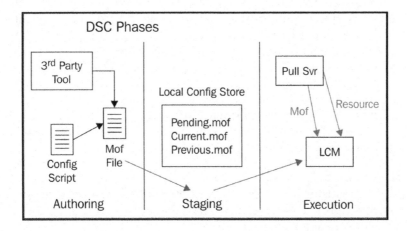

Authoring

In order to tell DSC what state the target node should be in, you have to describe that state in the DSC DSL syntax. The end goal of the DSL syntax is to create an MOF file. This listing and compilation process comprises the entirety of the **authoring** phase. Even so, you will not be creating the MOF files directly yourself. The MOF syntax and format is very verbose and detailed, too much for a human to reliably produce it. You can create an MOF file using a number of different methods—anything from *Notepad* to third-party tools, not just DSC tooling. Third-party vendors other than Microsoft will eventually implement their own compilers, as the operations to compile MOF are standardized and open for all to use, enabling authoring DSC files on any operating system.

For the purposes of this book, we will concentrate on how to create MOF files using PowerShell tooling. We will assume you are using a Windows 8.1 or Windows 2012 R2 OS with at least PowerShell V4 installed. If you are targeting the use of PowerShell V5, then we assume you are using Windows 10 or one of the production releases of WMF 5 on your platform of choice.

Syntax

DSC provides a DSL to help you create MOF files. We call the file that holds the DSL syntax the DSC configuration file. Even though it is a PowerShell script file (a text file with a `.ps1` extension), it can't do anything on its own. You can try to execute a configuration file all you want; it won't do anything to the system by itself. A DSC configuration file holds the information for the desired state, not the execution code to bring the node to a desired state. We talked about this separation of configuration information and execution logic earlier, and we are going to keep seeing this repeatedly throughout our use of DSC.

The DSC DSL allows both imperative and declarative commands. What this means is that configuration files can both describe what has to be done (declarative) as well as have a PowerShell code that is executed inline (imperative).

Declarative code will typically be DSC functions and resource declarations and will make up the majority of code inside your DSC configuration file. Remember, the purpose of DSC is to express the expected state of the system, which you do by declaring it in these files in the human-readable language.

Imperative code will typically make decisions based on the metadata provided inside the configuration file, for example, choosing whether to apply a configuration to a target node inside the $AllNodes variable or deciding which files or modules to apply based on some algorithm. You will find that putting a lot of imperative code inside your configuration files will cause maintenance and troubleshooting problems in the future. Generally, a lot of imperative code indicates that you are performing actions or deciding on logic that should be in a DSC resource, which is the best place to put imperative code. We will cover what indicators for this are and other important aspects of DSC resources in Chapter 4, *DSC Resources*.

Compilation

The DSC configuration file is compiled to an MOF format by invoking the declared DSC configuration block inside the DSC configuration file. When this is done, it creates a folder and one or more MOF files inside it. Each MOF file is for a single target node, containing all the configuration information needed to ensure the desired state on the target machine.

It's important to understand before we get too far into explaining MOF compilation that defining a DSC configuration script does not mean that you have to compile it to an MOF right away. The two actions are separate because the MOF file is either copied to the target node or the DSC pull server, and the DSC configuration file is kept in the source control or another safe place.

Sometimes, compilation is not needed at all, as in the case of the Azure DSC tooling. All you need to do with Azure and DSC is copy the DSC configuration script, and Azure will handle the rest.

If at this point you are looking for the example code of what this looks like, the *example workflow* section has what you are looking for. We will continue explaining MOF compilation here, but if you want to jump ahead and take a look at the example and come back here when you are done, that's fine.

You can have only one MOF file applied to any target node at any given time. Why one MOF file per target node? That is a good question. Due to the architecture of DSC, an MOF file is the one source of truth for that server. It holds everything that can describe that server so that nothing is missed.

You might be thinking that if there can be only one MOF file per target node, does that mean you can have only one DSC configuration file? There are two answers to this question. You can either have one DSC configuration block applied to a target node, or you can use DSC partial configurations. With the one DSC configuration block, you can use the power of the PowerShell language (pun intended) to filter which target nodes to apply settings to or do complicated logic operations to decide whether software is installed or not.

With DSC partial configurations, you can have separate DSC configuration blocks to delineate different parts of your installation or environment. This enables multiple teams to collaborate and participate in defining configurations for the environment instead of forcing all teams to use one DSC configuration script to track. For example, you can have a DSC partial configuration for an SQL server that is handled by the SQL team and another DSC partial configuration for the base operating system configuration that is handled by the operations team. Both partial configurations are used to produce one MOF file for a target node while allowing either DSC partial configuration to be worked on separately.

In some cases, it's easier to have a single DSC configuration script that has the logic to determine what a target node needs installed or configured rather than a set of DSC partial configuration files that have to be tracked together by different people. Whichever one you choose is largely determined by your environment. We will cover this subject in more detail in `Chapter 3`, *DSC Configuration Files*.

Staging

After authoring the configuration files and compiling them into MOF files, the next step is the **staging** phase. This phase slightly varies if you are using a push or pull model of deployment.

When using the push model, the MOF files are pushed to the target node and executed immediately. There isn't much staging with push, as the whole point is to be interactive and immediate. In PowerShell V4, if a target node is managed by a DSC pull server, you cannot push the MOF file to it using the `Start-DscConfiguration` cmdlet. In PowerShell V4, a target node is either managed by a DSC pull server or not. This distinction is somewhat blurred in PowerShell V5, as a new DSC mode allows a target node to both be managed by a DSC pull server and have MOF files pushed to it.

When using the pull model, the MOF files are pushed to the DSC pull server by the user and then pulled down to target nodes by DSC agents. Because the local LCMs on each target node pull the MOF when they hit the correct interval, MOF files are not immediately processed and thus are staged. They are processed only when the LCM pulls the MOF from the pull server. When attached to a pull server, the LCM performs other actions to stage or prepare the target node. The LCM will request all the required DSC resources from the pull server in order to execute the MOF in the next phase.

Whatever process the MOF file uses to get to the target node, the LCM processes the MOF file by naming it the `pending.mof` file and placing it inside the `$env:systemRoot/system32/configuration` path. If there was an existing MOF file executed earlier, it takes that file and renames it the `previous.mof` file.

Execution

After staging, the MOF files are ready for execution on the target node. An MOF is always executed as soon as it is delivered to a target node regardless of whether the target node is configured for push or pull management. The LCM runs on a configurable schedule, but this schedule controls when the LCM pulls the new MOFs from the DSC pull server and when it checks the system state against the described desired state in the MOF file. When the LCM executes the MOF successfully, it renames the `Pending.mof` file to `Current.mof` file.

The following diagram shows the execution phase:

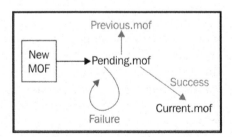

The **execution** phase operates the same no matter which deployment mode is in use, push or pull. However, different operations are started in the pull mode in comparison to the push mode, besides the obvious interactive nature of the push mode.

Push executions

In the push mode, the LCM expects all DSC resources to be present on the target node. Since the LCM doesn't have a way to know where to get the DSC resources used by the MOF file, it can't get them for you. Before running any push deployment on a target node, you must put all DSC resources needed there first. If they are not present, then the execution will fail.

Using the `Start-DscConfiguration` cmdlet, the MOF files are executed immediately. This kind of execution happens only when the user initiates it. The user can opt for the execution caused by the `Start-DscConfiguration` cmdlet to happen interactively and see the output as it happens or have it happen in the background and complete without any user interaction.

The execution can happen again if the LCM `ConfigurationMode` mode is set to the `ApplyAndMonitor` or `ApplyAndAutoCorrect` mode, but it will be applied only once if `ConfigurationMode` is set to `ApplyOnly`.

Pull executions

In the pull mode, the LCM contacts the pull server for a new configuration, and the LCM downloads a new one if present. The LCM will parse the MOF and download any DSC resources that are specified in the configuration file with respect to the version number specified there.

The MOF file is executed on a schedule that is set on each target node's LCM configuration. The same LCM schedule rules apply to a target node that is attached to a pull server as to the one that is not attached. The `ApplyAndMonitor` and `ApplyAndAutoCorrect` modes will continue to monitor the system state and change it if necessary. If it is set to the `ApplyOnly` mode, then LCM will check with the pull server to see whether there are new MOF files to download but will apply them only if the last execution failed. The execution happens continuously on a schedule that the LCM was set to use. In the next section, we will cover exactly how the LCM schedules configuration executions.

The example workflow

At this point, a simple example of the workflow you will use will be helpful to explain what we just covered. We will first create an example DSC configuration file. Then, we will compile it to an MOF file and show an example execution using the push deployment model.

A short note about composing configuration files: if you use the built-in PowerShell **Integrated Script Environment (ISE)**, then you will have IntelliSense provided as you type. This is useful as you start learning; the pop-up information can help you as you type things without having to look back at the documentation. The PowerShell ISE also provides on-demand syntax checking and will look for errors as you type.

The following text would be saved as a `TestExample.ps1` file. You will notice that this is a standalone file and contains no configuration data. Let's look at the following code snippet, which is a complete example of a DSC configuration file:

```
# First we declare the configuration
Configuration TestExample
{
  # Then we declare the node we are targeting
  Node "localhost"
  {
    # Then we declare the action we want to perform
    Log ImportantMessage
    {
      Message = "This has done something important"
    }
  }
}
# Compile the Configuration function
TestExample
```

For the sake of simplicity, we have saved more advanced topics such as this for Chapter 3, *DSC Configuration Files*.

We can see the `Configuration` keyword, which holds all the node statements and DSC resources statements. Then, the `Node` keyword is used to declare the target node we are operating on. This can either be hardcoded like in the example, or it can be passed in using the configuration data. And finally, the resource declaration for the action we want to take is added. In this example, we will output a message to the DSC event log when this is run on the localhost.

We use the term **keyword** here to describe `Configuration` and `Node`. This is slightly inaccurate, as the actual definitions of `Configuration` and `Node` are PowerShell functions in the `PSDesiredStateConfiguration` module. PowerShell functions can also be defined as cmdlets. This interchangeability of terms here is partly due to PowerShell's naming flexibility and partly due to informal conventions. It's sometimes a hot topic of contention. For the purposes of this book, substitute your preferred word here.

To compile this DSC configuration file into an MOF, we execute the following script from the PowerShell console:

```
PS C:\Examples> .\TestExample.ps1
    Directory: C:\Examples\TestExample
Mode                LastWriteTime     Length Name
----                -------------     ------ ----
-a---        5/20/2015    7:28 PM       1136 localhost.mof
```

As we can see from the result, compiling the configuration file to an MOF resulted in a folder with the name of the configuration block we just created and with one file called the `localhost.mof` file.

> Don't worry too much about reading or understanding the MOF syntax right now. For the most part, you won't be reading or dealing with it directly in your everyday use, but it is useful to know how the configuration block format looks in the MOF format.

Let's examine the following snippet:

```
/*
@TargetNode='localhost'
@GeneratedBy=James
@GenerationDate=05/20/2015 19:28:50
@GenerationHost=BLUEBOX
*/
instance of MSFT_LogResource as $MSFT_LogResource1ref
{
SourceInfo = "C:\\Examples\\TestExample.ps1::8::9::Log";
 ModuleName = "PSDesiredStateConfiguration";
 ModuleVersion = "1.0";
 ResourceID = "[Log]ImportantMessage";
 Message = "This has done something important";
};
instance of OMI_ConfigurationDocument
{
 Version="1.0.0";
 Author="James";
 GenerationDate="05/20/2015 19:28:50";
 GenerationHost="BLUEBOX";
};
```

We can see from this MOF that not only do we programmatically state the intent of this configuration (log a message), but we also note the computer it was compiled on as well as the user that did it. This metadata is used by the DSC engine when applying configurations and reporting statuses back to a pull server.

Then, we execute this configuration on a target node using the push deployment model by calling the `Start-DscConfiguration` cmdlet:

```
    PS C:\Examples> Start-DscConfiguration -Path C:\Examples\TestExample -
Wait -Verbose
    VERBOSE: Perform operation 'Invoke CimMethod' with following
parameters, ''methodName' =
    SendConfigurationApply,'className' =
MSFT_DSCLocalConfigurationManager,'namespaceName' =
    root/Microsoft/Windows/DesiredStateConfiguration'.
    VERBOSE: An LCM method call arrived from computer BLUEBOX with user sid
************.
    VERBOSE: [BLUEBOX]: LCM:  [ Start   Set       ]
    VERBOSE: [BLUEBOX]: LCM:  [ Start   Resource  ]  [[Log]ImportantMessage]
    VERBOSE: [BLUEBOX]: LCM:  [ Start   Test      ]  [[Log]ImportantMessage]
    VERBOSE: [BLUEBOX]: LCM:  [ End     Test      ]  [[Log]ImportantMessage]
in 0.0000 seconds.
    VERBOSE: [BLUEBOX]: LCM:  [ Start   Set       ]  [[Log]ImportantMessage]
    VERBOSE: [BLUEBOX]:                                [[Log]ImportantMessage]
This has done something important
    VERBOSE: [BLUEBOX]: LCM:  [ End     Set       ]  [[Log]ImportantMessage]
in 0.0000 seconds.
    VERBOSE: [BLUEBOX]: LCM:  [ End     Resource  ]  [[Log]ImportantMessage]
    VERBOSE: [BLUEBOX]: LCM:  [ End     Set       ]    in  0.3162 seconds.
    VERBOSE: Operation 'Invoke CimMethod' complete.
    VERBOSE: Time taken for configuration job to complete is 0.36 seconds
```

Notice the logging here. We used the `Verbose` parameter, so we see listed before us every step that DSC took. Each line represents an action DSC is executing, and each has a `Start` and `End` word in it, signifying the start and end of each execution even though an execution may span multiple lines. We will get into how to sort and use these logs more when we address troubleshooting DSC configurations later in this book.

Each `INFO`, `VERBOSE`, `DEBUG`, or `ERROR` parameter is written both to the console in front of us and also to the DSC event log. Everything done is logged for auditing and historical purposes. An important thing to note is that while everything is logged, not everything is logged to the same place. There are several DSC event logs: `Microsoft-Windows-DSC/Operational`, `Microsoft-Windows-DSC/Analytical`, and `Microsoft-Windows-DSC/Debug`. However, only the `Microsoft-Windows-DSC/Operational` event log is logged to by default; you have to enable the `Microsoft-Windows-DSC/Analytical` and `Microsoft-Windows-DSC/Debug` event log in order to see any events logged there. Any verbose messages are logged in `Microsoft-Windows-DSC/Analytical`, so beware if you use the `Log` DSC resource extensively and intend to find those messages in the logs.

Configuration data

Now that we have covered how deployments work (push and pull) in DSC and covered the workflow (authoring, staging, and execution) for using DSC, we will pause here for a moment to discuss the differences between configuration files and configuration data.

It is important to understand the concept of the separation of the **what** from the **where** that we covered in Chapter 1, *Introducing PowerShell DSC*, when considering how to deploy servers, applications, and environments using DSC.

The DSC configuration blocks contain the entirety of the expected state of the target node. The DSL syntax used to describe the state is expressed in one configuration file in almost a grocery list format. It expresses all configuration points of the target system and is able to express dependencies between configuration points.

DSC configuration data is separated from DSC configuration files to reduce variance and duplication. Some points that are considered data are software version numbers, file path locations, registry setting values, and domain-specific information, such as server roles or department names.

You may be thinking what the difference between the data you put in a configuration file and a configuration data file is. The data we put in a configuration file is structural data, data that does not change based on the environment. The data we put in configuration data files is environmental. For example, no matter the environment, a server needs IIS installed in order to serve web pages. The location of the source files for the web page may change depending on whether the environment is the development environment or the production environment. If you are wondering where these files reside and when you use them, we will cover each of them in term in the coming chapters.

The structural information (that we need IIS for) is contained in the DSC configuration file and the environmental information (source file locations) is stored in the configuration data file.

Configuration data can be expressed in DSC in several ways. Let's look at each of the ways in detail.

Hardcoded data

Configuration data can be hardcoded inside DSC configuration files, but this is not optimal in most cases. You will mostly use this for static sets of information or to reduce redundant code, as shown in the following code snippet:

```
configuration FooBar
{
  $features = @('Web-Server', 'Web-Asp-Net45')
  Foreach($feature in $features){
    WindowsFeature "Install$($feature)"
    {
      Name = $feature
    }
  }
}
```

Parameter-based data

Parameter-based data can be passed as parameters to a configuration block, as follows:

```
configuration FooBar
{
  param([switch]$foo,$bar)
  if($foo){
    WindowsFeature InstallIIS
    {
      Name = "Web-Server"
    }
  }elseif($bar){
    WindowsFeature InstallHyperV
    {
      Name = "Microsoft-Hyper-V"
    }
  }
}

FooBar -Foo
```

Hashtable data

The most flexible and preferred method is to use the `ConfigurationData` hashtable. This specifically structured hashtable provides a flexible way of declaring frequently changing data in a format that DSC will be able to read and then insert into the MOF file as it compiles it. This approach will be covered in greater detail later in `Chapter 3`, *DSC Configuration Files*, but it must be included in this chapter to fully describe the DSC architecture. Don't worry too much if the importance of this feature is not readily apparent. With the following command lines, we define a specifically formatted hashtable called `$data`:

```
$data = @{
  # Node specific data
  # Note that is an array of hashes. It's easy to miss
  # the array designation here
  AllNodes = @(
    # All the WebServers have this identical config
    @{
      NodeName            = "*"
      WebsiteName         = "FooWeb"
      SourcePath          = "C:\FooBar\"
      DestinationPath     = "C:\inetpub\FooBar"
      DefaultWebSitePath  = "C:\inetpub\wwwroot"
    },
    @{
      NodeName = "web1.foobar.com"
      Role     = "Web"
    },
    @{
      NodeName = "web2.foobar.com"
      Role     = "Web"
    },
    @{
      NodeName = "sql.foobar.com"
      Role     = "Sql"
    }
  );
}

configuration FooBar
{
  # Dynamically find the web nodes from configuration data
  Node $AllNodes.where{$_.Role -eq "Web"}.NodeName
  {
    # Install the IIS role
    WindowsFeature IIS
```

```
    {
      Ensure = "Present"
      Name   = "Web-Server"
    }
  }
}
# Pass the configuration data to configuration as follows:
FooBar -ConfigurationData $data
```

The first item's key is called the $AllNodes key, the value of which is an array of hashtables. The content of these hashtables is free form and can be whatever we need them to be, but they are meant to express the data on each target node. Here, we specify the roles of each node so that inside the configuration, we can perform a where clause and filter for only the nodes that have a web role.

If you look back at the $AllNodes definition, you'll see the three nodes we defined (web1, web2, and sql), but also notice one where we just put an * sign in the NodeName field. This is a special convention that tells DSC that all the information in this hashtable is available to all the nodes defined in this AllNodes array. This is an easy way to specify defaults or properties that apply to all nodes being worked on. We'll cover some strategies for this as we move forward in the book.

Local Configuration Manager

Now that we have covered how deployments work (push and pull) in DSC and the workflow (authoring, staging, and execution) for DSC, we will talk about how the execution happens on a target node.

The **Local Configuration Manager** (**LCM**) is the PowerShell DSC engine. It is the heart and soul of DSC. It runs on all target nodes and controls the execution of DSC configurations and DSC resources whether you are using a push or pull deployment model. It is a Windows service that is part of the WMI service host, so there is no direct service named LCM for you to look at.

The LCM has a large range of settings that control everything from the scheduling of executions to how the LCM handles configuration drift. LCM settings are configurable by DSC itself although using a slightly different syntax. This allows the LCM settings to be deployed just like DSC configurations in an automatable and repeatable manner.

These settings are applied separately from your DSC configurations, so you will have configuration files for your LCM and separate files for your DSC configurations. This separation means that LCM settings can be applied per server or on all servers, so not all your target nodes have to have the same settings. This is useful if some servers have to have a stricter scheduler and control over their drift, whereas others can be checked less often or be more relaxed in their drift.

Since the LCM settings are different from DSC settings but describe how DSC operates, they are considered DSC metadata. You will sometimes see them referred to as metadata instead of settings because they describe the entirety of the process and not just LCM-specific operations. These pieces of information are stored in a separate MOF file than what the DSC configuration block compiles to. These files are named with the `NodeName` field you gave them and appended with `meta.mof` as the file extension. Anytime you configure the LCM, the `*.meta.mof` files will be generated.

LCM settings

Common settings that you will configure are listed in the following table. There are more settings available, which can be viewed at `https://docs.microsoft.com/en-us/powershell/dsc/metaconfig`, but these are the ones that are most useful to know right away:

Setting	Description
AllowModuleOverwrite	Allows or disallows DSC resources to be overwritten on the target node. This applies to the DSC pull server use only.
ConfigurationMode	Determines the type of operations to perform on this host. For example, if set to ApplyAndAutoCorrect and if the current state does not match the desired state, then DSC applies the corrections needed.
ConfigurationModeFrequencyMins	The interval in minutes to check whether there is configuration drift.
RebootNodeIfNeeded	Automatically reboot the server if configuration requires it when applied.

RefreshFrequencyMins	Determines how often to check for a new configuration when LCM is attached to a pull server.
RefreshMode	Determines which deployment mode the target is in, push or pull.

The LCM comes with most of these settings set to logical defaults to allow DSC to operate out of the box. You can check what is currently set by issuing the following `Get-DscLocalConfigurationManager` cmdlet:

```
PS C:\Examples> Get-DscLocalConfigurationManager
ActionAfterReboot                 : ContinueConfiguration
AllowModuleOverwrite              : False
CertificateID                     :
ConfigurationID                   :
ConfigurationMode                 : ApplyAndMonitor
ConfigurationModeFrequencyMins    : 15
Credential                        :
DebugMode                         : {NONE}
DownloadManagerCustomData         :
DownloadManagerName               :
LCMCompatibleVersions             : {1.0}
LCMState                          : Idle
LCMVersion                        : 1.0
RebootNodeIfNeeded                : False
RefreshFrequencyMins              : 30
RefreshMode                       : PUSH
PSComputerName                    :
```

Configuration modes

An important setting to call out is the LCM `ConfigurationMode` setting. As stated earlier, this setting controls how DSC applies the configuration to the target node. There are three available settings:

- `ApplyOnly`
- `ApplyAndMonitor`
- `ApplyAndAutoCorrect`

These settings will allow you to control how the LCM behaves and when it operates. This controls the actions taken when applying the configuration as well as how it handles drift occurring on the target node. Let's look at each of these settings in detail.

ApplyOnly

When the `ApplyOnly` mode is set, DSC will apply the configuration and do nothing further unless a new configuration is deployed to the target node. Note that this is a completely new configuration, not a refresh of the currently applied configuration. If the target node's configuration drifts or changes, no action will be taken by DSC. This is useful for a one-time configuration of a target node or in cases where it is expected that a new configuration will be pushed at a later point, but some initial setup needs to be done now. This is not a commonly used setting.

ApplyAndMonitor

When the `ApplyAndMonitor` mode is set, DSC behaves exactly like `ApplyOnly`, except that after the deployment, DSC will monitor the current state for the configuration drift. This is the default setting for all DSC agents. It will report back any drift to the DSC logs or pull server but will not act to rectify the drift. This is useful when you want to control when change happens on your servers, but it reduces the autonomy DSC can have to correct changes in your infrastructure.

ApplyAndAutoCorrect

When the `ApplyAndAutoCorrect` mode is set, DSC will apply the configuration to the target node and continue to monitor for configuration drift. If any drift is detected, it will be logged and the configuration will be reapplied to the target node in order to bring it back into compliance. This gives DSC the greatest autonomy to ensure your environment is valid and act on any changes that may occur without your direct input. This is great for fully locked down environments where variance is not allowed but must also be corrected on the next scheduled run and without fail.

Refresh modes

While the `ConfigurationMode` mode determines how DSC behaves in regard to configuration drift, the `RefreshMode` setting determines how DSC gets the configuration information. In the beginning of this chapter, we covered the push and pull deployment models, and this setting allows you to change which model the target node uses.

By default, all installations are set to the push `RefreshMode`, which makes sense when you want DSC to work out of the box. Setting it to the pull `RefreshMode` allows the LCM to work with a central pull server.

The LCM configuration

Configuring the LCM is done by authoring an LCM configuration block with the desired settings specified. When compiled, the LCM configuration block produces a file with the meta.mof extension. Applying the meta.mof file is done using the Set-DscLocalConfigurationManager cmdlet .

You are not required to write your LCM configuration block in a file; it can alternatively be placed inside the DSC configuration file. There are several reasons to separate them. Your settings for the LCM could potentially change more often than your DSC configuration files, and keeping them separated reduces changes to your core files. You could also have different settings for different servers, which you may not want to express or tie down inside your DSC configuration files. It's up to you how you want to organize things.

Compiling the LCM configuration block to MOF is done just like a DSC configuration block by invoking the name of the LCM configuration you defined. You apply the resulting meta.mof file to the target node using the Set-DscLocalConfigurationManager cmdlet.

An example LCM configuration

An example LCM configuration is as follows, saved as ExampleLCMConfig.ps1. We could have put this inside a regular DSC configuration file, but it was separated for a clearer example, as shown here:

```
#Declare the configuration
Configuration SetTheLCM
{
  # Declare the settings we want configured
  LocalConfigurationManager
  {
    ConfigurationMode              = "ApplyAndAutoCorrect"
    ConfigurationModeFrequencyMins = 120
    RefreshMode                    = "Push"
    RebootNodeIfNeeded             = $true
  }
}

SetTheLCM
```

To compile this configuration into an MOF file, you execute the following configuration file in the PowerShell console:

```
PS C:\Examples> .\ExampleLCMConfig.ps1
    Directory: C:\Users\James\Desktop\Examples\SetTheLCM
Mode            LastWriteTime     Length Name
----            -------------     ------ ----
-a---     5/20/2015   7:28 PM        984 localhost.meta.mof
```

As we can see from the output, a `localhost.meta.mof` file was created inside a folder named for the configuration as a `SetTheLCM` folder. The filename reminds us again that the LCM settings are considered DSC metadata, so any files or operations on LCM get the **meta** moniker.

Looking at the contents of the MOF file, we see the same syntax as the MOF file generated by the DSC configuration file. We will keep seeing this standardized approach reused over and over again during our use of DSC, the importance of which we explained in `Chapter 1`, *Introducing PowerShell DSC*.

Let's take a look at the following snippet:

```
/*
@TargetNode='localhost'
@GeneratedBy=James
@GenerationDate=05/20/2015 19:28:50
@GenerationHost=BLUEBOX
*/
instance of MSFT_DSCMetaConfiguration as $MSFT_DSCMetaConfiguration1ref
{
RefreshMode = "Push";
 ConfigurationModeFrequencyMins = 120;
 ConfigurationMode = "ApplyAndAutoCorrect";
 RebootNodeIfNeeded = True;
};
instance of OMI_ConfigurationDocument
{
 Version="1.0.0";
 Author="James";
 GenerationDate="05/20/2015 19:28:50";
 GenerationHost="BLUEBOX";
};
```

We then execute the LCM configuration using the `Set-DscLocalConfigurationManager` cmdlet:

```
PS C:\Examples> Set-DscLocalConfigurationManager -Path .\SetTheLCM\ -
Verbose
VERBOSE: Performing the operation "Start-DscConfiguration:
SendMetaConfigurationApply" on target
"MSFT_DSCLocalConfigurationManager".
VERBOSE: Perform operation 'Invoke CimMethod' with following
parameters, ''methodName' =
SendMetaConfigurationApply,'className' =
MSFT_DSCLocalConfigurationManager,'namespaceName' =
root/Microsoft/Windows/DesiredStateConfiguration'.
VERBOSE: An LCM method call arrived from computer BLUEBOX with user sid
*********************.
VERBOSE: [BLUEBOX]: LCM:  [ Start  Set      ]
VERBOSE: [BLUEBOX]: LCM:  [ Start  Resource ]
[MSFT_DSCMetaConfiguration]
VERBOSE: [BLUEBOX]: LCM:  [ Start  Set      ]
[MSFT_DSCMetaConfiguration]
VERBOSE: [BLUEBOX]: LCM:  [ End    Set      ]
[MSFT_DSCMetaConfiguration]  in 0.0520 seconds.
VERBOSE: [BLUEBOX]: LCM:  [ End    Resource ]
[MSFT_DSCMetaConfiguration]
VERBOSE: [BLUEBOX]: LCM:  [ End    Set      ]   in  0.2555 seconds.
VERBOSE: Operation 'Invoke CimMethod' complete.
VERBOSE: Set-DscLocalConfigurationManager finished in 0.235 seconds.
```

The DSC pull server

The DSC pull server is your one-stop central solution for managing a large environment using DSC. In the beginning of this chapter, we talked about the two deployment modes of DSC: push and pull. A DSC pull server operates with target nodes configured to be in the pull deployment mode. We covered the DSC pull server superficially in Chapter 1, *Introducing PowerShell DSC*, and we will cover it again in Chapter 6, *Pulling DSC Configurations*, concerning specific deployment topics. In this section, we will describe it in depth from an architectural standpoint.

What is a DSC pull server?

A DSC pull server is an IIS website that exposes an OData endpoint that responds to requests from the LCM configured on each target node and provides DSC configuration files and DSC resources for download. That was a lot of acronyms and buzzwords, so let's take this one by one.

IIS is an acronym for **Internet Information Services**, which is the set of components that allows you to host websites on a Windows server. **OData** is an acronym for **Open Data Protocol**, which defines a standard for querying and consuming RESTful APIs. Explaining websites, REST, and APIs is a little more than what we can do here in this book, and you do not have to really know all these to use DSC. For the purposes of this book, think of API as the programmatic way the LCM on the target nodes asks the pull server what to do.

One last thing to cover before we move on. A DSC pull server can be configured to use **Server Message Block** (**SMB**) shares instead of HTTP to distribute MOF files and DSC resources. This changes the distribution mechanism of DSC Resources and MOF files, but not how the DSC server works. We will get into a more detailed explanation in `Chapter 6`, *Pulling DSC Configurations*.

What does the pull server do for us?

Since the LCM handles the scheduling and executing of the MOF files, what does the pull server do? The pull server operates as a single management point for all DSC operations. By deploying MOF files to the pull server, you control the configuration of any target node attached to it. Let's examine each function the DSC pull server has.

Automatic and continuous configuration

As a central location for all target nodes to report to, a pull server provides an automatic deployment of configurations. Once a target node's LCM is configured, it will automatically pull configurations and dependent files without requiring input from you. It will also do this continuously and on schedule without requiring extra input from you.

Repository

The pull server is the central repository for all the MOF files and DSC resources that the LCM uses in order to schedule and execute. With the push model, you are responsible for distributing the DSC resources and MOF files to the target nodes yourself. A DSC pull server provides them to the target nodes on demand and ensures that they have the correct version.

Reporting

The pull server tracks the status of every target node that uses it, so it also has another role called a reporting server. You can query the server for the status of all the nodes in your environment and the pull server will return information on their last run. A reporting server stores the pull operation status and configuration and node information in a database. Reporting endpoints can be used to periodically check the status of the nodes to see whether their configurations are in sync with the pull server or not.

The PowerShell team has transitioned from calling this a compliance server to a reporting server during the PowerShell V5 development cycle.

Security

A pull server can be set up to use HTTPS or SMB with NTFS permissions for the MOF and DSC resource repositories. This controls access to the DSC configuration files and DSC resources and also encrypts them over the wire.

At some point, you will most likely have to provide credentials for one of your settings or DSC resources. Certificates can be used to encrypt the credentials being used in the DSC configurations. It would be foolish to enter the credentials inside the DSC configuration files, as they would be in plain text that anyone could read. By setting up and using certificates to encrypt the credentials, only the servers with the correct certificates can read the credentials.

Setting up a DSC pull server

You would think that with so many dependencies, setting up a DSC pull server would be hard. Actually, it's a perfect example of using DSC to configure a server! We are going to get a jump on `Chapter 3`, *DSC Configuration Files*, here by showing an example DSC configuration file that configures a server as a DSC pull server. Again, don't worry if some of this is still not clear; we will cover how to make DSC configuration files in more detail later.

 You do *not* have to set up a pull server to use DSC with this book. You can complete the rest of the book's examples using push deployments. This is up to you to do if you want. We cover setting it up here so that we can explain how it works.

Pull server settings

A pull server has several configuration points for each of the roles it performs. These can either be set manually or through DSC itself, as discussed in the following table:

Name	Description
EndpointName	Configures the name of the OData endpoint.
Port	The port the service listens on.
CertificateThumbPrint	The SSL certificate thumbprint the web service uses.
PhysicalPath	The installation path of the DSC service.
ModulePath	The path to the DSC resources and modules.
ConfigurationPath	The working directory for the DSC service.

Installing the DSC server

The following example is taken from the example provided by the PowerShell team in the `xPSDesiredStateConfiguration` module. Just as when we showed an example DSC configuration in the authoring phase, don't get too caught up on the following syntax. Examine the structure and how much this looks like a list for what we need. Running this on a target node sets up everything needed to make it a pull server, ready to go from the moment it is finished.

In the interest of showing an actual example, we are skipping several setup steps that you must complete in order to actually use the example. We will go into detail in Chapter 6, *Pulling DSC Configurations*, with all steps required to make this work for you. Here, we aim to show you how easy it is to describe a set of disparate components and achieve a fully configured server out of them.

The first step is to make a text file called the SetupPullServer.ps1 file with the following content:

```
# Declare our configuration here
Configuration SetupPullServer
{
# Import a DSCResource here. We will cover this more in chapter 3
Import-DSCResource -ModuleName xPSDesiredStateConfiguration
# Declare the node we are targeting
Node "localhost"
{
  # Declare we need the DSC-Service installed
  WindowsFeature DSCServiceFeature
  {
    Ensure = "Present"
    Name   = "DSC-Service"
  }
  # Declare what settings the pull server should have
  xDscWebService PSDSCPullServer
  {
    Ensure               = "Present"
    State                = "Started"
    EndpointName         = "PSDSCPullServer"
    Port                 = 8080
    CertificateThumbPrint = "AllowUnencryptedTraffic"
    PhysicalPath         =
"$env:SystemDrive\inetpub\wwwroot\PSDSCPullServer"
    ModulePath           =
"$env:PROGRAMFILES\WindowsPowerShell\DscService\Modules"
    ConfigurationPath =
"$env:PROGRAMFILES\WindowsPowerShell\DscService\Configuration"
    DependsOn            = "[WindowsFeature]DSCServiceFeature"
  }
 }
}
```

The next step is to invoke the **DSC Configuration** cmdlet to produce an MOF file. By now, we don't need to show the output MOF file, as we have covered that already. We then run the `Start-DscConfiguration` cmdlet against the resulting folder and the pull server is set up. Remember, we will cover this in detail in `Chapter 6`, *Pulling DSC Configurations*.

A good thing to remember when you eventually try to use this DSC configuration script to make a DSC pull server is that you can't make a client operating system a pull server. If you are working on a Windows 8.1 or 10 desktop while trying out these examples, some of them might not work for you because you are on a desktop OS. For example, the `WindowsFeature` DSC resource works only on the server OS, whereas the `WindowsOptionalFeature` DSC resource operates on the desktop OS. You will have to check each DSC resource to find out what OS or platforms they support, just like you would have to check the release notes of the software to find out the supported system requirements.

Adding MOF files to a pull server

Adding an MOF file to a pull server is slightly more time consuming than using an MOF with the **push mode**. You still compile the MOF with the same steps we outlined in the *Authoring* section earlier in this chapter.

We will walk through an overview of the process of deploying MOFs here, but we will go into far greater detail in `Chapter 6`, *Pulling DSC Configurations*, where we discuss pull servers exclusively. We will also cover some PowerShell functions that will automate most of this work for you.

Pull servers require MOFs to use checksums to determine when an MOF has changed for a given target node. They also require the MOF filename to be the `ConfigurationID` file of the target node. A unique identifier is much easier to work with than the names a given target node is using. This is typically done only once per server and is kept for the lifetime of the server. It is usually decided when configuring the LCM for that target node.

The first step is to take the compiled MOF and rename it with the unique identifier we assigned it when we were creating the configuration for it. In this example, we will assign a newly created GUID, as shown here:

```
    PS C:\Examples> Rename-Item -Path .\TestExample\localhost.mof -NewName
"$([GUID]::NewGuid().ToString()).mof"
    PS C:\Examples> ls .\TestExample\
        Directory: C:\TestExample
    Mode                LastWriteTime       Length Name
    ----                -------------       ------ ----
```

```
    -a---          5/20/2015   10:52 PM        1136 b1948d2b-2b80-4c4a-9913-
ae6dcbf23a4d.mof
```

The next step is to run the `New-DSCCheckSum` cmdlet to generate a checksum for the MOF files in the `TestExample` folder, as shown here:

```
    PS C:\Examples> New-DSCCheckSum -ConfigurationPath .\TestExample\ -
OutPath .\TestExample\ -Verbose
    VERBOSE: Create checksum file
'C:\Examples\TestExample\\b1948d2b-2b80-4c4a-9913-
ae6dcbf23a4d.mof.checksum'
    PS C:\Examples> ls .\TestExample\
        Directory: C:\TestExample
    Mode                LastWriteTime     Length Name
    ----                -------------     ------ ----
    -a---          5/21/2015   10:52 PM        1136 b1948d2b-2b80-4c4a-9913-
ae6dcbf23a4d.mof
    -a---          5/22/2015   10:52 PM          64 b1948d2b-2b80-4c4a-9913-
ae6dcbf23a4d.mof.checksum
    PS C:\Examples> gc .\TestExample\b1948d2b-2b80-4c4a-9913-
ae6dcbf23a4d.mof.checksum
    A62701D45833CEB2A39FE1917B527D983329CA8698951DC094335E6654FD37A6
```

The next step is to copy the checksum file and the MOF file to the pull the server MOF directory. This is typically located in the `C:\Program Files\WindowsPowerShell\DscService\Configuration` path on the pull server, although it's configurable, so it might have been changed in your deployment.

Adding DSC resources to a pull server

In the push mode, you can place a DSC resource module folder in a PowerShell module path (any of the paths defined in the `$env:PSModulePath` path), and things will work out fine. A pull server requires that DSC resources be placed in a specific directory and compressed into a ZIP format with a specific name in order for the pull server to recognize and be able to transfer the resource to the target node.

Here is our example DSC resource in a folder on our system. We are using the experimental `xPSDesiredStateConfiguration` resource provided by Microsoft, but these steps can apply to your custom resources as well:

```
PS C:\Examples> ls .
    Directory: C:\Examples
    Mode                LastWriteTime         Length Name
    ----                -------------         ------ ----
    d----         5/20/2015   10:52 PM
xPSDesiredStateConfiguration
```

The first step is to compress the DSC resource folder into a ZIP file. You may be tempted to use the .NET `System.IO.Compression.Zipfile` classes to compress the folder to a ZIP file. In DSC V4, you cannot use these classes as they create a ZIP file that the LCM cannot read correctly. This is a fault in the DSC code that reads the archive files. However, in DSC V5, they have fixed this so that you can still use `System.IO.Compression.zipfile`. A potentially easier option in PowerShell V5 is to use the built-in `Compress-Archive` cmdlet to accomplish this. The only way to make a ZIP file for DSC V4 is to use either the built-in compression facility in Windows Explorer, a third-party utility such as *7-Zip*, or the COM `Shell.Application` object in a script:

```
PS C:\Examples> ls .
    Directory: C:\Examples
    Mode                LastWriteTime         Length Name
    ----                -------------         ------ ----
    d----         5/20/2015   10:52 PM
xPSDesiredStateConfiguration
    d----         5/20/2015   10:52 PM
xPSDesiredStateConfiguration.zip
```

Once you have your ZIP file, we rename the file to `MODULENAME_#.#.#.#.zip`, where `MODULENAME` is the official name of the module and `#.#.#.#` refers to the version of the DSC resource module we are working with.

> If you start getting confused with version numbers, folder structures, and deployment folders, fear not. We will cover DSC resource internals in more detail in `Chapter 5`, *Pushing DSC Configurations*, and deployment internals in `Chapter 6`, *Pulling DSC Configurations*.

This version is not the version of the DSC resource inside the module but the version of the DSC resource root module. You will find the correct version in the top-level `psd1` file inside the root directory of the module.

Let's take a look at the following example:

```
PS C:\Examples> ls .
    Directory: C:\Examples
Mode                 LastWriteTime     Length Name
----                 -------------     ------ ----
d----         5/20/2015   10:52 PM
xPSDesiredStateConfiguration
d----         5/20/2015   10:52 PM
xPSDesiredStateConfiguration_3.2.0.0.zip
```

As with MOF files, DSC needs a checksum in order to identify each DSC resource. The next step is to run the `New-DscCheckSum` cmdlet against our ZIP file and receive our checksum:

```
PS C:\Examples> New-DSCCheckSum -ConfigurationPath
.\xPSDesiredStateConfiguration_3.2.0.0.zip -OutPath . -Verbose
    VERBOSE: Create checksum file 'C:\Examples\xPSDesiredStateConfiguration
_3.2.0.0.zip.checksum'
    PS C:\Examples> ls .
        Directory: C:\TestExample
    Mode                 LastWriteTime     Length Name
    ----                 -------------     ------ ----
    -a---         5/21/2015   10:52 PM       1136
xPSDesiredStateConfiguration _3.2.0.0.zip
    -a---         5/22/2015   10:52 PM         64
xPSDesiredStateConfiguration _3.2.0.0.zip.checksum
```

The final step is to copy the ZIP file and checksum file up to the `C:\Program Files\WindowsPowerShell\DscService\Modules` path on the pull server.

In order to make the previous steps easier, Microsoft published a set of PowerShell scripts in the `xPSDesiredStateConfiguration` DSC resource to automate these steps. We will cover how to use this in Chapter 6, *Pulling DSC Configurations*.

Once completed, the previous steps provide a working pull server. You configure your target nodes using the steps outlined in the previous section on LCM, and your target nodes will start pulling configurations. If you have more questions about this or want a more automated solution to making your pull server and adding your target nodes, we will be covering this in Chapter 6, *Pulling DSC Configurations*.

Deployment considerations

By this point, we have covered the architecture and the two different ways that we can deploy DSC in your environment. When choosing the deployment method, you should be aware of some additional considerations and observations that have come through experience using DSC in production.

General observations

You will generally use the DSC push mode deployments to test new configurations or perform one-off configurations of servers. While you can use the push mode against several servers at once, you lose the benefits of the pull server.

Setting up a DSC pull server is the best option for a large set of nodes or environments that frequently build and destroy servers. It does have a significant learning curve in setting up the DSC resources and MOF files, but once done, it is reliably repeatable without additional effort.

When using pull servers with PowerShell V4, each target node is assigned a configuration ID that is required to be unique and is expected to stay with that server for its lifetime. There is currently no built-in tracking of configuration IDs inside DSC or in the pull server, and there are no checks to avoid duplicate collisions. This is by design, as it allows greater deployment flexibility.

You can choose to have a unique ID for every target node in your environment or have one single ID for a group of systems. An example of sharing a configuration ID is a web farm that creates and destroys VMs based on demand during certain time periods. Since they all have the same configuration ID, they all get the same configuration with significantly less work on your part (not having to make multiple MOF files and maintain lists of IDs for temporary nodes).

Maintaining a list of used IDs and which targets they refer to is currently up to you. Some have used the active directory IDs for the target node as an identifier. This is awkward to support, as often we run configurations on target nodes before they are joined to an AD domain. We recommend that you use a GUID as an identifier and keep the configuration data files where the node identifiers are kept: in a source control system.

When using pull servers with PowerShell V5, a `RegistrationKeys.txt` file needs to be maintained that holds the registration information from the clients. This allows client nodes to use configuration names instead of configuration IDs, but it introduces another place to keep track of client information. We will cover its setup and use in `Chapter 6`, *Pulling DSC Configurations*.

LCM gotchas

The LCM service runs under the system account and has high privilege access to the system. However, the system account is not a user account, which causes trouble when you assume DSC can perform an action just like you did a moment ago. Common gotchas include accessing network file shares or accessing parts of the system that require user credentials. In PowerShell V4, these will typically fail with a generic **Access Denied**, which will most likely lead you down the wrong path when troubleshooting. Unfortunately, the only way to know this beforehand is to hope that the DSC resource or application you are executing documented the permissions they needed to run in PowerShell V4. Some DSC resources have parameters that accept a `PSCredential` object for this very purpose, so ensure that you inspect examples or the DSC resource itself to find out how to best handle access permissions in PowerShell V4. Trial and error will prove things one way or the other for you here.

This awkwardness is fixed in PowerShell V5, where a new parameter called `PSDSCRunAsCredential` is added to each DSC resource by the **DSC engine**. When specified, this parameter will indicate to DSC that the DSC resource needs to run under alternate credentials. This handles all the problems mentioned in the previous paragraph.

As described in the *Execution* phase in the *The general workflow* section, when first deploying using push or pull and trying out new configurations or troubleshooting existing ones, the frequent executions often cause problems. If the configuration run is interrupted or stopped mid-run, a `pending.mof` file is often left in place. This signals to DSC that a configuration is either in flight or that something else occurred and it should not run. When you try to run another configuration, you get an error saying that a configuration is currently in flight. To solve this, you need to delete the `pending.mof` file before running the `Update-DscConfiguration` or `Start-DscConfiguration -Force` cmdlet.

Deployment mode differences

When used with a DSC pull server, the LCM does a lot of work for you. It will pull down the required DSC resources for your DSC configuration file automatically instead of you having to copy them there yourself. It will also report the status back to the pull server, so you can see the status of all your targets in one place.

When used in the push mode, the LCM does all the work of applying your DSC configuration file for you, but it does not do as much when in the pull mode. It does not auto-download dependent DSC resources for you.

Summary

In this chapter, we identified the three phases of DSC use and two different deployment models. We then covered how the phases and models work together to comprise the architecture of DSC. And lastly, we covered how the LCM and pull server work separately and together.

In the next chapter, you will learn about the syntax of DSC configuration scripts and data files, how to debug and troubleshoot authoring them, and their general best practices.

3
DSC Configuration Files

"Success is not final, failure is not fatal: it is the courage to continue that counts."
- Winston S. Churchill

Throughout the first two chapters, we covered the foundations of configuration management and how DSC works using them. We delved inside the innards of DSC, covering the inner architecture and how the various pieces work together to maintain the state of your environment. By this point, you should have a solid understanding of the *what* and the *why*, and now we start understanding the *how*. We will address the core interface or API you will use with DSC: the DSC configuration script.

In this chapter, we will cover the following topics:

- Defining a DSC configuration script file
- Defining a DSC configuration data file
- Creating reusable DSC configurations
- Debugging and troubleshooting configuration script files

Defining a DSC configuration script file

Now that we're past the abstract concepts and the explanatory architecture, we can start addressing how to use DSC in real-world situations. Thus far in the book, we have been referring to the DSC configuration script files without really getting into the details of what they are. There isn't a specific file or file extension called a **DSC configuration script** file, it's the term used to describe the PowerShell script file that defines a special type of function: **configuration**.

You should be familiar with the general format of a DSC configuration block, as we have covered a few examples so far. Here is a simple one we will use as we move through the chapter. We will expand it to perform more advanced configurations and update it to allow multiple target nodes and use external configuration data:

```
Configuration InstallExampleSoftware
{
  Node "localhost"
  {
   WindowsFeature DotNet
   {
    Ensure = 'Present'
    Name = 'NET-Framework-45-Core'
   }
  }
}
```

While the preceding example is a DSC configuration block, it is not a DSC configuration script file. A DSC configuration block is the set of instructions used to compile the information to an MOF file. This file is a PowerShell script file (a file with the .ps1 or .psm1 extension) that is required to have at least one configuration block defined inside it. Inside the configuration block are the DSC resource import declarations and one or more node declarations. Inside the node declaration is one or more DSC resource blocks, where you define what state is expected on each node. So a DSC configuration block has the actual code, and the configuration script file is your mechanism to making MOF files.

The DSC configuration script files are allowed to have PowerShell code defined before or after the DSC configuration block, which means that a DSC configuration script could be inside a larger script or in a standalone script. We will see examples later on of using DSC configuration script files with and without additional code and the pros and cons of both approaches. To keep things simple, for the rest of the book, we will use the term DSC configuration script file to mean both a configuration block and a configuration script file.

Authoring DSC configuration files

In previous chapters, we stated that you can author configuration files in any text editor you want and how important that is for both cross-platform use and tooling choice freedom. In practice, your choice of text editor largely depends on your preferences and the interactive experience you want as you type. The best thing about authoring files for DSC is that you can pick and choose whichever text editor you want to use at any point in time in your workflow. You don't have to stick with one or the other as you progress in your use of DSC.

When you are first starting out with DSC, or really any new technology, you will benefit from tools that provide you with immediate feedback on whether you are correct or not in the code you are writing. These features are the key to your first forays into authoring configuration files as they provide immediate usefulness without having to look back at the documentation outside the editor. This is invaluable as a first line of defense against bugs and common errors when first starting out, and we will explore more of this in the last section of this chapter as debugging DSC on target nodes is an involved process and not always easy.

Historically, the PowerShell ISE provided you with the best learning experience as it was the only editor available that provided that immediate feedback. It has syntax highlighting for DSC language features and cmdlets as well as for other PowerShell language features. The ISE IntelliSense autocompletes all DSC cmdlets and language features and additionally provides inline help tooltips for DSC resource parameter sets. The ISE parser will automatically evaluate your script in real time for syntax errors and missing parameters.

Since the first edition of this book, *Visual Studio Code* has been released and reached version 1 status. It has rapidly become the default editor of choice for many scripters regardless of the language. The extension model allows many useful extensions to be added, one of which is the PowerShell extension from the PowerShell team. This extension lights up the same syntax highlighting and IntelliSense features as the ISE but releases at a much faster rate than the ISE can. This means bugs are addressed more quickly, and new features come out more frequently than the ISE can as it's tied to the OS release model.

Since we are writing text files, the list of third-party editors is huge and potentially includes anything out there. We are going to mention one in particular here, as its features merit mention all by themselves. *Sublime Text* has advanced textual editing that includes multiple selections, configurable keyboard shortcuts, powerful file and function search and replacement, and a command pallet that allows execution of any feature of *Sublime Text* without the menu navigation. For a better explanation and more examples, go to its website and try it out.

What do I use? Most of the time, use *Sublime Text* and fall back on PowerShell ISE if things go wrong.

DSC automatic variables

When crafting your DSC configuration script and DSC configuration data files, there are a few variables you will use that are predefined and special. These variables are reserved in the sense that DSC will populate the variables with values you provide from your configuration data files at runtime. They provide special functions or features that you can use inside your configuration scripts.

Seeing what these variables look like will be helpful when reading these descriptions, so we will show an example to refer to for each variable as we move through them individually. We will see these example again in the *Defining a DSC configuration data file* section.

AllNodes

The first variable to cover is the $AllNodes variable. $AllNodes refers to the entire collection of nodes defined in a ConfigurationData set. $AllNodes is an array of hash tables that contain the information for all target nodes. The hash table can contain any set of information you need as long as each hash table has a key called NodeName:

```
@{
    AllNodes = @(
    @{
        NodeName = "server1"
    },
    @{
        NodeName = "server2"
    }
    );
}
```

DSC requires NodeName because each hash table represents a target node. This allows us to specify information for a specific node on a granular level. Imagine a set of servers that has to have a file placed in a different path depending on some aspect of the server, so each server has a different path. In each hash table in the $AllNodes array, we can specify a property that has the file path and will be applied to the correct server. More on this in a moment.

The $AllNodes array can be filtered to select only the desired target nodes thanks to the .Where() and .ForEach() methods added in PowerShell V4. You can get as fancy as you want using normal PowerShell filtering syntax to select which nodes are configured at both a global and a granular level. For example, you could have an entry in each target node hash table in the $AllNodes array that defines a **role** for each server and filter on that. Only servers with the **web** role will have IIS installed on them.

If each hash table entry in the $AllNodes array is specific to a target node, what happens if you have a piece of information that can vary between servers but you want a **default** value applied to every server? If you specify a hash table with a value of * for the NodeName key, then all the values in this hash table act as defaults for all target nodes. This allows us to specify a default value but **override** it for a particular target node at will. For example, say, you need to ensure that a specific version of software is installed on all the target nodes, but one server needs to stay locked at a specific version for backward compatibility.

When used properly, the $AllNodes array allows a powerful level of control and flexibility in your deployments.

Node

The next variable to cover is the $Node variable. $Node refers to the specific target node being worked on. It is a particular entry inside the $AllNodes array. Think of the $Node variable as an iteration on the values of the $AllNodes array, so anything inside this variable applies to one node at a time. This doesn't mean that execution of the contents of the $Node variable happens serially across target nodes; it is more a mental model to keep in mind when looking at the configuration scripts.

The $Node variable is a single hash table that has all the values you provided for that target node in your $AllNodes array. For example, we will use the following piece of code pulled from an example we'll use later on, to show how to use ConfigurationData inside our DSC configuration scripts:

```
Package InstallExampleSoftware
{
 Ensure = "Present"
 Name = $Node.ExampleSoftware.Name
 ProductId = $Node.ExampleSoftware.ProductId
 Path = $Node.ExampleSoftware.Path
}
```

It uses the data we define in `ConfigurationData` that we pass to the DSC configuration block. Using the preceding example, this is how we would define it:

```
@{
  AllNodes = @(
  @{
  NodeName = "server1"
  ExampleSoftware = @{
  Name = "ExampleSoftware"
  ProductId = "{b652663b-867c-4d93-bc14-8ecb0b61cfb0}"
  SourcePath = "c:\packages\thesoftware.msi"
  }
  },
  @{
  NodeName = "server2"
  }
  );
}
```

This is the granular level we were just talking about in the `$AllNodes` section. This hash table is free form and can contain any information you want. It can contain nested hash tables or typed information. This is the place where you can fully describe the state of each server as you want it to be. Anything is up for grabs to include, but be careful as there are some rules and syntax you must know when trying to place information here; we will cover this in the *Defining a DSC configuration data file* section later in this chapter.

ConfigurationData

The `$ConfigurationData` variable is a hash table that accepts any data you want. Why would we need another variable that can accept any data? The main difference between this variable and the `$Node` variable is that the `$ConfigurationData` variable is global. It does not contain target node-specific information but information that is applicable to the environment as a whole.

Why is this needed? Looking back at our explanation for the `$AllNodes` variable, we decided whether to install IIS if a server had the `Role` property defined inside each target node hash table. This was something that was applicable per server and changed depending on which server you were examining. There are some things (settings, values, applications, and so on) that are applicable to all servers no matter what and that you want applied on all servers.

An example of this is an application that must be present on all servers and have the same configuration set in its configuration file. Set the values in the `ConfigurationData` hash table once, and it will be available to each target node you run this on instead of having to specify the values in each target node hash in the `$AllNodes` array.

To show how this is specified, we'll steal another example from later on in this chapter but will reduce it just to show the use of `$ConfigurationData`:

```
# data file
@{
 AllNodes = @(
 @{
 NodeName = "server1"
 },
 @{
 NodeName = "server2"
 }
 );
 NonNodeData = @{
 ConfigFileContents = (Get-Content "Config.xml")
 }
}
# end of data file

# beginning of the example configuration
Configuration MyConfiguration
{
 Node $AllNodes.NodeName
 {
 File ConfigFile
 {
 DestinationPath = "c:\foo.txt"
 Contents = $ConfigurationData.NonNodeData.ConfigFileContents
 }
 }
}
# ending of the example configuration
```

The preceding example will not work if you copy and paste it and try to run it, as we have not covered how to pass configuration data to a configuration block yet; this is only an example.

In our data file, we store the contents of _config.xml_ in a variable called $ConfigFileContents and use that to create a file on each target node. Since this is something that is created on all our servers, we only have to specify it once in the $ConfigurationData section.

In practice, this is for data that does not change much and is generally static. This variable is not used as much, as the power of the inheritance and granularity of the $AllNodes array allows a lot of flexibility while reducing the amount of repeated information.

DSC resource import declarations

One last area we need to cover before we get into the syntax of DSC configuration script files is DSC resource imports. When we write our DSC configuration blocks, DSC needs to know what external DSC resources are used in order to validate parameters, ensure the syntax is correct, and record version information about the DSC resources being used.

We use the Import-DSCResource command to tell DSC that the specified DSC resources must be loaded in order to parse this configuration file. These DSC resources must be present on the system in one of the paths listed in the PowerShell module path variable $env:PSModulePath, but they aren't executed when you compile the configuration script to MOF. They are inspected for the parameters needed by each DSC resource so that the DSC configuration script can be validated and then compiled to MOF.

Import-DSCResource

Import-DSCResource is a dynamic keyword, not a cmdlet, contrary to what the verb-noun format suggests. Being a dynamic function, it behaves slightly differently from what you'd expect. Its parameters are not positional, so you have to specify them in order for it to work. It does not exist outside the configuration block, so you can't call it from the PowerShell commandlet line in isolation. This makes discovery using the normal PowerShell tools hard; you can't run Get-Help or Get-Member on it, so you will have to rely on PowerShell documentation. There are only a few parameters for Import-DSCResource: Name, ModuleName, and ModuleVersion.

The `Name` parameter accepts the `ClassName` of the DSC resource or its full name. This is generally the name of the DSC resource that is listed when running `Get-DSCResource`. You can specify one or more values to this parameter. It is preferred to use `ModuleName` because when `Name` is provided, DSC has to iterate over every DSC resource in the module path and search for the resource specified. This is a costly operation that has to happen for each name specified. It will also load the first matching resource, which means if there are different versions, the first one wins and it will miss the other versions. Another option is to use both `ModuleName` and `Name` when you want to specify that only one DSC resource is being used in a specific module. While this may not speed up resolution, it may be clearer to someone coming back to your DSC configuration script as to what exactly is being used.

The `ModuleName` parameter accepts the name of the module containing the DSC resources to be used. This parameter also accepts one or more string values of names to search for, but it also accepts hash tables. The hash table can specify both the name of the module and the version of the module to find. This ensures the correct version is used for your deployment. The flexibility and power of this parameter are coupled with the fact that it is more efficient than the `Name` parameter at finding and parsing the DSC resource specified in the module path.

The `ModuleVersion` parameter is used in WMF 5 and higher to indicate which version of a DSC resource to use. This parameter allows you to be specific about which version your DSC configuration will use. You would most likely use this parameter to **pin** your DSC configuration to a certain version of a DSC resource in order to ensure that you are not broken by new updates or parameter changes. If you are using WMF 4, then you would use the `ModuleName` parameter, as described earlier.

DSC configuration syntax

Now that we have covered how to author the configuration files and special variables and how to import DSC resources, we can cover the syntax of using these elements inside DSC configurations.

In the *Defining a DSC configuration script file* section, we stated that you can have more than one configuration block in a given DSC configuration script file. In the field, you will want to have only one DSC configuration block per file and little to no extra code inside the file besides the DSC configuration block. This is a best practice for many reasons, but first and foremost, it's to support the main purpose of any CM product: *to reduce points of change or variance*.

If we have multiple DSC configuration blocks inside a configuration file, we have multiple points of change that need to be accounted for. If there are multiple configuration blocks in a file, from a readability standpoint, it's hard to know what is going on in the whole file at a glance. It's difficult to determine whether the multiple configuration blocks have a relationship or whether they just happen to be grouped together in the same file. Since there is no tooling to show us without compiling an MOF, it's our responsibility to know.

You may decide to take on the added complexity of having multiple DSC configuration blocks in separate scripts and conditionally pushing them to target nodes using `Start-DscConfiguration`. If you don't know this approach is yet, we will talk more about pushing DSC configurations in `Chapter 5`, *Pushing DSC Configurations*. In a constrained environment where you have complete control and know your environment well, this may work for you as it keeps things organized. It requires a great deal of control and discipline to keep everything straight. Take care to ensure that you do not need to apply two of your DSC configurations at once; if both are applied, they may cancel out each other and cause unintended breakage. You can have DSC partial configurations, which can express multiple configuration blocks for a single target node, but this is only available in PowerShell V5 and is covered in detail later in this chapter. A more appropriate feature to use is the DSC composite resource, which we will cover later in this chapter.

You're probably wondering how one file could possibly describe the entirety of a configuration state for thousands of target nodes. The short answer is the flexible and powerful filtering we can do inside the `$AllNodes` array and the declarative and flexible DSC configuration data files. We can categorize target nodes and decide what state they should have at runtime, and in doing so, keep the separation of the data (the parts that change) from the configuration (the steps to set the states that do not change). We will cover the filtering and other mechanisms available to us inside the DSC configuration script file here and will address what we can do with configuration data in the upcoming *Defining a DSC configuration data file* section.

Earlier in this chapter, we showed you an example DSC configuration block and said we would use it to go into further detail about how it is constructed, and now is the time to do that. We are going to start with the following DSC configuration block, which ensures that a specific version of the .NET framework is installed on the target host, and by the end of the chapter, we will modify it to install an MSI package as well. This shouldn't look too strange to you at this point because we have shown several examples so far. Don't worry if it does, as we will go through each part in detail now:

```
Configuration InstallExampleSoftware
{
Node $AllNodes.Where({$_.Roles -contains 'FooBar'}).NodeName
{
WindowsFeature DotNet
```

```
    {
    Ensure = 'Present'
    Name = 'NET-Framework-45-Core'
    }

    File ConfigFile
    {
    DestinationPath = "c:\foo.txt"
    Contents = $ConfigurationData.NonNodeData.ConfigFileContents
    }

    Package InstallExampleSoftware
    {
    Ensure = "Present"
    Name = $Node.ExampleSoftware.Name
    ProductId = $Node.ExampleSoftware.ProductId
    Path = $Node.ExampleSoftware.Path
    DependsOn = @('[WindowsFeature]DotNet')
    }
    }
}
```

This is the general format or anatomy of the configuration block you will use in your production scripts. While you may or may not use the indenting or brace format of the preceding example, the important thing is that you and your team agree on a code formatting style and stick with it. This will improve the readability of your code and increase the effectiveness of code review and historical examination of changes in the code. The following conventions were used to increase readability in this book and ensure all important parts are clear:

- Opening and closing braces were put on the next line for each function declaration
- The statements within the braces were indented and the closing brace was put on the same indentation level as the header of the function on a line of its own
- Parameter statements had their equal signs aligned to the longest parameter name
- Normal PowerShell coding style guidelines for any inline code written inside these blocks were followed

If you are not used to this, it may seem like a lot of ceremony without function. You will want to keep a tight coding style or format to ensure readability of the script in the months to come. You don't want to come back to the script months later and wonder what it does because of poor formatting or organization. Indenting, newlines, and spacing all seem trivial and inconsequential and best left to programmers to bicker about, but they are the key to ensuring your script is maintainable and will adapt to future modifications. Do not underestimate the value of a well-formatted script when you have to read it months later to find out what is going on with your boss looking over your shoulder.

The configuration keyword

A DSC configuration block starts with declaring the **configuration** keyword and a name for the configuration block. It follows PowerShell function name declaration rules, but otherwise, there are no requirements on what to name it.

Choose the name of the DSC configuration block carefully as it will not only be how you refer to what configuration is applied, but by default, it will also be the name of the output folder where the MOF files are placed after compilation. You can change the name and path using the OutputPath parameter. Technically, it does not have to be unique as the additional metadata written to the MOF file on compilation helps identify what exactly is deployed to target nodes, but it helps to be as descriptive as possible.

The DSC configuration block can be treated like a PowerShell function declaration in that it accepts parameter statements and contains code inside it. This is important to note, as this means you can control how the DSC configuration block behaves both by the parameter statements defined as well as the defining custom parameters.

There are two built-in parameters that are always present in any configuration block you define: the ConfigurationData and the OutputPath parameters. We just mentioned the OutputPath parameter. The ConfigurationData parameter allows you to specify the environmental data to your function, which we covered in the DSC automatic variables section. You can define custom parameters by adding a param statement to your configuration block:

```
Configuration InstallExampleSoftware
{
param(
$computer,
$ExampleSoftwareName,
$ExampleSoftwareProductId,
$ExampleSoftwarePath,
$ConfigFileContents)
```

```
Node $computer
{
WindowsFeature DotNet
{
Ensure = 'Present'
Name = 'NET-Framework-45-Core'
}

File ConfigFile
{
DestinationPath = "c:\foo.txt"
Contents = $ConfigFileContents
}

Package InstallExampleSoftware
{
Ensure = "Present"
Name = $ExampleSoftwareName
ProductId = $ExampleSoftwareProductId
Path = $ExampleSoftwarePath
DependsOn = @('[WindowsFeature]DotNet')
}
}
}
```

You would execute the preceding `configuration block` as follows:

```
InstallExampleSoftware -computer "foo1" -ExampleSoftwareName 'FooSoftware'
-ExampleSoftwareProductId '4909a5d0-b3c3-4a98-be90-a0dcee7c4eef' -
ExampleSoftwarePath 'e:\source\foosoftware.msi' -ConfigFileContents (Get-
Content "Config.xml")
```

For the most part, you will likely prefer to not use custom parameter statements and rely on the more powerful $AllNodes or $Node variables instead, as they provide superior flexibility and do not require you to provide them inline. We will cover examples that prove this statement in the *Defining a DSC configuration data file* section later in this chapter.

The Node keyword

The **Node** keyword is confusing at first glance because we've already said there is a special variable called $Node earlier in the chapter. It is further confusing because in our previous example, we have both the Node keyword and the $Node variable in use. It's not so confusing, however, once you know that one is a PowerShell keyword and the other is a reserved variable.

Remember, the $Node variable is used to grab specific configuration data for the target node. As shown in the example, you use it like any other PowerShell object, accessing properties and values using normal syntax. The Node keyword selects the nodes using the filter statement we provide and builds the $Node variable for each target node. In the example, we provide this filter:

```
Node $AllNodes.Where({$_.Roles -contains 'FooBar'}).NodeName
```

There are a couple things going on here; let's take it one by one. First is the Node keyword, which takes an array of strings that represent the names of the target nodes. We provide the array of names using a PowerShell filter called Where() which accepts a script block. Inside that script block, we evaluate each item in the $AllNodes array and inspect whether it matches our filter. In this case, we are looking for all items that have a role called FooBar and are getting the value for the key NodeName.

This is the power we were talking about earlier, when we explained how DSC puts all the configuration state information for one target node inside one file. We can put all the information we need inside the configuration data files, and inside the DSC configuration block, we can inspect and apply filters on it and decide what gets applied when and where. You will notice that the configuration block doesn't need to change when our target node list changes. It only needs to change when our example property role changes, which makes sense because a change of this importance would require a change in our deployment methodology. Even then, it's not too big a change because it's either an additive or a subtractive change; we either add a new node block for a new role or remove a node block for a role we don't need anymore. The Roles property is an example here; it can be anything you need.

Before we move on, we should go back to that Node keyword statement again. This statement can be as complex or as simple as you need. You can get away with just passing the $AllNodes array as is:

```
Node $AllNodes.NodeName
```

Or, you can just have a specific hostname:

```
Node "server1.company.com"
```

It's up to you how complex or simple you want it. A general rule is to keep it as simple as possible to increase readability and decrease the chance of bugs in your filtering logic. If you notice that your filter statement is more than a line or two, you might want to look at splitting your declaration into two node blocks. It is a good indication that there is enough difference there to warrant the break.

DSC resource statements

Inside the Node keyword block are the actual statements that will determine the configuration state of your target nodes. This is where you'll use the DSC DSL and DSC resources to describe the different operations, settings, software, and other aspects of your nodes. This is the last and most important step in the syntax of DSC configuration script files, as this is the part that is parsed by DSC and compiled to MOF using DSC resources. There are a lot of moving parts here but not much to explain in general as this will be very implementation-specific. It would not be much use to you to regurgitate help file documentation for each DSC resource, but we will cover some best practices here.

It is very easy to hardcode or write down the exact text of configuration data next to the DSC resource parameters that are using it. You must identify these hardcoded values and extract them to configuration data variables ($AllNodes, $Node, or $ConfigurationData). We covered the separation of environmental data and structural data in Chapter 2, *DSC Architecture*, in the *Configuration data* section, and this is where it comes into play. We want to take all the environmental data out of our DSC configuration script file and inside the node blocks is where it most often crops up. Fortunately, DSC makes this easy to extract using the DSC special variables. We will move more into the format of specifying the configuration data in the *Defining a DSC configuration data file* section of this chapter.

A common mistake is to put the PowerShell code inside the node block that performs some kind of decision logic for the target node. You might need to parse a string, figure out a version number, or resolve a path, and so on. There are many different things you might try to accomplish inside the node block because it's so easy to drop down to PowerShell and get it done. You must resist this temptation because adding logic that needs to be executed on the target node here breaks the utility and power of the DSC engine. DSC allows idempotent configuration of a target node no matter how many times it is run on the target node. The logic put into the DSC configuration block or node block is not part of the DSC resources, and so it is not executed on the target node but instead on the computer you compiled the MOF on. Remember, the DSC resource is the part that does the actual work of determining and applying the state, and the code that you put in the node block is never seen by the DSC resources. When you go to run DSC on the target node again, your code will not be re-evaluated.

For example, you write some code to determine what version software to install on a target node based on a file on a remote server. When you compile your DSC configuration to MOF, that value is stored, as is in the MOF file. When applied to the target node, that value is used. If run again, that value does not change because the MOF was not regenerated.

There are some cases where code can be placed inside a node block and not be a problem. Code or conditional logic inside this area that makes decisions based on your deployment processes can be very useful and powerful here, for example, code that determines whether a software package is installed on test servers or production servers or code that determines which set of servers are web servers or database servers, or both. These are examples of environmental choices whose data is stored in your `ConfigurationData` files, but the decision to use it lies in your DSC configuration script.

If you are not supposed to put any code inside the Node or configuration blocks, where should it be put? If you have code in these places, it is a clear sign that you should be creating a DSC resource that handles this logic or decision-making. The DSC resource is the best place to understand how to apply this logic in an idempotent manner. In the next chapter, we will cover how to create DSC resources, so stay tuned.

DSC configuration script file example

Now that we have covered the different parts of a DSC configuration block syntax, we can finally create a DSC configuration script. As we said earlier, we are going to modify it to install an MSI package as well as to ensure the .NET 4.5 framework is installed. We are going to use the package DSC resource to accomplish this. We are also going to change things up (such as the real world often does) and make this a bit more complicated by ensuring our target nodes all have a state file using the file DSC resource and an environment variable that points to the location of the state file using the environment DSC resource. Before we start writing our DSC configuration script file, let's examine each resource and determine the information needed to use it. The package DSC resource accepts the `Name`, `ProductId`, and `Path` to the MSI as parameters, along with some others we won't need to use in our example. This information is likely to change frequently as the software is updated or the source location is changed, so it makes sense to take advantage of the DSC special variables to keep this information out of our DSC configuration script file.

If you are looking at the `ProductId` parameter and scratching your head at what it is, you wouldn't be the first one. `ProductId` refers to the `ProductCode` of the MSI you are installing. Why the PowerShell team used `ProductId` and not the actual term `ProductCode` is unknown, but there is probably a good reason somewhere. You can obtain the `ProductCode` by querying the MSI itself using PowerShell, opening the MSI in an MSI reader program such as `Orca.msi`, or installing the MSI on a test system and inspecting the registry for the value. Included in the book source code is some PowerShell code to do this. The file DSC resource requires that at least `DestinationPath` be specified, but since we are trying to create a file, we need to specify file for Type. The environment DSC resource requires `Name` and `Value` to operate, so we fill in those with the name of the variable we want and the location to the state file.

The file and environment DSC resources will be applied to all our servers, but we will only install the MSI package to those with the FooBar role. This means we will split these DSC resource statements into two node blocks, so we can filter appropriately.

The last thing to discuss is the parts that make this a script file. We are going to be compiling this DSC configuration block into MOF files frequently, every time an environment variable changes. We won't want to perform the steps we did in Chapter 2, *DSC Architecture*, over and over again on the command line. The purpose of both PowerShell and DSC is to automate, after all! So, we will put our DSC configuration block inside a PowerShell script file and wrap the invocations of the configuration block. PowerShell script files accept parameter statements that give you the ability to specify custom parameters, which allow us to specify things such as the path in which to put the MOF files and environmental data.

So, we will begin our script with a set of parameters that represent our OutputPath and ConfigData. Then, we will specify our DSC configuration block and then end the script with the configuration block invocation. We will continue to build on this script as we move along in the chapter, and the final version of it is included in the book source code:

```
# beginning of script
[CmdletBinding()]
param(
 [Parameter()]$OutputPath = [IO.Path]::
 Combine($PSScriptRoot, 'InstallExampleSoftware'),
 [Parameter()]$ConfigData
)
Configuration InstallExampleSoftware
{
 Node $AllNodes.NodeName
 {
 WindowsFeature DotNet
 {
 Ensure = 'Present'
 Name = 'NET-Framework-45-Core'
 }
 }

 Node $AllNodes.Where({$_.Roles -contains 'FooBar'}).NodeName
 {
 Environment AppEnvVariable
 {
 Ensure = 'Present'
 Name = 'ConfigFileLocation'
 Value = $Node.ExampleSoftware.ConfigFile
 }
```

```
File ConfigFile
{
DestinationPath = $Node.ExampleSoftware.ConfigFile
Contents = $ConfigurationData.NonNodeData.ConfigFileContents
}

Package InstallExampleSoftware
{
Ensure = 'Present'
Name = $Node.ExampleSoftware.Name
ProductId = $Node.ExampleSoftware.ProductId
Path = $Node.ExampleSoftware.SourcePath
DependsOn = @('[WindowsFeature]DotNet')
}
}
}

InstallExampleSoftware -OutputPath $OutputPath -ConfigurationData
$ConfigData
# script end
```

All the elements we planned to include are present. We declared our configuration block, set our DSC resource imports, declared our Node filter statements and listed the DSC resource blocks we needed. And in the package DSC resource, we specified the configuration data, so we kept a clear separation of environment data from our structural data.

We have a production quality script that is maintainable and separated from environmental data, but if you tried to run it as is, it would fail. We don't know how to pass configuration data to the file yet! We are going to address how to make and use configuration data now.

Defining a DSC configuration data file

In the previous sections, we covered using DSC configuration script files with DSC configuration data, but we have not covered exactly how to specify configuration data or how it is stored separately from the configuration scripts. In this section, we will cover this and the rules applying to what configuration data can be specified as well as some best practices on using it.

When we refer to DSC configuration data, we are referring to any environmental data supplied to the DSC configuration function. This may be slightly confusing, as we mentioned a DSC special variable called $ConfigurationData earlier in this chapter. Try to remember that when we refer to the DSC configuration data term, we are referring to the entirety of the data supplied to the configuration function, not just the data available through the special variable called $ConfigurationData.

DSC configuration data can be supplied either through a hash table or as a PowerShell manifest file (a file with a .psd1 extension) passed to the configuration function parameter. For the majority of the time, you will be using data files instead of the hash table approach, as these increase flexibility by allowing you to switch data files when compiling to MOF.

Some of the examples you might see online when first learning about DSC show passing the data directly to the DSC configuration block and defining that data in the same file. Although probably done to simplify the example, it defeats the point of CM that we covered in the first chapter and provides bad examples for new users. In this book, we will cover in detail how to pass configuration data to DSC configuration blocks from external files, but you should keep in mind that you can also do this from inside your script using an ordinary hash table.

Authoring DSC configuration data files

As with DSC configuration scripts, you can use any text editor to author them. Since there is little else needed other than some syntax highlighting, you can choose anything you desire. By convention, we use the .psd1 extension to signify that this is a data manifest file. You could technically name it anything you want, as you are responsible for loading the file, but in practice, this is not good form. It is best to keep with certain expected conventions, as doing that aids discovery and maintainability later on.

Configuration data syntax

The DSC ConfigurationData hash table must have an AllNodes key whose value is an array, with hash tables with one key named NodeName. This is a hard requirement; the key must be spelled correctly, as DSC looks for that specific key. The error message DSC outputs when this key is incorrect is hard to figure out at first in order to be sure to be correct in this to save some headaches later on. A very contrived example is as follows:

```
[PS]> $ConfigData = @{
>>> AllNodes = @(
>>> @{
```

```
>>> Node = "foo"
>>> }
>>> )
>>> }
[PS]>
[PS]> configuration InstallExampleSoftware
>>> {
>>> Node "localhost"
>>> {
>>> WindowsFeature DotNet
>>> {
>>> Ensure = 'Present'
>>> Name = 'NET-Framework-45-Core'
>>> }
>>> }
>>> }
[PS]>
[PS]> InstallExampleSoftware -ConfigurationData $ConfigData
ValidateUpdate-ConfigurationData : all elements of AllNodes
need to be hash table and has a property 'NodeName'.
At
C:\Windows\system32\WindowsPowerShell\v1.0\Modules\
PSDesiredStateConfiguration\PSDesiredStateConfiguration.psm1:1816
char:30
+ ... $dataValidated = ValidateUpdate-ConfigurationData
$ConfigurationData
+ ~~~~~~~~~~~~~~~~~~~~~~~~~~~~~~~~~~~~~~~~~~~~~~~~~~~~~~
 + CategoryInfo : InvalidOperation: (:)
 [Write-Error], InvalidOperationException
 + FullyQualifiedErrorId : ConfiguratonDataAllNodesNeedHashtable,
 ValidateUpdate-ConfigurationData
[PS]>
```

The AllNodes array will contain one or more hash tables that are required to have one key called NodeName. Again, including this key and spelling it correctly is important for the same reasons as discussed previously. A special hash table may be included that uses * as the value for NodeName instead of an actual node name. This special hash table acts as the default value for all the other hash table nodes. This allows you to specify sensible defaults or values that apply to all target nodes, while still allowing the individual target node hash tables to override the values:

```
@{
 AllNodes = @(
 @{
 NodeName = "server1"
 Roles = @('Foobar')
 ExampleSoftware = @{
```

```
Name = "ExampleSoftware"
ProductId = "{b652663b-867c-4d93-bc14-8ecb0b61cfb0}"
SourcePath = "c:\packages\thesoftware.msi"
ConfigFile = "c:\foo.txt"
}
},
@{
NodeName = "server2"
}
);
NonNodeData = @{
ConfigFileContents = (Get-Content "Config.xml")
}
}
```

There are two ways in which you can assign configuration data to a DSC configuration block: by a variable or by a file. Variable syntax usage is fairly straightforward and easy to specify but is hard to maintain in the long term. The data is separate from the DSC configuration block but is still present in the file, so we have not gotten much separation and insulation from change. If the data changes, we still have to edit our configuration file, so we really haven't separated much. Data file syntax is slightly more complex but is more flexible and easier to maintain in the long run. It fully separates the data from the configuration file.

The variable syntax

You can assign the hash table to a variable and pass the variable to the configuration parameter, as follows:

```
$TheData = @{
AllNodes = @(
@{
NodeName = "server1"
Roles = @('Foobar')
ExampleSoftware = @{
Name = "ExampleSoftware"
ProductId = "{b652663b-867c-4d93-bc14-8ecb0b61cfb0}"
SourcePath = "c:\packages\thesoftware.msi"
ConfigFile = "c:\foo.txt"
}
},
@{
NodeName = "server2"
}
);
NonNodeData = @{
```

```
ConfigFileContents = (Get-Content "Config.xml")
  }
}
InstallExampleSoftware -ConfigurationData $TheData
```

You can also assign the hash table directly to the configuration function:

```
InstallExampleSoftware -ConfigurationData @{
  AllNodes = @(
  @{
  NodeName = "server1"
  Roles = @('Foobar')
  ExampleSoftware = @{
  Name = "ExampleSoftware"
  ProductId = "{b652663b-867c-4d93-bc14-8ecb0b61cfb0}"
  SourcePath = "c:\packages\thesoftware.msi"
  ConfigFile = "c:\foo.txt"
  }
  },
  @{
  NodeName = "server2"
  }
  );
  NonNodeData = @{
  ConfigFileContents = (Get-Content "Config.xml")
  }
}
```

The data file syntax

A DSC configuration data file is a PowerShell manifest file (a file with a `.psd1` extension) that contains a single hash table. This hash table follows the same rules as the preceding hash table, with the exception of not being able to specify a variable name inside the file.

To create a data file, create a new file with a `.psd1` extension and start adding the hash table like the ones in the following example. Note the catchall wildcard `NodeName` in the first hash table, whose values apply to all other hash tables, as discussed in the DSC special variables section earlier. Also, note that the `server2` hash table overrides the default `ExampleSoftware` entry and specifies a new path for the MSI:

```
# beginning of data file
@{
  AllNodes = @(
  @{
  NodeName = "server1"
```

```
Roles = @('Foobar')
ExampleSoftware = @{
Name = "ExampleSoftware"
ProductId = "{b652663b-867c-4d93-bc14-8ecb0b61cfb0}"
SourcePath = "c:\packages\thesoftware.msi"
ConfigFile = "c:\foo.txt"
}
},
@{
NodeName = "server2"
Roles = @('Foobar')
ExampleSoftware = @{
Name = "ExampleSoftware"
ProductId = "{b652663b-867c-4d93-bc14-8ecb0b61cfb0}"
SourcePath = "e:\packages\thesoftware.msi"
ConfigFile = "e:\foo.txt"
}
},
@{
NodeName = "server3"
Roles = @('Wakka')
}
);
NonNodeData = @{
ConfigFileContents = (Get-Content "Config.xml")
}}
# ending of data file
```

We can now use this data section with the DSC configuration script we defined in the *Defining a DSC configuration script file* section, and it will work. We do this by saving the preceding hash table to a text file and passing that file to the configuration function we defined:

```
InstallExampleSoftware -ConfigurationData c:\exampledatafile.psd1
```

By specifying the data inside a configuration data file, you gain the flexibility of separating data from logic. We covered this in Chapter 2, *DSC Architecture*, and here we really see its power. Imagine an environment of a thousand servers divided into test, staging, and production. You could have one configuration data file per environment: test.psd1, staging.psd1, and production.psd1 and have one DSC configuration script called install.psd1. Each of the .psd1 files has a list of target nodes in it along with all the environment-specific configuration information in it. When compiling to MOF, all environment-specific information is coded and handled.

Allowable DSC configuration content

DSC configuration data files follow the same restricted language set of rules that PowerShell data sections have. A PowerShell data section is a block of text that contains only data and a limited subset of the general PowerShell language.

The allowed code is limited to the following:

All PowerShell operators, with the exception of -match:

- `If`, `else`, and `elseIf` statements.
- The following automatic variables:
  - `$PSCulture`
  - `$PSUICulture`
  - `$True`
  - `$False`
  - `$Null`
  - Comments
  - Pipelines
- Statements separated by semicolons.
- Any cmdlets that you permit explicitly in a data section by using the `SupportedCommand` parameter.

This effectively means that there is little code you can put inside a DSC configuration data file by default. While this sounds like a bad limitation, in practice, it's a good thing as it prevents you from trying to put too much logic in what should be a data only file. Remember, every time we covered why you should be putting the decision-making logic inside DSC resources: it all applies here.

There is one case where you might want some small bits of code to be inside DSC configuration data files. Since we are dealing with environmental data, you may have different application configuration files, artifacts, or an installation file path to include in your data files depending on which environment or aspects of a target node you are operating on. Choosing which sets of data to include in your file may be something you need to do from time to time. For example, a production web server may have a different `web.config` file than the development web server, possibly in different locations as well. Keeping in mind the list we just covered, we will notice that we can't include cmdlet names inside the file. If this is the case, how can we use conditional logic?

The trick is in changing how we load the DSC configuration data file. We've already covered loading external data files by passing their path to the configuration function parameter `ConfigurationData`, and we can build on that to pass any configuration data we want.

Creating reusable DSC configurations

So far, we have been working with singular DSC configuration script files and DSC configuration blocks. We have taken an approach of one DSC configuration block per script file and one script file per environment. We covered why this was a best practice in the earlier sections, and at this point, you've probably tried out a couple on your own using what we have done so far. You are likely realizing that these script files can grow very large, containing hundreds of lines of code with large sections of just DSC resource declaration statements.

This is a common problem with CM. The world is complex and messy, and declaring it in text files sounds easy at first, but it becomes difficult to maintain if all you have is one big ball of lines without any organization. If you have developed scripts or code in any language, you are familiar with a common solution to the **big ball of mud** problem, encapsulation. Encapsulation involves extracting the common or related parts to reusable components and then referencing those components in all the different places they are needed. This reduces the complexity of maintaining the code while increasing the flexibility of its use across your code base. We can apply this technique to DSC in a few different ways to varying degrees of success.

Other CM products, such as Puppet and Chef, provide several features that address this need with things like file inheritance or function includes. They allow you to bundle a set of steps to bring a target node into compliance in a reusable package that can be referenced in many other configuration scripts. The actual implementation and feature set vary with which vendor you choose.

Since DSC is still a young product, it is missing some of the features that other products that have been out there longer have. This isn't a criticism, just a statement of what features are provided out-of-the-box with DSC. There are some ways we can get the encapsulation we desire using the features DSC has now, using either nested DSC configurations or DSC composite resources. We'll cover those now.

Nested DSC configurations

The easiest way to start organizing your DSC configuration script is to use **Nested DSC configurations**. Nested DSC configurations use the encapsulation technique by organizing related code inside one DSC configuration block, then referencing that DSC configuration block inside another DSC configuration block, which is a set of DSC resource statements and code grouped together into a single DSC configuration block. You can then reference this DSC configuration block inside another DSC configuration block.

Nested DSC configuration syntax

Think of using nested DSC configurations as writing PowerShell functions. Each PowerShell function encompasses a certain purpose just like a DSC configuration block encompasses a certain set of configuration instructions. If we look at the example in code_example_05.ps1, we can see that setting the environment variable and creating the config file are related and tied together. If we encapsulate them together, we can just reference a single block of code instead of a list of DSC resources. Let's use code_example_5.ps1 and apply the nested DSC configuration method to it:

```
[CmdletBinding()]
param(
 [Parameter()]$OutputPath = [IO.Path]::Combine($PSScriptRoot,
'InstallExampleSoftware'),
 [Parameter()]$ConfigData
)

Configuration ImportantSoftwareConfig
{
 param($ConfigFile, $ConfigFileContents)

 Environment AppEnvVariable
 {
 Ensure = 'Present'
 Name = 'ConfigFileLocation'
 Value = $ConfigFile
 }

 File ConfigFile
 {
 DestinationPath = $ConfigFile
 Contents = $ConfigFileContents
 }
}

Configuration InstallExampleSoftware
```

```
{
Node $AllNodes.NodeName
 {

WindowsFeature DotNet
 {
Ensure = 'Present'
Name = 'NET-Framework-45-Core'
 }
 }

Node $AllNodes.Where({$_.Roles -contains 'FooBar'}).NodeName
 {
ImportantSoftwareConfig SetImportantValues
 {
ConfigFile = $Node.ExampleSoftware.ConfigFile
ConfigFileContents = $ConfigurationData.NonNodeData.ConfigFileContents
 }

Package InstallExampleSoftware
 {
Ensure = 'Present'
Name = $Node.ExampleSoftware.Name
ProductId = $Node.ExampleSoftware.ProductId
Path = $Node.ExampleSoftware.SourcePath
DependsOn = @('[WindowsFeature]DotNet')
 }
 }
}
InstallExampleSoftware -OutputPath $OutputPath -ConfigurationData
$ConfigData
```

We immediately see the benefit of encapsulating a set of configuration instructions inside separate DSC configurations when we examine InstallExampleSoftware. All the work needed to get the **important** environment variable set is encapsulated inside the ImportantSoftwareConfig nested DSC configuration, and the main InstallExampleSoftware is able to deal with the rest of the configuration. We now clearly see that setting the environment variable and creating the config file are related and dependent on each other, and we can reference this block wherever we need to. It is now a reusable piece of code.

Nested DSC configuration limitations

There are some limitations to nested DSC configurations. As we see in the previous example, we have created a reusable piece of code, but it's still in the same file as the original DSC configuration block. We haven't reduced the lines of code needed in the file; we've just moved them around. We have increased the modularity of the code (the code can be used in several places by just referencing the method signature), but we still have a file with lots of lines of code. This may become hard to read as the file gets larger. Frequently, you will have to understand the entire file to know what will be executed, which gets harder and harder as the line count increases.

Your first instinct is most likely to cut the `ImportantSoftwareConfig` DSC configuration block and put it in a separate file. Once you do that, you will notice more limitations. There aren't any import statements for nested DSC configurations, so you will have to dot-source the separate file in your main configuration file, as shown in the following snippet:

```
./importantsofwareconfig.ps1

Configuration InstallExampleSoftware
{
 Node $AllNodes.Nodename
<#...#>
}
```

This introduces more work for you. You have to locate the dependent configuration file and ensure that it exists before you continue. If you make a lot of them, it will become harder for you to keep track of all the files.

Even if you get the **dot-sourcing** approach to work, there are some functional problems with it. There have been isolated bug reports that some parameters aren't parsed when a nested DSC configuration exists outside the main configuration file. These reports seem to have been cleared up by the latest WMF 4 release, which occurred on May 28, 2015, so make sure you are at least on that release if you intend to use them.

Using `DependsOn` does not work for nested configurations at all in WMF 4, as reported here in the **PowerShell Connect** bug tracker: `https://connect.microsoft.com/PowerShell/feedback/details/812943/dsc-cannot-set-dependson-to-a-nested-configuration`. This has been corrected in WMF 5.0, and to some extent, though there are still some reported bugs in the patched version of WMF 4.0 on *WS2012 R2*.

Thankfully, these limitations are addressed by the feature we introduce in the next section, called **DSC composite resources**.

DSC composite resources

Why are we mentioning resources in the chapter on DSC configuration files when we are covering DSC resources in the next chapter? This is a good question that is awkward to answer because of the confusing name choices that were made to describe this feature. Once we get the definitions out of the way, things will become much clearer.

A DSC composite resource is a DSC configuration block that is bundled up in a DSC resource PowerShell module folder structure that can be reused in other DSC configuration script files. While the authoring and syntax are slightly different, the usage of a DSC composite resource is exactly like a DSC resource. I assume the naming stemmed from this similarity in implementation.

Why use DSC composite resources?

When you convert a set of DSC configuration blocks into a reusable DSC composite resource, you abstract the complexity of configuration that targets nodes or pieces of software and improves the manageability of your configuration scripts.

If this sounds confusing, it's because it is confusing to explain without an example to look at. If you look at the DSC configuration script in *Defining a DSC configuration script file* section of this chapter, you will see several DSC resources being used to declare the desired state of a target node. We split them into two node blocks because only some of the target nodes should have ExampleSoftware installed on them and all of them should have .NET installed, a specific environment variable set, and a specific file created. Let's imagine that we need to install another piece of software, called TheRealSoftwareStuff, software that has its own list of dependencies that are different from ExampleSoftware. We would have a long list of statements with a complicated DependsOn dependency list.

We've mentioned DependsOn several times without specifically calling it out. DependsOn is a parameter all DSC resources implement. This allows DSC to execute the DSC resources in an expected order. If DependsOn is not specified, then DSC does not guarantee the order in which it executes the DSC resources defined.

Adding to the middle of this list would require reordering the entire dependency tree and copying and pasting entries until it looked right, which we could get wrong. Wouldn't it be simpler and less error-prone if we were able to group the dependencies and steps into separate blocks? If we could do that, our dependency tree would suddenly become a lot smaller, and only the parts that matter to the software we are installing would be present.

We are going to take the example in the script file example, add `TheRealSoftwareStuff` software to it and then split it up into DSC composite resources. If you're thinking I didn't explain anything about the earlier remark of how DSC composite resources have to be packaged specially and it's hard to get right, don't worry; I will get to that. It's easier to understand if we look first at why you would want to do this. I won't copy the original here, as you can look at the *Defining a DSC configuration script file* section for that. Here is the modified script before we start to encapsulate the code. This example can be used with the following:

```
# beginning of script
[CmdletBinding()]
param(
 [Parameter()]$OutputPath = [IO.Path]::
 Combine($PSScriptRoot, 'InstallExampleSoftware'),
 [Parameter()]$ConfigData
)

Configuration InstallExampleSoftware
{
 Node $AllNodes.NodeName
 {
 WindowsFeature DotNet
 {
 Ensure = 'Present'
 Name = 'NET-Framework-45-Core'
 }
 }

 Node $AllNodes.Where({$_.Roles -contains 'FooBar'}).NodeName
 {
 Environment AppEnvVariable
 {
 Ensure = 'Present'
 Name = 'ConfigFileLocation'
 Value = $Node.ExampleSoftware.ConfigFile
 }

 File ConfigFile
 {
 DestinationPath = $Node.ExampleSoftware.ConfigFile
 Contents = $ConfigurationData.NonNodeData.ConfigFileContents
 }

 Package InstallExampleSoftware
 {
 Ensure = 'Present'
 Name = $Node.ExampleSoftware.Name
```

```
ProductId = $Node.ExampleSoftware.ProductId
Path = $Node.ExampleSoftware.SourcePath
DependsOn = @('[WindowsFeature]DotNet')
}
}

Node $AllNodes.Where({$_.Roles -contains 'RealStuff'}).NodeName
{
WindowsFeature IIS
{
Ensure = 'Present'
Name = 'Web-Server'
}

WindowsFeature IISConsole
{
Ensure = 'Present'
Name = 'Web-Mgmt-Console'
DependsOn = '[WindowsFeature]IIS'
}

WindowsFeature IISScriptingTools
{
Ensure = 'Present'
Name = 'Web-Scripting-Tools'
DependsOn = @('[WindowsFeature]IIS',
'[WindowsFeature]IISConsole')
}

WindowsFeature AspNet
{
Ensure = 'Present'
Name = 'Web-Asp-Net'
DependsOn = @('[WindowsFeature]IIS')
}

Package InstallRealStuffSoftware
{
Ensure = 'Present'
Name = $Node.RealStuffSoftware.Name
ProductId = $Node.RealStuffSoftware.ProductId
Path = $Node.RealStuffSoftware.Source
DependsOn = @('[WindowsFeature]IIS', '[WindowsFeature]AspNet')
}
}

}
```

```
InstallExampleSoftware -OutputPath $OutputPath -ConfigurationData
$ConfigData
# script end
```

It's obvious that this will get quite long as we keep adding software and other features. If we need to insert a new IIS feature, it has to be inserted in the dependency chain of the IIS feature set as well as before the MSI package install. We also need to remember to keep the chain of steps between the `ExampleSoftware` install and `RealStuffSoftware` separated and not mix any steps between the two. In a long script, this may not be apparent when you come back to it after months of successful use.

We can reduce this complexity by grouping these declarations into DSC composite resources. In the new approach, shown as follows, we replace the long list of declarations with one DSC composite resource declaration. Note that we put the configuration data we used earlier as parameters to the parameter declarations. We will read more about this when we get to the syntax in the next section:

```
# beginning of script
[CmdletBinding()]
param(
 [Parameter()]$OutputPath = [IO.Path]::Combine($PSScriptRoot,
'InstallExampleSoftware'),
 [Parameter()]$ConfigData
)

Configuration InstallExampleSoftware
{
 Import-DSCResource -Module ExampleSoftwareDscResource
 Import-DSCResource -Module RealStuffDscResource

 Node $AllNodes.NodeName
 {
 WindowsFeature DotNet
 {
 Ensure = 'Present'
 Name = 'NET-Framework-45-Core'
 }
 }

 Node $AllNodes.Where({$_.Roles -contains 'FooBar'}).NodeName
 {
 ExampleSoftwareDscResource InstallExampleSoftware
 {
 Name = $Node.ExampleSoftware.Name
 ProductId = $Node.ExampleSoftware.ProductId
 Path = $Node.ExampleSoftware.Source
 ConfigFile = $Node.ExampleSoftware.ConfigFile
```

```
ConfigFileContents =
$ConfigurationData.NonNodeData.ConfigFileContents
}
}


Node $AllNodes.Where({$_.Roles -contains 'RealStuff'}).NodeName
{
RealStuffDscResource InstallRealStuffSoftware
{
Name = $Node.RealStuffSoftware.Name
ProductId = $Node.RealStuffSoftware.ProductId
Path = $Node.RealStuffSoftware.Source
}
}


}

InstallExampleSoftware -OutputPath $OutputPath -ConfigurationData
$ConfigData
```

The DSC composite resource syntax

The syntax for a DSC composite resource is exactly the same as a DSC configuration block. This makes sense because they are, in effect, the same thing. This is great because it allows you to copy and paste your existing working DSC configuration blocks and encapsulate them inside reusable components without much modification.

The exception to the statement that the syntax is the same is that you do not include the node block inside a DSC composite resource declaration. Since the DSC composite resource is being used inside the **main** DSC configuration block, it inherits the target node it's being applied to.

Remember when we covered the syntax of a DSC configuration block and said that you could use parameters with a DSC configuration block just like a normal PowerShell function? And that you normally wouldn't because the other DSC features, such as the DSC special variables, are so much more powerful that you don't really need them? Well, with DSC composite resources, the opposite is true. The parameter statement is the entry point for your DSC composite resource and the only way to get configuration data or other information inside it. Any data or variables you expect to use inside the DSC composite resource have to come through the parameter statements.

The DSC composite resource folder structure

A DSC composite resource relies on a set of folders and files that have to be in their exact correct places in order to work successfully.

 Before continuing, ensure that you are familiar with creating PowerShell v2 modules.

A DSC composite resource can be described as a PowerShell module inside a root PowerShell module. The root PowerShell module is required to declare this as a DSC composite resource to the DSC engine; it itself does not usually contain any code, nor does it actually contain any DSC configuration blocks. Inside the root module is a subfolder called DSCResources. The folder must be named exactly this for the DSC composite resource to be parsed correctly. Inside the DSCResources folder is one or more PowerShell module folders. Each module represents an actual DSC composite resource.

For the most part, all the normal PowerShell module files are present, with the exception of the file that actually contains the DSC configuration blocks. This file must have a schema.psm1 extension instead of just a .psm1 extension.

In the following code block is an example folder structure for a DSC composite resource. In this example, we have two DSC composite resources packaged together:

```
$env:PSModulePath
 |- <RootModuleName>
 |- <RootModuleName>.psd1 (PowerShell Module Manifest file, Required)
 |- <RootModuleName>.psm1 (PowerShell Module file, Optional)
 |- DSCResources
 |- <DSCCompsiteResource1>
 |- <DSCCompsiteResourceName1>.psd1 (DSC Composite Resource manifest file,
Required)
 |- <DSCCompsiteResourceName1>.schema.psm1 (DSC Composite Resource
PowerShell module, Required)
 |- <DSCCompsiteResource2>
 |- <DSCCompsiteResourceName2>.psd1 (DSC Composite Resource manifest file,
Required)
 |- <DSCCompsiteResourceName2>.schema.psm1 (DSC Composite Resource
PowerShell module, Required)
```

If this still isn't clear to you, then you are not alone. Let's try this again and apply the preceding example to the `ExampleSoftware` and `TheRealSoftwareStuff` software we are trying to install:

```
$env:PSModulePath
 |- <KickingCompanyResources>
 |- KickingCompanyResources.psd1
 |- KickingCompanyResources.psm1
 |- DSCResources
 |- ExampleSoftwareDscResource
 |- ExampleSoftwareDscResource.psd1
 |- ExampleSoftwareDscResource.schema.psm1
 |- RealStuffDscResource
 |- RealStuffDscResource.psd1
 |- RealStuffDscResource.schema.psm1
```

So, we start out at the `root` module, `KickingCompanyResources`. We named our `root` module after our company, but there really are no official rules here. Microsoft initially recommended that the community prefix their DSC resources and DSC composite resources with a `c` and that Microsoft prefix their experimental ones with an `x`. Since this wasn't a requirement in DSC, the actual implementation of these suggested that naming schemes have had spotty adoption. When Microsoft moved their DSC resource kit to GitHub (this is covered later in the book), it highlighted how all DSC resources with an `x` are prefixed but are released to the `PSGallery` with the `x` still there. There is also a ticket explaining that Microsoft will eventually move away from suggesting prefixes (`https://github.com/PowerShell/DscResources/issues/27`). It is clear that the naming conventions are still being worked out.

Generally speaking, it's prudent to name your `root` module something sensible that also makes sense in the context of the operations you are performing. Here, we are packaging two resources that operate on software written by the `KickingCompany`, so it makes sense to be so bold as to name them with the company name.

Inside the `root` module folder, we see the PowerShell manifest file and the PowerShell module file. The module file can be left blank; it's not required and not used for a DSC composite resource. The manifest file must contain the normal module manifest data to help identify it. This is easily created using the `New-ModuleManifest` cmdlet, or you can do it by hand:

```
[PS]> New-ModuleManifest -Path .\ExampleSoftwareDscResource.psd1
[PS]> Get-Content .\ExampleSoftwareDscResource.psd1
#
# Module manifest for module 'ExampleSoftware'
#
```

```
# Generated by: James Pogran
#
# Generated on: 1/1/2015
#
@{
# Script module or binary module file associated with this manifest.
# RootModule = ''

# Version number of this module.
ModuleVersion = '1.0'

# ID used to uniquely identify this module
GUID = 'a80febb6-39d1-4129-88ae-7572561e43c8'

# Author of this module
Author = 'James Pogran'
<#
...
#>
}
```

Next, we have the `DSCResources` folder, which contains the two folders, `ExampleSoftwareDscResource` and `RealStuffDscResource`. Here is where we start deviating from the normal PowerShell module structure. Each has a normal PowerShell manifest file, in which the most important field is the `RootModule` entry. However, it has to point to the `schema.psm1` file, not just to a file with a `.psm1` extension. The `schema.psm1` file contains the DSC configuration block and nothing else.

Still not super clear? You're still not alone. It was confusing enough to remember each time I used DSC composite resources that I created a short PowerShell function to encapsulate the above steps into a simple command-line execution. The function itself is a little too long to include in this chapter, but it can be found in `https://powershell.org/` GitHub repo here: `https://github.com/PowerShellOrg/DSC/blob/master/Tooling/DscDevelopment/New-DscCompositeResource.ps1`.

DSC composite resource drawbacks

We have spent significant time explaining the benefits of code reuse, avoiding duplication, and improving maintainability by writing clean code throughout this book. If DSC composite resources enable these things, then how could there be a section with *drawbacks* in its title?

In the original WMF 4 release, you couldn't use the `DependsOn` property to express a dependency between two DSC composite resources. You could use `DependsOn` inside the DSC composite resource in a normal manner but could not link two DSC composite resources together. This has been corrected in the WMF 5 release. The fix was backported to the latest WMF4 release.

DSC composite resources were sometimes hard to develop. Iterative development (some call this trial and error) was painful as DSC would cache the any DSC resource, and it seemed like it never let go of the DSC composite resources. Make a change and copy the new DSC composite resource and you could spend a lot of time hitting your head against the wall while your configuration runs fail, only to remember about the cache and have it work wonderfully when you reset it (refer to the next section for more on how to remedy this). Some of this is alleviated in WMF5 with the advent of the `DebugMode` setting for the LCM (we'll look at this in the *Debugging and troubleshooting configuration script files* section).

Partial DSC configurations

In WMF 5.0, DSC allows DSC configurations to be delivered in fragments and from multiple sources, then the LCM puts the fragments together before applying them as a single DSC configuration. This allows sharing the control of DSC configurations between teams or organizations within the same company. **Team A** could be in charge of the base operating system configuration, while **Team B** could be in charge of the exchange configuration, **Team C** SharePoint, and so on. Each partial configuration from each team is combined and applied to the target nodes that match the classification in the `ConfigurationData`. Furthermore, these partial DSC configurations could be pulled from different DSC pull servers, allowing different areas to house installation sources or other artifacts that can't be centrally located.

You can use partial DSC configuration in either push or pull modes or a combination of the two. The syntax of a partial DSC configuration is as follows:

```
PartialConfiguration ExamplePartialConfig
{
 Description = 'Configuration to add the example to the thing'
 RefreshMode = 'Push'
}
```

The RefreshMode decides whether Push or Pull is used, and the name of the block (here ExamplePartialConfig) has to match exactly the names of the DSC configurations that are pushed or pulled to the target node.

 The name of the partial configuration must match the actual name or the DSC configuration as it's specified in the DSC configuration script, not the name of the MOF file, which should be either the name of the target node or an ID.

This is configured just like a DSC resource statement inside a WMF 5 DSC configuration block:

```
[DSCLocalConfigurationManager()]
configuration PartialConfigExample
{
 Node localhost
 {
 PartialConfiguration ExamplePartialConfig
 {
 Description = 'Configuration to add the example to the thing'
 RefreshMode = 'Push'
 }
 }
}
```

The configuration and use of either Push or Pull will be covered in Chapter 5, *Pushing DSC Configurations*.

Debugging and troubleshooting configuration script files

So, you ran a DSC configuration against a target node using either Start-DscConfiguration or a Pull Server and you want to look at the logs for its execution; where do you go? If you ran it with Start-DscConfiguration and the verbose parameter, then you have a log in your console, but that goes away when you close your console and you don't have this available with a Pull Server.

Worry not, for DSC provides a rich set of information from each operation it performs, although it's not always easy to access this information.

Status at a glance

A new feature for WMF 5 is storing status information in each target node which helps in identifying the current status of a node and, recent failures of any DSC runs. You get this by issuing the `Get-DSCConfigurationStatus` command. This command returns high-level information about whether or not a DSC run was successful. Here is an example of the status returned:

```
PS C:\> Get-DscConfigurationStatus

Status StartDate Type Mode RebootRequested NumberOfResources
------ --------- ---- ---- --------------- -----------------
Failure 11/24/2015 3:44:56 Consistency Push True 36
```

It shows more detailed information, such as the following:

- All of the resources that failed
- Any resource that requested a reboot
- Meta-configuration settings at the time of the configuration run

```
PS C:\> (Get-DscConfigurationStatus).ResourcesNotInDesiredState

ConfigurationName : MyExampleFoo
DependsOn :
ModuleName : PSDesiredStateConfiguration
ModuleVersion : 1.1
PsDscRunAsCredential :
ResourceID : [File]ExampleFoo
SourceInfo : c:\foo\wakka\ExampleFoo\ExampleFoo.ps1::9::51::File
DurationInSeconds : 0.19
Error : SourcePath must be accessible for current configuration. The
related file/directory is:
 \\Server10\Common\foo.txt. The related ResourceID is [File]ExampleFoo
FinalState :
InDesiredState : False
InitialState :
InstanceName : ServiceDll
RebootRequested : False
ReosurceName : File
StartDate : 5/15/2017 10:05:09
PSComputerName :
```

If `Get-DSCConfigurationStatus -All` is specified, then all previous configuration run information is shown.

Using DSC event logs

Like most Windows software, DSC writes all event information to a Windows event log, which can be viewed with many applications, including Event Viewer and PowerShell.

DSC logs these events to the `Microsoft-Windows-DSC` event log, which has the following channels:

- Microsoft-Windows-DSC/Operational
- Microsoft-Windows-DSC/Debug
- Microsoft-Windows-DSC/Analytic

Enabling verbose logging

The Analytic and Debug channels are not enabled by default and have to be enabled on each target node before any events are written to them:

```
#enable analytic and debug DSC channels
wevtutil.exe set-log "Microsoft-Windows-Dsc/Analytic" /q:true /e:true
wevtutil.exe set-log "Microsoft-Windows-Dsc/Debug" /q:True /e:true
```

What do DSC event logs contain?

DSC events are split over the three event log channels depending on the importance and purpose of the message. The three event log channels are as follows:

- All informational and error messages are logged to the Operational channel
- The Analytic channel receives verbose events, which typically mean more events in general and events that are more granular in the information they provide
- The Debug channel receives debug level events from the DSC operations

This is helpful because it separates the information into easily filterable buckets that make logical sense to group together. This is also less helpful, however, because it may mean you have to look in multiple places to find all the information required to troubleshoot a problem.

Gathering events from a single DSC operation

We can use Windows Event Viewer or PowerShell to view all events from all DSC channels. Event Viewer is good for interactive sessions, but is not great for automated scenarios and is not easily exportable. The PowerShell approach requires more typing, but is easier to export to formats that allow easier inspection.

Event Viewer

On Windows 2008 and above, Event Viewer was upgraded with advanced filtering capabilities. We can use the custom view feature to select all the events from the three DSC channels and present it in one view for the purpose of investigating, following the given steps:

1. Open up the Windows **Event Viewer** and navigate to the **Custom View** node in the **Action** pane.
2. Right-click on the **Custom View** node and select **Create Custom View**.
3. Click on each event type you want. For now, select all of them.
4. Click on the dropdown for the event logs and navigate to the DSC channels.
5. Select all the DSC channels.
6. Click on **OK**. View the DSC events in a single pane.

PowerShell

We can use the `Get-WinEvent` cmdlet to gather DSC events. We can query the DSC channels and store the events in an array and then use the `Group-Object` cmdlet to arrange them by the `ID` property:

```
# collect all logs from all channels
$dscEvents = @(
 Get-WinEvent "Microsoft-windows-DSC/operational"
 Get-WinEvent "Microsoft-Windows-DSC/Analytic" -Oldest
 Get-WinEvent "Microsoft-Windows-DSC/Debug" -Oldest
)
```

If you are wondering whether you can skip using `Oldest` with the Analytic and Debug logs, you can't. The error that appears when you try this is as follows:

```
[PS]> Get-WinEvent "Microsoft-Windows-Dsc/Analytic"
Get-WinEvent : The Microsoft-Windows-DSC/Analytic event log can be read
only in the forward chronological order
because it is an analytical or a debug log. To see events from the
Microsoft-Windows-DSC/Analytic event log, use the
```

```
Oldest parameter in the command.
At line:1 char:1
+ Get-WinEvent "Microsoft-Windows-Dsc/Analytic"
+ ~~~~~~~~~~~~~~~~~~~~~~~~~~~~~~~~~~~~~~~~~~~~~~~~
 + CategoryInfo : InvalidArgument: (Microsoft-Windows-DSC/Analytic:String)
[Get-WinEvent], Exception
 + FullyQualifiedErrorId : SpecifyOldestForLog,
 Microsoft.PowerShell.Commands.GetWinEventCommand
```

Further querying can be performed on the resulting data by sorting and grouping the result objects:

```
# Group all logs based on the job ID
$operations = $dscEvents | Group-Object {$_.Properties[0].value}
```

For example, you can find all events that have the error severity level by searching for the error:

```
$operations | Where-Object {$_.Group.LevelDisplayName -contains "Error"}
```

Or, you could examine the message from a single event:

```
$operations[0].Group.Message
```

Or, you could find all events from a specific job ID:

```
($operations | Where-Object {$_.Name -eq 2025}).Group
```

Using the xDscDiagnostics module to analyze DSC logs

After reading the previous explanation, you may throw up your hands in frustration at the amount of work that needs to be done to view any useful information. The `xDscDiagnostics` PowerShell module provided by Microsoft directly addresses this frustration. It wraps many of the tasks into two cmdlets that can help you identify DSC events on both the local machine, as well as remotely against a target node. This is a great help in diagnosing and pinpointing issues with DSC.

For the purposes of this module, we will define a DSC operation as the set of events that describe a DSC execution from start to finish. For example, the events generated from `Start-DSCConfiguration` will be separate from those generated from `Test-DSCConfiguration`.

Get-xDSCOperation

The `Get-xDSCOperation` cmdlet works on both local and remote target nodes and returns an object that contains the collection of events produced by each DSC operation run on the target node. Each object returned is a `Microsoft.PowerShell.xDscDiagnostics.GroupedEvents` object, which is the collection of all events for a specific DSC execution. This object reports the sequence ID, the time the DSC operation began, the name of the target node being queried, the success or failure result, and all events produced by the DSC operation.

Trace-xDSCOperation

The `Trace-xDSCOperation` cmdlet works on both local and remote target nodes and returns a collection of events related to a specified sequence ID. Typically, you will run `Get-xDSCOperation` and choose a specific sequence ID to run `Trace-xDSCOperation` against.

On the other hand, `Get-xDSCOperation` provides a general overview of what happened during a DSC operation and `Trace-xDSCOperation` provides specific detail. Most notable of these details is the message field, which reports the exact text or error reported by DSC when executing that operation.

Resetting the DSC engine cache

The DSC engine caches any DSC resources or DSC composite resources stored in any of the `PSModule` locations. DSC does this to speed up the discovery, parsing, and execution of the various elements inside DSC, but this can cause problems if you are activating developing DSC configurations using DSC resources or DSC composite resources that are also in active development. DSC will keep these resources cached until the DSC processes are restarted.

The only way to make or force DSC to reset its cache is to restart the process hosting the DSC engine. The easiest, but least preferable way to do this is rebooting the server. When you restart, the DSC engine will have cleared its cache and read in your current resources. To reset the cache without restarting the server, you must stop and start the host process. How you go about doing this differs in DSC V4 and V5.

In DSC V4, you perform a brute force approach:

```
[PS]> Get-Process *wmi* | Stop-Process -Force;
[PS]> Restart-Service winrm -Force
```

In DSC V5, there is a provided way:

```
[PS]> $dscProcessID = Get-WmiObject msft_providers |
 Where-Object {$_.provider -like 'dsccore'} |
 Select-Object -ExpandProperty HostProcessIdentifier
[PS]> Get-Process -Id $dscProcessID | Stop-Process
```

While this is effective, there is a way to avoid having to do this brute force approach in DSC V5. In the next paragraph, we'll take a look at how to configure DSC to not cache DSC resources.

Enabling the debug mode

We can avoid having to reset the DSC cache frequently by enabling the debug mode in DSC. However, this mode is only available in DSC V5, so if you are still using V4, you will have to keep refreshing the cache.

To enable the debug mode, we use the same methods we described in the previous chapter to configure the LCM:

```
LocalConfigurationManager
{
 DebugMode = $true
}
```

Fixing a stuck DSC run

You may come across a situation where a DSC configuration run has been executed but failed at some point in the process. Perhaps you have fixed the problem or simply want to run it again, but DSC provides the following error:

```
Cannot invoke the SendConfigurationApply method.
The SendConfigurationApply method is in progress and must return
before SendConfigurationApply can be invoked.
+ CategoryInfo : NotSpecified: (root/Microsoft/...gurationManager:String)
[], CimException
+ FullyQualifiedErrorId : MI RESULT 1
+ PSComputerName: box1
```

This means that DSC thinks there is an execution run currently in progress and it's trying to protect you by not running another execution run. If more than one execution is allowed to run at the same time, then DSC cannot guarantee that the desired state is in effect. So, we need to tell DSC to ignore the failed last run and start a new one. We do this by following the same procedure to refresh the DSC cache with one additional step. We also remove the `pending.mof` file so that DSC does not have any record of a past run that failed. Don't worry; the last run is still recorded for the target node's state if you set up the DSC compliance server part of the DSC pull server, as shown here:

```
[PS]> Remove-Item $env:systemRoot/system32/configuration/pending.mof -
Force;
[PS]> Get-Process *wmi* | Stop-Process -Force;
[PS]> Restart-Service winrm -Force
```

In WMF5, we could use `Start-DSCConfiguration -Force` to avoid having to do this.

Summary

In this chapter, we covered the syntax of configuration script and data files and how to create and execute them. We covered how to create usable components using DSC composite resources and their pros and cons. We ended our chapter on how to debug and troubleshoot executing DSC configurations.

In the next chapter, we will be covering how to find and use DSC resources. We will also delve into how to create your own custom DSC resources to handle your own unique deployment needs. Then, we will cover some differences in implementation in DSC MOF-based and class-based resources.

4
DSC Resources

"You must do the thing you think you cannot do."
- Eleanor Roosevelt

In this chapter, you will learn the definition and syntax of a DSC resource. This entails both the code/syntactic elements as well as the folder structure and placement. We will spend significant time covering the purpose of a DSC resource and best practices to develop custom DSC resources; we'll do this by showing examples of badly authored DSC resources and working on them until they are well-defined DSC resources. We will then explain class-based DSC resource differences and how you should handle them compared to their V4 counterparts.

In this chapter, we will cover the following topics:

- What are DSC resources?
- How do you find DSC resources?
- Creating a PowerShell MOF-based DSC resource.
- Creating a PowerShell class-based DSC resource.

What are DSC resources?

DSC resources are PowerShell modules that contain both the schema and implementation to determine and set the target node state. The schema is defined in MOF files, and the implementation code is defined in PowerShell script modules. Beginning with PowerShell V5, DSC resources can also be implemented using only PowerShell script files.

This is all well and good for a definition, but we are getting ahead of ourselves. At its simplest definition, a DSC resource is a PowerShell script that can be run against a target node that only changes the system state when it differs from the desired state. Schema MOFs and module folders aside, the core of a DSC resource is the idempotent code that determines the state of the target node and adjusts it until it is in line with what is expected. This code is implemented in PowerShell, so you're already familiar with the language used, which is a huge boost in starting to customize your own DSC resources.

Since DSC resources are authored using PowerShell code, the power is in your hands. It's the same PowerShell code you know and love. This boosts productivity out of the gate, leaving you with the freedom to focus on the actual code that performs the changes, instead of worrying about learning a new way of doing things.

DSC resources are responsible for both testing the current state of a target node and bringing the target node to the expected state. They follow the concepts of idempotency by only changing the system state if it is not in compliance, and they can be run as many times as desired. Even if they are run many times, DSC resources will only change the state if it is not in compliance with the desired state.

DSC resources are the smallest units of change in PowerShell DSC, so, by their very nature, they are much more focused and narrow in the subject matter they address. You will not find a single all-encompassing DSC resource that installs and configures the entirety of a Microsoft SQL Server four-node cluster with *alwayson* availability, but, instead, you'll find several focused DSC resources that each cover unique and specific task to accomplish. One DSC resource handles installation and basic configuration, while another handles configuration of the cluster and addition of the four nodes, and yet another handles creating or removing databases.

This specification of DSC resources allows you to perform complicated orchestration of multi-node deployments. Rather than a resource that installs a whole SQL cluster across nodes, several individual DSC resources install each component of a SQL cluster, which can be chained across nodes and reboots to accomplish the task. The point is that DSC resources, such as PowerShell Cmdlets, do one thing and in a repeatable, idempotent fashion.

We will delve into more about how DSC resources accomplish this as we progress through this chapter.

What makes a good DSC resource

At this point, we've covered what DSC resources are. Even with this knowledge, it is good to step back and consider what makes a *good* DSC resource. Remember when we were covering DSC configuration scripts in the previous chapter and we spent some time on best practices to create them? The same approach applies here.

Idempotent

It is up to you to uphold the tenets of idempotency that we have been learning over the course of this book in each DSC resource you author. The DSC resource is the last stop in the line of executions that determines whether the current state of the target node is the desired state we described in the DSC configuration script. You must write the code that tests and sets this state in a way that will change the state of the target node only once: the time when the system is not in the desired state.

Significant care must be taken when accomplishing this. You must not change the state of the system if it is in the state we desire. Users of PowerShell DSC expect to be able to run DSC as many times as they want and receive no unintended side-effects from doing so. This is accomplished by running near-obsessive testing of the current state to ensure we are changing things when we have to.

Do one thing well

A good DSC resource will do one thing, and it will do that one thing well. When crafting your DSC resources, you should choose the smallest tasks possible to tackle. For example, consider SQL Server. A DSC resource could be written to install and configure a SQL Server that, even if it got very complicated, could manage both installation and configuration in one resource. However, installing SQL Server is not a simple task when you take into account that it can be installed in a cluster or as part of a recovery set or a great many other options. How do you handle the long list of options to install SQL Server compared to the equally long list of configuration settings?

Consider the configuration of SQL Server. It is likely that the configuration options of SQL Server will change across versions, but the installation steps won't differ as much. Differing configuration steps or options can be handled in smaller DSC resources, reducing the amount of work each has to do while enabling flexibility of choosing when to execute.

Reuse code, but don't go overboard

Since DSC resources are PowerShell modules, it is easy to use their built-in discovery methods to share functions and other code artifacts between DSC resources. You must resist overusing this approach, as it can bite you as time goes on. Let's say two DSC resources called `ExampleResource1` and `ExampleResource2` are in the same module called `ExampleFooResource`. `ExampleResource1` has a function that `ExampleResource2` borrows to retrieve the same information in order to do its work.

We've created a dependency, which is now our responsibility to uphold for the life of the DSC resource. If we change the function in `ExampleResource1`, it has to change in `ExampleResource2` too. If we don't have some way of tracking this dependency, it can be become hard to troubleshoot how to break this dependency until the DSC resource is used. If it is a lesser-used function and we don't have a testing practice set up, it could be quite some time before we find out the breakage. While this is not optimal, if you had to copy and paste the code instead of reusing it, you would have to deal with updating code in several files whenever you fixed a bug or updated a functionality.

The point being made here is to be aware of the trade-offs when you develop DSC resources.

Contribute back

Once you have a solid custom DSC resource that works and is well-tested (refer to the following section for advice on testing DSC resources), we highly recommend contributing it to the community. There are several places to contribute your code to.

Microsoft has a wonderful how-to section on its GitHub repo on how to get started with contributing DSC resources: `https://github.com/PowerShell/DscResources/blob/master/CONTRIBUTING.md`.

The `PowerShell.org` site hosts its own GitHub repo you can contribute to at `https://github.com/PowerShellOrg`.

Creating PowerShell MOF-based custom DSC resources

We have touched on how to create PowerShell MOF-based DSC resources briefly as we have worked our way through this book, and here, we will dive into the details of doing that in depth. We will cover the folder structures and files needed as well as the mindset and best practices necessary in order to make custom DSC resources that are effective and useful to you.

 This section was titled *PowerShell V4 custom DSC resources* in the first edition of this book. Since then, the term *MOF-based* has been solidified as the correct term to use for this type of DSC resource. This makes sense, as you will see that an MOF-based DSC resource is supported from PowerShell V4 up to V6 (at the time of writing this).
Before continuing, ensure that you are familiar with creating PowerShell v2 modules. Knowing how to create and use PowerShell modules is the key to understanding how DSC resources are made.

MOF-based DSC resource folder structure

An MOF-based DSC resource has a strict folder structure. By convention, each PowerShell module that contains one or more DSC resources is stored in the `$env:ProgramFiles\WindowsPowerShell\Modules` folder. You can store DSC resources in any of the standard `$env:PSModulePath` paths, or you can store them in a location of your choosing as long as you append the location to the `$env:PSModulePath` variable before compiling the resource.

The strict folder structure for MOF-based DSC resources is as follows:

```
$env:ProgramFiles\WindowsPowerShell\Modules
    |- ExampleModule
    |- ExampleModule.psd1
    |- DSCResources
    |- Example_InstallFoo
    |- Example_InstallFoo.psd1 (optional)
    |- Example_InstallFoo.psm1 (required)
    |- Example_InstallFoo.schema.mof (required)
    |- Example_ConfigureFoo
    |- Example_ConfigureFoo.psd1 (optional)
    |- Example_ConfigureFoo.psm1 (required)
    |- Example_ConfigureFoo.schema.mof (required)
```

A folder called DSCResources inside the root folder, with other folders that are also DSC resources themselves, and files with schema separate from the code module files. Like with the DSC composite resource, you must be wondering why they make this so hard! It is difficult to keep track at first, but once you have done one or two DSC resources, it's not really that hard to keep track. It is easier to understand once you see that each DSC resource is made up of one or more PowerShell modules.

A DSC resource contains one or more PowerShell modules inside a root PowerShell module. This root PowerShell module declares the DSC resource and has the information required for the DSC engine to load the modules into memory. The root module typically does not contain any code itself, as it won't be available without significant effort to the submodules. Each submodule in the DSCResources folder represents an actual DSC resource. Inside each module folder is a .psm1 file and a .mof file. The .psm1 file is the file that contains all of the executable code that DSC uses to determine and set the state on the target node. The .mof file contains schema data that describes the parameters in use for a particular DSC resource.

Let's look at an example DSC resource provided by Microsoft instead of a contrived example such as the preceding folder structure. We will look at xTimeZone as it is a relatively simple resource that has one submodule and a few files. Inside the root module folder, we can see the DSCResources folder that holds all the submodules, as shown here:

```
[PS]> ls $env:ProgramFiles\WindowsPowerShell\Modules\xTimeZone
Directory: C:\Program Files\WindowsPowerShell\Modules\xTimeZone
Mode LastWriteTime Length Name
---- ------------- ------ ----
d---- 7/9/2015 10:11 PM DSCResources
-a--- 7/9/2015 10:11 PM 969 xTimeZone.psd1
-a--- 7/9/2015 10:11 PM 1988 xTimeZone.Tests.ps1
```

As you can see listed in the preceding structure, the main DSC resource folder also contains a folder called DSCResources. The DSCResources folder contains all the actual DSC resource modules. The root folder, in this case xTimezone, is our container module. It holds all the information needed to discover and parse DSC resources, namely the xTimeZone.psd1 file. This is the basic PowerShell module format and function here, so there's nothing new. The DSCResources subfolder is a special folder; the DSC engine looks for that folder, and if present, it will know to enumerate that directory for DSC resources to load.

If you see more files on your copy of xTimeZone than we list here, the reason for the difference is that we removed extraneous files to simplify our example. Looking at the DSCResources folder, we see the following structure:

```
[PS]> ls $env:ProgramFiles\WindowsPowerShell\Modules\xTimeZone\DSCResources
Directory: C:\Program
Files\WindowsPowerShell\Modules\xTimeZone\DSCResources
Mode LastWriteTime Length Name
---- ------------- ------ ----
d---- 7/9/2015 10:11 PM xTimeZone
```

As we can see in the preceding listing, the DSCResources folder contains all the actual DSC resource module folders. In this case, we see a folder called xTimeZone, which is the same name of the root module. In our next example, we'll see one that diverges from this and find out why it does, but, for now, let's continue down the path we're on.

Looking at the xTimeZone folder, we see two files, at which point we come to the last stop in our tour of a DSC resource:

```
[PS]> ls
$env:ProgramFiles\WindowsPowerShell\Modules\xTimeZone\DSCResources\xTimeZon
e
Directory: C:\Program
Files\WindowsPowerShell\Modules\xTimeZone\DSCResources\xTimeZone
Mode LastWriteTime Length Name
---- ------------- ------ ----
-a--- 7/9/2015 10:11 PM 3194 xTimeZone.psm1
-a--- 7/9/2015 10:11 PM 173 xTimeZone.schema.mof
```

These two folders contain the actual meat of a DSC resource and hold all information needed for the DSC engine to parse and use a DSC resource on a target node. The xTimeZone.psm1 file holds the PowerShell code that operates on the target node. The xTimeZone.schema.mof file holds the MOF schema that defines the parameter statement for the DSC resource. We will cover these two files in detail in the following section.

MOF-based DSC resource syntax

The PowerShell MOF-based DSC resource syntax can be described by dividing it into the DSC resource definition file and the DSC resource PowerShell module file.

The DSC resource definition file

A DSC resource definition file is an MOF schema file that has a specific CIM syntax, whose name is `<DSCResourceName>.schema.mof`. In the previous section, our example of `xTimeZone` had an MOF schema file called `xTimezone.schema.mof`. It is at first very obtuse and unfriendly to look at but becomes easier to read the more you work with it. The MOF files are supposed to be easy for the machine to read and not you, so there is some initial effort in understanding the syntax and format for them. Don't worry too much about this as you aren't meant to look at it yourself much. MOF schema files are expected to be automatically created and updated using the DSC tooling that Microsoft has released.

The main purpose of a DSC resource MOF schema file is to provide the name and version of the DSC resource and declare the parameters the DSC resource will accept. An example of a DSC resource MOF schema file is as follows:

```
[ClassVersion("1.0.0"), FriendlyName("InstallFoo")]
class Example_InstallFoo: OMI_BaseResource
{
 [Key] string Name;
 [Required] string PhysicalPath;
 [write,ValueMap{"Present", "Absent"},Values{"Present", "Absent"}] string
Ensure;
};
```

If you are reading CIM syntax, class names, and writeable values and starting to sweat, don't worry. Your fears will be allayed in the *Creating PowerShell class-based custom DSC resources* section.

There is still some benefit in going over the syntax of the MOF schema file, as you might have to troubleshoot issues in parsing when creating your own DSC resources or troubleshooting DSC resources created by others. If this section is getting through to you, you can reference it later when the time comes.

Naming

There are two DSC resource names to keep track of: the CIM **class name** (sometimes referred to as the fully qualified name) and the **friendly name**. The CIM class name is the name that DSC uses internally to refer to a DSC resource, and the friendly name is typically a shorter and easier-to-read version for a human.

You have to be careful in specifying these names, as your choice of which one to include determines how your users ask for your DSC resource. If you specify the same name for both, then a user uses that name when they ask for the DSC resource to be imported. If you specify the CIM class name but not the *friendly name*, then the user has to specify the CIM class name. If you specify the friendly name, then the user must use that to import your DSC resource and cannot use the CIM class name. If all this sounds confusing, do like the author does and keep it simple by setting both names the same when authoring DSC resources.

We can simplify naming the DSC resource in the MOF example we used earlier, as shown here:

```
[ClassVersion("1.0.0"), FriendlyName("InstallFoo")]
class InstallFoo: OMI_BaseResource
{
 [Key] string Name;
 [Required] string PhysicalPath;
 [write,ValueMap{"Present", "Absent"},Values{"Present", "Absent"}] string
Ensure;
};
```

Why the complicated naming? It was explained that these different names account for situations where DSC resources are named the same and allow the user to specify which ones to load and use. As we will see in the class-based DSC resource section, this concept has been simplified greatly and is easier to use.

Versioning

The second piece of information to include is the DSC resource version. Versioning your DSC resources is very important during the lifetime of use of your DSC resource. Along with the DSC resource name, users can specify an exact version to load. This ensures they will get the exact DSC resource they are expecting.

Parameters

The most important piece of information in the DSC MOF schema file is the property declarations.

CIM uses the term **property**, and PowerShell uses **parameter** to refer to the same thing. It's easy to get confused by this, and some people use the term interchangeably.

As we will cover in The DSC PowerShell module file coming up, the parameters or properties the DSC resource accepts have to match each of the `TargetResource` functions. This rule also applies to the MOF schema file.

The parameter statement has the same information as the parameter statement in the `TargetResource` functions, but it looks drastically different. This is because it is using the more verbose CIM syntax, which is less pleasant to the eyes than the PowerShell syntax. There are a few rules to keep in mind when specifying the parameter set here, and we will cover them in the next section, when we author our own DSC resources.

Qualifiers

Each parameter can have one or more qualifiers: `Key`, `Required`, `Read`, and `Write`. These qualifiers describe what the parameter is and what it is allowed to do, listed as follows:

The `Key` qualifier indicates that the parameter is mandatory and is used to uniquely identify the DSC resource in the DSC configuration script file. This means that the value for this parameter has to be unique in the script file and has to be singular as well; it cannot be an array or a collection. It must also be a string or numeric value; it cannot be any other type. All DSC resources are required to have at least one `Key` property. For DSC resources with more than one `Key` property defined, DSC uses a combination of all `Key` properties put together as the `Key` qualifier used.

The `Required` qualifier indicates that the parameter is mandatory but is not required to be unique for the DSC resource.

The `Write` qualifier is used to pass information and values to the DSC resource but is not required for the successful execution of the DSC resource. If used, this parameter is not mandatory.

The `Read` qualifier is used only in the `Get-TargetResource` function, as it returns information only.

The DSC PowerShell module file

The DSC PowerShell module file (or implementation file) is the file where the actual code that determines a target node's state resides. The DSC PowerShell module file has the same name as what was declared as the CIM class name in the DSC resource definition file.

Each DSC resource module file (the PowerShell `.psm1` file) is required to contain three functions with specific names in order to work. Each function is required to have the same parameters that were defined in the DSC resource definition file. Any deviation in parameter set declarations (typos, missing, or added parameters, conflicting types, and so on) between functions is not allowed.

Adding up all the places in which you must keep track of parameter statements ultimately makes four places you need to keep track of. If this sounds like a recipe for syntax errors and forgotten parameters to you, then you aren't alone. Keep this in mind when we get to the next section on class-based DSC resources.

Get-TargetResource

The `Get-TargetResource` function is responsible for reporting on the current state of the system. This function will never change the system; it is read-only. Instead, it inspects the system state and returns a PowerShell hash containing the information obtained.

This function is required to implement all `Key` and `Required` properties defined in the DSC resource definition file. The `Write` (non-mandatory) parameters do not have to be included. In practice, many people include all properties in an effort to not miss out on including important ones.

A `Get-TargetResource` function is required to return a single PowerShell hashtable that contains the information collected from the target system. This hashtable must contain all parameters that were defined in the DSC resource definition file as well as their corresponding values.

Test-TargetResource

The `Test-TargetResource` function is similar to the `Get-TargetResource` function in that it inspects the current state of the system, but it takes things one step further. After inspecting the current state of the system, it compares it to the expected values provided by the user. Depending on the way the values are specified, it tests to see whether they match.

This function is required to implement all `Key`, `Required`, and `Write` parameters defined in the DSC resource definition file. `Key` and `Required` properties are required to be defined as mandatory parameters.

The `Test-TargetResource` function always returns a Boolean value of either `$true` or `$false`. If the target node is in the desired state, the function should return `$true`. If the target node is not in the desired state, it should return `$false`.

Set-TargetResource

The `Set-TargetResource` function actually brings the state of the system to the desired state. This is the place where idempotency comes into play; the PowerShell code here is responsible for detecting the current state and only changing it if it does not match what is expected.

This function is required to implement all `Key`, `Required`, and `Write` parameters defined in the DSC resource definition file. `Key` and `Required` properties are required to be defined as mandatory parameters.

A `Set-TargetResource` function does not return any value to the calling code. This function either succeeds or fails; it does not indicate any state in between. Failure is indicated by throwing an exception with message text indicating the failure. Success is indicated by the function completing without error.

Optionally, a `Set-TargetResource` function can support the `WhatIf` PowerShell behavior and provide a summary of what would be changed on a target node without actually changing the target node state. The function can support this by implementing PowerShell's `SupportsShouldProcess` feature.

If the target node must be restarted after `Set-TargetResource` has successfully implemented the changes it was instructed to do, it can indicate this to the DSC engine by setting the global variable `$global:DSCMachineStatus` to 1 before exiting.

Authoring custom DSC resources

Now that we have covered the syntax and structure of DSC resources, we can finally cover how to make your own DSC resources. The fun begins!

Creating DSC resources manually

The secret to creating DSC resources manually is to not create DSC resources manually. Seriously, there are easier ways and you needn't put yourself through the pain. As with most things that have a lot of easy-to-reproduce structure, we can use tools to perform most of the grunt work for us. This is not just to avoid doing extra work; this removes the possibility of getting something wrong due to human error.

Creating DSC resources automatically

While you can create DSC resources manually by creating the files and folders required by hand, you do not have to. Microsoft released a PowerShell module as part of their DSC resource Kit that automates the creation of DSC resources called `xDscResourceDesigner`.

Using the `xDscResourceDesigner` module requires a little up front thought and planning, but it returns that investment in making DSC resources that are syntactically correct and properly arranged easily and without much fuss.

Before you start to create your DSC resource, you must make a decision on the following points:

- Decide the name, friendly name, and version of the DSC resource you are creating
- Decide the location you are going to create the files in
- Decide the parameters you are going to use in your DSC resource

Once you have this information decided in creating the DSC resource, using the `xDscResourceDesigner` module is as easy as these two steps:

1. Create a variable for each `DSCResourceProperty` (or, as we have been calling them, parameters) using the `New-xDscResourceProperty` cmdlet.
2. Pass the array of variables created to the `New-DscResource` cmdlet. Putting all together, here is an interactive session that creates the `xExampleResource` with two parameters:

```powershell
[PS]> $Ensure = New-xDscResourceProperty -Name "Ensure" -Type "String" -
Attribute Write -ValidateSet "Present","Absent" -Description "Ensure
Present or Absent"
 [PS]> $ExampleSetting = New-xDscResourceProperty -Name "ExampleSetting" -
Type "String" -Attribute Key -Description "Set an Example Setting"
 [PS]> New-xDscResource -Name "xExampleResource" -Property
$Ensure,$ExampleSetting -Path
"$env:ProgramFiles\WindowsPowerShell\Modules\xExampleResource" -
ClassVersion 1.0 -FriendlyName "Example" -Force
Directory: C:\Program Files\WindowsPowerShell\Modules
Mode LastWriteTime Length Name
---- ------------- ------ ----
 d---- 7/9/2015 9:57 PM xExampleResource
Directory: C:\Program Files\WindowsPowerShell\Modules\xExampleResource
Mode LastWriteTime Length Name
---- ------------- ------ ----
 d---- 7/9/2015 9:57 PM DSCResources
```

```
Directory: C:\Program
Files\WindowsPowerShell\Modules\xExampleResource\DSCResources
Mode LastWriteTime Length Name
---- ------------- ------ ----
d---- 7/9/2015 9:57 PM xExampleResource
```

The preceding code creates the following resource:

```powershell
[PS]> ls
$env:ProgramFiles\WindowsPowerShell\Modules\xExampleResource\DSCResources\x
ExampleResource
Directory: C:\Program
Files\WindowsPowerShell\Modules\xExampleResource\DSCResources\xExampleResou
rce
Mode LastWriteTime Length Name
---- ------------- ------ ----
-a--- 7/16/2015 9:57 PM 3004 xExampleResource.psm1
-a--- 7/16/2015 9:57 PM 594 xExampleResource.schema.mof
```

Looking at xExampleResource.schema.mof, we see that New-xDscResource did all the heavy lifting for us and not only set up the CIM class for us, but also correctly set all the parameter statement information we needed:

```powershell
[ClassVersion("1.0"), FriendlyName("Example")]
 class xExampleResource : OMI_BaseResource
 {
 [Write, Description("Ensure Present or Absent"),
ValueMap{"Present","Absent"}, Values{"Present","Absent"}] String Ensure;
 [Key, Description("Set an Example Setting")] String ExampleSetting;
 };
```

Inspecting xExampleResource.psm1, we see that New-xDscResource created stub TargetResource functions for us with the example code. More importantly, it added the parameters in the correct formats for each function:

```powershell
function `Get-TargetResource`
 {
 [CmdletBinding()]
 [OutputType([System.Collections.Hashtable])]
 param
 (
 [parameter(Mandatory = $true)]
 [System.String]
 $ExampleSetting
 )
```

```
#Write-Verbose "Use this cmdlet to deliver information about command
processing."
 #Write-Debug "Use this cmdlet to write debug information while
troubleshooting."
<#
 $returnValue = @{
 Ensure = [System.String]
 ExampleSetting = [System.String]
 }
$returnValue
 #>
 }

 function `Set-TargetResource`
 {
 [CmdletBinding()]
 param
 (
 [ValidateSet("Present","Absent")]
 [System.String]
 $Ensure,
 [parameter(Mandatory = $true)]
 [System.String]
 $ExampleSetting
 )
#Write-Verbose "Use this cmdlet to deliver information about command
processing."
 #Write-Debug "Use this cmdlet to write debug information while
troubleshooting."
 #Include this line if the resource requires a system reboot.
 #$global:DSCMachineStatus = 1
 }

 function `Test-TargetResource`
 {
 [CmdletBinding()]
 [OutputType([System.Boolean])]
 param
 (
 [ValidateSet("Present","Absent")]
 [System.String]
 $Ensure,
 [parameter(Mandatory = $true)]
 [System.String]
 $ExampleSetting
 )
#Write-Verbose "Use this cmdlet to deliver information about command
processing."
```

```
#Write-Debug "Use this cmdlet to write debug information while
troubleshooting."
<#
$result = [System.Boolean]
$result
#>
}
Export-ModuleMember -Function *-TargetResource
```

So, we have seen the cmdlets from the xDscResourceDesigner module are really useful in making the authoring of custom DSC resources easier and quicker, while, at the same time, maintaining correct syntax and structure. This is all well and fine if we know all the parameters and properties we want to use in our DSC resource ahead of time. What happens if we use these cmdlets, write a bunch of code, and then find out we needed another parameter? Do we have to manually add it ourselves and risk getting the syntax wrong? Never fear; Update-xDscResource is here!

To use Update-xDSCResource, all we have to do is create a new variable for our new parameter and point Update-xDscResource at it, and it will update the existing DSC resource with our new parameter, as shown here:

```powershell
[PS]> $ExampleFooBar = New-xDscResourceProperty -Name "FooBar" -Type
"String" -Attribute Write -Description "Set an Example FooBar"
[PS}> Update-xDscResource -Name "xExampleResource" -Property
$ExampleFooBar,$Ensure,$ExampleSetting -ClassVersion 1.0 -Force
```

Looking at the MOF schema file, we see our new parameter added:

```powershell
[ClassVersion("1.0"), FriendlyName("Example")]
class xExampleResource : OMI_BaseResource
{
[Write, Description("Set an Example FooBar")] String FooBar;
[Write, Description("Ensure Present or Absent"),
ValueMap{"Present","Absent"}, Values{"Present","Absent"}] String Ensure;
[Key, Description("Set an Example Setting")] String ExampleSetting;
};
```

If you look back at our `Update-xDscResource` statement, you'll notice that we specified our previous variables as well as our new one. This is the one inconvenience with using `Update-xDSCResource`; you have to provide the same set of parameters as you did when you first created the DSC resource when you want to update it with new ones. This is not too much of an imposition when you are actively making a DSC resource, but it becomes more of a problem when you come back to a DSC resource after months have elapsed. Most likely, you won't have saved the text you used to create the DSC resource and will have to create it all over again.

While you are in active development of a DSC resource, you could keep the commands you used to create it for easier updating later in a text file. You could also serialize your parameter statement to a file using the `Export-Clixml` cmdlet and then reimport it at a later time using `Import-Clixml`:

```powershell
[PS]> $params = $Ensure,$ExampleSetting,$FooBar
[PS]> $params | Export-Clixml -Path .\myDscParams.xml
 # time passes
[PS]> $params = Import-Clixml -Path .\myDscParams.xml
[PS]> Update-xDscResource -Name "xExampleResource" -Property $params -
ClassVersion 1.0 -Force
```

How you choose to handle this depends largely on how much you expect your DSC resource properties to change in the future.

Creating PowerShell class-based custom DSC resources

As we have been moving along with this chapter, we have made some observations about PowerShell MOF-based DSC resources. We have seen that DSC resource MOF schema files are verbose and obtuse. CIM schema requires many lines to express a simple parameter statement, and the wording used is confusingly different than the wording used inside the PowerShell scripts. Managing both MOF schema files and PowerShell scripts files with essentially the same information is prone to human error and mistakes.

Microsoft listened to this feedback and came back with PowerShell class-based DSC resources.

PowerShell classes

PowerShell V5 introduced a new feature called a PowerShell class. If you are familiar with programming in any language, you will recognize this new feature. If not, don't worry about it too much as you can get pretty far with some basic programming knowledge that you already learned using PowerShell. This is the one of the original design goals in Jeffrey Snover's Monad manifesto-to create PowerShell as a gateway step to C# for those so inclined.

Since you're already adept at using PowerShell, you know that anything and everything PowerShell operates on and produces is a class, specifically a class in the .NET Framework. Run `Get-Process`, and you get a collection of the `System.Diagnostics.Process` objects.

We won't get too far into discussing classes here, as that is a subject on which many books have already been written. For our purposes, think of a class as a grouping of properties and functions inside one place that can be created to perform specific functions. PowerShell classes are designed to provide similar functionality.

PowerShell classes are very similar to PowerShell functions (a design that is not by accident), so they are easy to understand once you grasp some simple concepts. Let's use a common example—a class that defines a point, something that represents a location on the computer screen. We would need to describe this point's location using x and y coordinates and also have some way to adjust those coordinates to move the point to a new location. This is accomplished in a PowerShell class, as follows:

```powershell
class Point
 {
 $X = 0
 $Y = 0
[void] Move($xOffset, $yOffset)
 {
 $this.X += $xOffset
 $this.Y += $yOffset
 }
 }
```

Not too scary, right? It looks like a PowerShell function for the most part. We declare properties with normal PowerShell variable syntax and declare the class method using the PowerShell function syntax. We can create a point object and move it, as follows:

```powershell
$point = [Point]::new()
 $point.Move(10, 20)
 $point
```

Again, this book can't begin to cover the programming concepts you would need in order to get started. It is enough to describe the concepts we are going to use with DSC resources.

Class-based DSC resources

We have stated that class-based DSC resources provide several benefits over PowerShell MOF-based DSC resources. The main reasons for these benefits are the folder structure and file improvements that class-based DSC resources use.

The folder structure of class-based DSC resource

A class-based DSC resource has a much simpler folder structure than a module-based DSC resource. The submodule folder structure underneath a root DSCResources folder with extra .psd1 files and multiple schema and .psm1 files that need to be matched are gone. In its place are a simple one folder structure and two PowerShell files, a .psd1 and .psm1 file, as follows:

```powershell
[PS]> ls
$env:ProgramFiles\WindowsPowerShell\Modules\xExampleClassBasedDSCResource
Directory: C:\Program
Files\WindowsPowerShell\Modules\xExampleClassBasedDSCResource
Mode LastWriteTime Length Name
---- ------------- ------ ----
-a--- 7/9/2015 10:11 PM 3194 xExampleClassBasedDSCResource.psm1
-a--- 7/9/2015 10:11 PM 173 xExampleClassBasedDSCResource.psd1
```

What about grouping similar DSC resources into one distributable package like we discussed earlier? Does moving to class-based resources do away with that? Not at all. Instead of multiple folders and files, all your DSC resources go into one file. Since each DSC resource is a self-contained class, it's not as messy as you think, and it actually organizes things better than the previous approach.

Class-based DSC resource syntax

While the class-based DSC resource folder structure is much more relaxed, the syntax for a class-based DSC resource is rather strict, or slightly more so. This makes sense, as we are collapsing a lot of functionality into one file and need a reliable way of parsing the files to get the same information we got previously in several separate files.

- **Declaring the class**: Instead of a PowerShell function declaration, we use a PowerShell class declaration to define our DSC resource:

```powershell
[DscResource()]
 class FooBar
 {
 <# Class code here #>
 }
```

  Instead of function, we use class, so there's not too much difference. We added a new attribute called `DscResource`, but if you are familiar with PowerShell V2 parameter attributes, using attributes to denote supported functionality should be easy to transition to. We use the `DscResource` attribute to indicate that this class is a DSC resource. This is done so that the DSC engine can locate and parse classes as DSC resources.

- **Schema**: A class-based DSC resource schema defines the properties of the class that can be used by the user of the DSC resource. Instead of a separate MOF file, the properties are defined inside the class using the PowerShell attribute syntax on top of PowerShell variable declarations.
  - Declaring DSC properties is a simple as this:

```powershell
[DscResource()]
 class FooBar
 {
 [DscProperty(Key)]
 [string]$Wakka
[DscProperty(Mandatory)]
 [string]$Path

 <# Class code here #>
 }
```

- There is one attribute that can be used here, DscProperty, but several values that can be passed to it to indicate what type of DSC properties are being used here:

```
Property | MOF equivalent | Description
---------|----------------|------------
DscProperty(Key) | Key |The property is a key for the DSC
resource and required
DscProperty(Mandatory) | Required | The property is
required
DscProperty(NotConfigurable) | Read | The property is
read-only and is populated by the Get() function
DscProperty() | Write | This is a configurable property
that is not required
```

- **Methods**: Declaring a class and a few properties are not all that is required for a class-based DSC resource. Remember Get-TargetResource, Test-TargetResource, and Set-TargetResource in the module-based DSC resource in the previous section? In the class-based DSC resource, we have simplified this into three methods with the same prefix, all in the same class. Let's build on the previous example and add the required methods:

```powershell
[DscResource()]
 class FooBar
 {
 [DscProperty(Key)]
 [string]$Wakka
<# Class code here #>
[FooBar] Get() {}
 [bool] Test() {}
 [void] Set() {}
 }
```

 As before with the module-based DSC resources, each method returns a specific value or none at all.

- **Get**: This method returns an instance of the class instead of a hashtable, with the properties populated with the discovered values. In our preceding example, the Get method returns an instance of the FooBar class. If we were to implement the Get method, it would look like this:

```powershell
```

```
[FooBar] Get()
{
$present = $this.TestForWakka($this.Path)
if ($present)
{
$this.Wakka = $this.Path
}
else
{
$this.Wakka = $null
}
return $this
}
```

The internal code is contrived, so forgive the silliness, but it proves the point. This tests a few things and sets the properties with values based on those tests. Note the use of the special variable $this; it's an automatic class variable that refers to the instance of the class itself. You can use it to access methods and properties defined in the class.

- **Test**: This method is the equivalent of the `Test-TargetResource` function and returns a Boolean indicating the state of the target node. If the node is in the expected state, it returns `$true`. If it is not in the expected state, it returns `$false`.

- **Set**: This method is the equivalent of the `Set-TargetResource` function. The `Set` method executes the code necessary to bring the target node to compliance. Like the module-based DSC resource, it does not return a value and indicates success by not throwing an exception instead.

  Implementing the `Set` method will vary greatly according to your problem domain, but here is an example of a `Set` method that operates on the information it finds on the target node:

```powershell
[void] Set()
{
$fileExists = $this.TestFilePath($this.Path)
if($this.ensure -eq [Ensure]::Present)
{
if(-not $fileExists)
{
$this.CopyFile()
}
}else{
if($fileExists)
```

```
{
Remove-Item -LiteralPath $this.Path -Force
}
}
}
```

Advantages of a class-based DSC resource

So, how does having PowerShell classes benefit us with DSC resources? A PowerShell class defines both the schema and implementation of the DSC resource in the same file, greatly simplifying the authoring and use of DSC resources. Instead of the verbose folder structure we covered in the *Creating PowerShell custom DSC resources in C#* section, we have a single class that handles everything for us.

PowerShell MOF-based DSC resources require a specific folder structure and many files in order to work correctly. There is a lot of boilerplate code and repetition in declaring the properties and functions in order to make things work. The separate MOF schema file has to be kept in sync with the PowerShell module file implementing the Get, Set, and Test-TargetResource functions, which means manual human intervention. This is an error-prone process that is easily forgotten about when trying to make a DSC resource work.

Perhaps the easiest to overlook but most important part of a class-based DSC resource is the type safety provided. Type safety is a programming term that means a certain object, method, or property can only ever be the thing we assigned it. The methods and properties of a DSC class only return the information we expect, which returns runtime errors due to programming mistakes.

In PowerShell V4, there was no way to directly invoke the Get-TargetResource functions using DSC against a target node yourself, so the function had little utility in interactive use. In V4, it wasn't used internally by the DSC engine as much as it is in V5, so there were not very many people who bothered to implement the function.

Instead, they declared the function and had it return an empty hash. In PowerShell V5, you can directly invoke the Get-TargetResource function using Invoke-DscResource, which brings a lot of utility and purpose to this function. It is assumed that this function will really shine when there is a **reporting** feature to DSC. Currently, there isn't a way to report on the current state of target nodes using DSC. This information is stored after a DSC run is performed on a target node.

Disadvantages of a class-based DSC resource

The main disadvantage of class-based DSC resources is that you cannot use them in an environment that has both PowerShell V4 and PowerShell V5 installed, while module-based DSC resources work fine in either version. This makes transitioning hard as it is unlikely you will be able to upgrade an entire environment to PowerShell V5 at once. This will influence your decisions on making custom DSC resources now, as you will have to anticipate and plan for the version of PowerShell that is on the target host in the future.

This is especially important if you are making a DSC resource you want to share with the community. If you choose to implement it as a class-based DSC resource, then you are potentially limiting the number of people who can use your resource until WMF 5 becomes the most commonly installed version.

Miscellaneous minor problems with using class-based DSC resources are shown in the following list:

- The types that you create in a class are not available outside the module yet. This means that, if you have several common variables, enums, or methods, you have to create them in each class you make. There isn't a global way to address them outside the module they live in.
- You cannot have class-based and MOF-based DSC resources inside the same DSC resource module.
- You cannot unload classes from a running PowerShell session using `Remove-Module`, which can cause a failure to reload a class-based DSC resource when the LCM is set to the `ForceModuleImport` debug mode.

Creating single-instance custom DSC resources

For all that DSC resources are powerful and useful, there are some ways in which you could hurt yourself in their use. One way you could do just that is by using a DSC resource more than once in a DSC configuration. This may sound innocuous at first, but if these two DSC resource declarations had different values for the same parameter, then DSC would continually change the state of the system with each run.

For example, if you defined the xComputer DSC resource twice for the same target node, you would change the name of the target node twice in the DSC run. This sounds silly and would be something you would catch right away. Consider coming back to a couple hundred-lines-long DSC configuration script after several months. Would you remember every DSC resource used in it? Or, consider the same DSC configuration script, except it's maintained by several teams of people who don't necessarily look at the entire script before adding a new DSC resource statement. This is a slightly contrived example, but it proves the point and can show you what can happen in long DSC configuration scripts that are edited by many humans. Contrived examples such as these happen infrequently in real life, where good continuous integration and testing practices are in place.

To implement a single-instance custom DSC resource, add a key property to your DSC resource called IsSingleInstance and limit it to only accept Yes as a value. If you attempt to use a DSC resource twice in the same DSC configuration, compilation will fail, with an error telling you a conflict was detected between resources.

An example Single Instance MOF-based DSC resource is as follows:

```powershell
[ClassVersion("1.0.0.0"), FriendlyName("xFooBarBaz")]
 class xFooBarBaz : OMI_BaseResource
 {
 [Key, Description("Specifies the resource is a single instance, the value
must be 'Yes'"), ValueMap{"Yes"}, Values{"Yes"}] String IsSingleInstance;
 [Required, Description("Specifies the FooBarBaz.")] String FooBarBaz;
 };
```

Each Get, Set, or Test-TargetResource function inside your DSC resource code file would have the following parameter statement:

```powershell
function Set-TargetResource
 {
 [CmdletBinding(SupportsShouldProcess=$true)]
 param
 (
 [parameter(Mandatory = $true)]
 [ValidateSet('Yes')]
 [String]$IsSingleInstance,
 [parameter(Mandatory = $true)]
 [ValidateNotNullOrEmpty()]
 [String]$FooBarBaz
 )
```

If you were implementing a single instance class-based DSC resource, you would implement the same parameters as we did in the MOF-based one, except with class properties:

```powershell
[DscResource()]
 class xFooBarBaz
 {
 [ValidateSet('Yes')]
 [DscProperty(Key)]
 [ValidateNotNullorEmpty()]
 [String] $IsSingleInstance
[DscProperty(Mandatory)]
 [ValidateNotNullorEmpty()]
 [String] $FooBarBaz = $null
```

Creating PowerShell custom DSC resources in C#

You can create custom DSC resources in PowerShell using MOF schema and in PowerShell using PowerShell classes, but what if you wanted to use another language? Well, you can create DSC resources in C#, which is incidentally how most of the built-in original DSC resources were created.

Why would you create a custom DSC resource in C#? There are several reasons, some being personal preference. A C# DSC resource would have native access to the .NET framework without the intermediary PowerShell interpretation. It could also have better access to concepts such as **generics** or other frameworks that can't be easily used directly in PowerShell. You might also be more familiar with C# than you are with PowerShell and be more comfortable there.

In practice, the potential benefits are mostly outweighed by the time and complexity cost to make a C# custom DSC resource. As you are about to see, setting up the environment to develop this is difficult for someone who doesn't already have a C# development environment setup, and it adds extra steps to make and deploy the DSC resource. Ultimately, these trade-offs are up to you to decide.

Create the MOF schema

In making a C# custom DSC resource, you follow the same conventions as an MOF-based custom DSC resource, with the exception of the PowerShell .psm1 code file being replaced by the C# DLL.

You start with creating the MOF schema file:

```
[ClassVersion("1.0.0"), FriendlyName("xExampleThing")]
 class xExampleThing : OMI_BaseResource
 {
 [Key, Description("path")] String Path;
 [Write, Description("Should the file be present"),
ValueMap{"Present","Absent"}, Values{"Present","Absent"}] String Ensure;
 };
```

Create the Visual Studio project

The following steps will help you to create a Visual Studio project:

1. Open Visual Studio.
2. Create a C# project.
3. Select **Class Library** from the project template list.
4. Name the project to match the DSC resource you are creating (in this case, it's xExampleThing).
5. Click on **OK**.
6. Once the project has loaded, add a reference to System.Automation.Management.dll in your project from the GAC.

Create the C# cmdlet code

Add a new class file to the project named xExampleThing for your DSC resource. The actual file name doesn't strictly matter, but it helps in keeping track of things. Inside this file, you will create three classes: GetTargetResource, SetTargetResource, and TestTargetResource. Each class will follow the rules to implement PowerShell cmdlets in C#, with getters and setters and ProcessRecord() methods. The implementation of the C# code here is out of scope of our subject; look for documentation on creating PowerShell cmdlets in C# for more information. Note how each class has the ProcessRecord() method return the data type that the TargetResource function is expecting. Therefore, the GetTargetResource method returns what the Get-TargetResource function in a PowerShell .psm1 file would have returned:

```c#
namespace CSharpCustomDSCResource
 {
 using System;
 using System.Collections.Generic;
```

```
using System.IO;
using System.Management.Automation; // Windows PowerShell assembly.
[OutputType(typeof(System.Collections.Hashtable))]
[Cmdlet(VerbsCommon.Get, "TargetResource")]
public class GetTargetResource : PSCmdlet
{
[Parameter(Mandatory = true)]
public string Path { get; set; }
/// <summary>
/// Implement the logic to return the current state of the resource as a
hashtable with keys being the resource properties
/// and the values are the corresponding current value on the machine.
/// </summary>
protected override void ProcessRecord()
{
// Code implementation
}
}
[OutputType(typeof(void))]
[Cmdlet(VerbsCommon.Set, "TargetResource")]
public class SetTargetResource : PSCmdlet
{
[Parameter(Mandatory = true)]
public string Path { get; set; }
[Parameter(Mandatory = false)]
[ValidateSet("Present", "Absent", IgnoreCase = true)]
public string Ensure {
get
{
// set the default to present.
return (this._ensure ?? "Present") ;
}
set
{
this._ensure = value;  ,
}
}
private string _ensure;
/// <summary>
/// Implement the logic to set the state of the machine to the desired
state.
/// </summary>
protected override void ProcessRecord()
{
// Code implementation
}
}
[Cmdlet("Test", "TargetResource")]
```

```
[OutputType(typeof(Boolean))]
public class TestTargetResource : PSCmdlet
{
[Parameter(Mandatory = true)]
public string Path { get; set; }
[Parameter(Mandatory = false)]
[ValidateSet("Present", "Absent", IgnoreCase = true)]
public string Ensure
{
get
{
// set the default to present.
return (this._ensure ?? "Present");
}
set
{
this._ensure = value;
}
}
private string _ensure;
/// <summary>
/// Return a Boolean value which indicates wheather the current machine is
in desired state or not.
/// </summary>
protected override void ProcessRecord()
{
// Code implementation
}
}
}
```

Once the file is saved, building the project in Visual Studio will result in a C# DLL that you can add to your DSC resource.

Packaging the C# custom DSC resource

As stated earlier, the conventions are the same with C# custom DSC resources as MOF-based custom DSC resources, and that applies to the folder structure as well. The only thing actually different is that you put the DLL in place of the .psm1 file:

```powershell
$env:ProgramFiles\WindowsPowerShell\Modules
|- xExampleThingDSCResource
|- xExampleThingDSCResource.psd1
|- DSCResources
|- xExampleThing
```

```
|- xExampleThing.psd1 (optional)
|- xExampleThing.dll (required)
|- xExampleThing.schema.mof (required)
```

Once that is done, deployment is the same as any other DSC resource described in this book.

Testing custom DSC resources

There are a few methods available to you to test the custom DSC resources you have created, whether they are PowerShell V4- or V5-based.

Using xDscResourceDesigner

We covered using `xDscResourceDesigner` in the previous section on creating module-based DSC resources, but automating DSC resource creation is not the only trick up this module's sleeve. The two cmdlets, `Test-xDscResource` and `Test-xDscSchema`, provided by this module aid in testing your custom DSC resources.

`Test-xDscResource` and `Test-xDscSchema` will check your custom DSC resource to make sure that the data types are the same between your DSC MOF schema file and your DSC PowerShell script `Get`, `Set`, and `Test-TargetResource` functions, and that the mandatory parameters are the same for all three functions, and that any parameters that are marked as `Mandatory` in the scripts are set to `Required` in the schema file.

You use `Test-xDscSchema` by providing it with a schema file to test:

```powershell
[PS]> Import-Module
$env:ProgramFiles\WindowsPowerShell\Modules\xDscResourceDesigner
 [PS]> test-xdscschema
"xWebAdministration\DSCResources\MSFT_xWebsite\MSFT_xWebsite.schema.mof"
 True
```

You use `Test-xDscResource` by passing it the path of the DSC resource you want to test:

```powershell
[PS]> import-module
$env:ProgramFiles\WindowsPowerShell\Modules\xDscResourceDesigner
[PS]> Test-xDscResource -Name 'xWebAdministration\DSCR
 esources\MSFT_xWebsite'
 True
```

In both `Test-xDscSchema` and `Test-xDscResource`, we had to provide exact paths to look for the DSC resource we were testing. It was not enough to just provide a path to the PowerShell module holding the DSC resources.

Pester

Pester is the name of an open source project that has become the de facto standard in testing PowerShell code, so much so that it is a Microsoft sponsored project that is being included in Windows 10. We can use Pester to write repeatable tests that run against our DSC resources as we develop them.

Pester and testing in general are expansive topics, so, if you need a starting point or a good refresher, the Pester WiKi page (`https://github.com/pester/Pester/wiki`) is the perfect place to start.

Here is an example Pester script that tests `ExampleResource` we have been using in our examples using the cmdlets from the `xDscResourceDesigner` module. This script will test our DSC resources and output any errors as we develop them:

```powershell
Import-Module
$PSScriptRoot\DSCResources\xExampleResource\xExampleResource.psm1
Describe 'ExampleDscResource Passes Standard DSC resource Tests' {
 It 'should be syntactically correct' {
 $res = Test-xDscSchema -Path
$PSScriptRoot\DSCResources\xExampleResource\xExampleResource.schema.mof
 $res | Should Be $true
 }
It 'should be a well formed resource' {
 $res = Test-xDscResource -Name xExampleResource
 $res | Should Be $true
 }
 }
```

Invoking a Pester run is done by importing the Pester module and executing the `Invoke-Pester` cmdlet, as follows:

```powershell
[PS]> Invoke-Pester
'$env:ProgramFiles\WindowsPowerShell\Modules\xExampleResource\xExampleResou
rce.tests.ps1'
 Describing ExampleDscResource Passes Standard DSC resource Tests
 [+] should be syntactically correct 147ms
 [+] should be a well formed resource 751ms
 Tests completed in 898ms
```

```
Passed: 2 Failed: 0 Skipped: 0 Pending: 0
```

You can also skip using the `Invoke-Pester` cmdlet and just invoke the PowerShell script file directly, if you are using the latest Pester release.

Microsoft recommendations

On the PowerShell blog, `http://blogs.msdn.com/b/powershell/archive/2014/11/18/ powershell-dsc-resource-design-and-testing-checklist.aspx`, Microsoft published a list of recommended steps to test your custom DSC resources. This is a very long list of suggestions that would be good for you to peruse and adapt to your testing process.

How do you find DSC resources?

There are several DSC resources that come *in the box* with a PowerShell install. These DSC resources are enough to get you started and cover most basic system and software configuration tasks; however, you are not expected to survive on these alone. Remember, we want to be as specific and custom as possible with a DSC resource, or it is of little use for us. At some point, you will want to find more DSC resources than those that come installed by default, but where do you go to get them?

Ruby has `https://rubygems.org/`, Perl has **CPA**, Node has npm, but what does DSC have? When DSC was still *new*, there were many places to find official and community-provided DSC resources, but there wasn't one place that everyone agreed to use. This is expected with a new software product; things are new and in flux and both the community and Microsoft haven't sorted out the best approaches for distribution yet. Things like this happen over time as various approaches are tried out and put through the gauntlets of production systems.

It took a long time for systems such as **Comprehensive Perl Archive Network (CPAN)** and npm to work out the kinks and be accepted as the default resources for both the companies that made them as well as the community that uses them. With this in mind, it's no surprise that Microsoft started out with one approach and is now moving toward a different approach. Over time, both the community and Microsoft have settled on using the `PSGallery` as a distribution mechanism, but we are getting ahead of ourselves; let's cover each available option one by one.

Microsoft DSC resource Kits

Microsoft's first approach was the DSC resource Kit. This harkens back to the Windows resource kits of old that first started coming out in the Windows NT days. The Windows resource kit was a bundle of several utilities that may not have had the same support guarantees as the built-in tools of Windows but provided needed functionality that system administrators came to rely on nonetheless.

The DSC resource Kit is similar in approach in that it contains several DSC resources bundled together into one ZIP file that you download from the Microsoft Script Center. However, they do not come with any support guarantees and are very much a *use at your own risk* type of option. This sounds like a dangerous idea and not something you would expect from Microsoft. You're used to getting production quality tools ready to use in your environment from Microsoft on day 1 of their release. This was a good approach for Microsoft in the past, but in today's world, delivering this kind of quality means months to even years of development and testing. Instead, Microsoft is following an agile cadence in releasing these DSC resources and producing a new release every month or so. By releasing these DSC resource Kits earlier in the development cycle, Microsoft delivers the tools faster to end users and also gets feedback earlier (when it can actually be acted upon and not months down the line when decisions are immovable). The users get the DSC resources they need sooner but have to balance that with testing these DSC resources themselves.

However convenient they are these, resource kits are hard to deploy in your environments. They were released in *waves* over the course of a year, each release happening every month or so. Users received a human typed list of changes and features added but no real way to see the differences between releases. Extensive testing had to be employed to ensure the new DSC resource at least behaved as well or better than the last release. These waves frequently had missing DSC resources that were present in the previous release, or they deprecated a DSC resource without telling the end user in the release notes, causing a surprise when the time came to use it. This made it quite evident that the process of releasing a resource kit wave involved a human zipping a folder by hand and writing up release notes after the fact, rather than an automated process that executed in tandem with development.

The largest negative aspect for this approach (as if the previous observations weren't enough), and most likely the reason Microsoft has de-emphasized this approach, is that it still took a long time for these resource kits to get to end users. It was a month or more between waves, and then the only way an end user knew there was a new release was to see it on the Windows PowerShell blog or through social media. While the PowerShell community is great at disseminating information quickly, this informal approach is not something to rely on as an update notification measure, and not one Microsoft really expected to stay as is. At the time of writing this, these kits are still available on the Script Center website but are not kept up to date.

Installing DSC resource Kits

Installing DSC resource Kits is a simple, if very manual, process:

1. Download the resource kit ZIP file from the Microsoft Script Center.
2. Extract it to a deployment location.
3. Copy the deployment folder to the `$env:ProgramFiles\WindowsPowerShell\Modules` folder on all target nodes.

These steps are repeated for every new release and every new target machine.

Microsoft PowerShell DSC GitHub repository

The DSC resources provided in the resource kits were developed at an agile cadence, which meant that the community received the DSC resources faster than the traditional development schedules could handle. This speed also meant that bugs were caught by the community instead of through internal testing. The PowerShell community is a powerful force full of some very smart people; when they are presented with a problem, they find a solution. Ultimately, they found solutions to these bugs but had nowhere to submit them.

Seeing the need to have the official DSC resources developed in the open and in a manner that could accept contributions from the community, the Microsoft PowerShell team open sourced all the existing DSC resources that were previously only available inside the resource kits and put them up on GitHub at `https://github.com/powershell/DscResources` or, as we will refer to it from now on, PowerShell or DSC resources.

Gone are the days of finding a solution to a problem in an existing DSC resource and not being able to share your solution with the community. With a little bit of Git knowledge, you can commit your fix to the PowerShell or DSC resources repositories and see your fix directly used by anyone using that module.

If at this point you're seeing Git and GitHub and wondering what the author is going on about, you shouldn't worry, as you are not alone. Git is a version control system for software code and is currently the soup of the day of VCS software. If Git is new to you, you should take some time to learn about it before you try to commit your fixes or features to the community. There are many books and resources online to help you learn Git, and going to `https://git-scm.com/` will get you on your way.

If you do not feel like learning Git at this point, do not worry; this book will assume some basic Git knowledge only for this section and will not be needed for the rest of the chapter.

When we refer to the PowerShell or DSC resources GitHub repository, we actually mean repositories. The PowerShell team created a GitHub organization and created a repository per DSC resource module. While this resulted in many repositories (currently 52 and counting) and sounds like a hard-to-manage solution, this approach makes sense. You want each DSC resource module to be a unique unit where bug reports and feature requests can be made without confusing things for other DSC resources. A repository per DSC resource module also allows separate versioning per DSC resource, which is a must when dealing with so many different moving parts. You want to be able to say that an increment to the version of the `xTimeZone` DSC resource does not mean the user has to update the `xWinEventLog` DSC resource as well.

This does make consuming these DSC resources slightly cumbersome. You could maintain a separate clone locally of each DSC resource repository and keep it up to date yourself. Doing this, however, makes you in charge of tracking versioning and tags and determining when a given DSC resource is *stable*.

Another approach is to use the PowerShell or DSC resources repository. This repository is a mostly empty repository that contains Git submodules, or links, to all the individual DSC resource repositories. When cloning `https://github.com/PowerShell/DscResources`, you tell Git to recursively check out all the Git submodules as well as the main repository:

```
[PS]> git clone https://github.com/PowerShell/DscResources --recurse -
submodules
```

Git submodules and their use are a hot topic in developer circles. There is a lot of opinion and disagreement out there on how to use them or whether to use them at all, which is mostly out of the scope of this book to address. What is germane to our use case is that Git submodules are point-in-time links to a certain Git commit. This means that when checking out the PowerShell or DSC resources repository, we do get all DSC resources but at the latest Git commit they have been pinned at. If active development is going on in a given DSC resource repository, it won't be reflected in the PowerShell or DSC resources repository because it has not been updated to point at the newer commit.

The point in time where the repository is pinned is the last release for that specific DSC resource. So, when cloning PowerShell or DSC resources, you are sure to get all the currently released code at that point in time. This gives you a measure of surety that you are getting stable code. In order to live life on the bleeding edge, you would either have to fork the PowerShell or DSC resources repository and keep the Git module links up to date yourself or go directly to each DSC resource in GitHub and check out the latest.

If this all sounds like a lot to learn at once, keep faith; we are approaching the easiest way to handle this.

Installing DSC resources from GitHub

While GitHub is a great development experience and a great way to see how the DSC resources you are using are being worked on, this does not lend well to some operational deployment models. You will have to either clone the main PowerShell or DSC resources repository or keep up with all the available DSC resource repositories on GitHub. Then, once these are all cloned, you'll have to take the local copy and distribute it out to your target nodes or your DSC pull servers yourself. Sure, you can automate some of this and get a pretty good script going, but if this all feels like a *solved problem* that you shouldn't be worrying about, you are not alone. The Microsoft PowerShell Gallery addresses this issue.

Microsoft PowerShell Gallery

The Microsoft PowerShell Gallery is a central repository for PowerShell modules and DSC resources and is the premier choice for consuming and deploying DSC resources. The PowerShell Gallery contains useful PowerShell modules and DSC resources that you can use on all your target servers. Not all of the content in the Gallery will be from Microsoft; some of it will be community contributed content. It is recommended that you test and inspect all content downloaded from the Gallery.

When we use the word `repository` here, we mean software repository, not software version control such as when we were talking about Git in the previous section.

To use the PowerShell Gallery, you must use a new feature of PowerShell called `PackageManagement`. `PackageManagement` is a software package manager that manages packages. All jokes aside, `PackageManagement` is a powerful solution to the problem of finding, downloading, and installing PowerShell modules onto Windows target nodes.

PackageManagement

At its core, `PackageManagement` handles the searching for and resolving of software packages and installing those packages on target nodes. The beauty of `PackageManagement` is that it delegates the details of package resolution and installation to submodules that handle the specifics of each software package and platform. This enables `PackageManagement` to leave the implementation details to the `last mile` and worry about the larger issues at stake, resulting in faster, more nimble releases and allowing a large plugin community to grow to address any need.

`PackageManagement` is currently targeted for release with PowerShell V5, but it supports downlevel versions of Windows and PowerShell. The following instructions have been tested as working on PowerShell V4, but as it is still in development, there may be steps changed or parts of this list that will be out of date at the time of publication. In that case, refer to the `PackageManagement` documentation or the PowerShell Gallery for more information.

Installing PackageManagement

`PackageManagement` comes pre installed in any PowerShell V5 installation, but there are downlevel packages available for the other PowerShell versions. Refer to `http://www.powershellgallery.com/` for installation details for downlevel packages.

Each PowerShell V5 installation package is a Windows Update standalone installer package or MSU. MSU responds to standardized command-line automation or through a user interface, so deploying PowerShell V5 manually or through software deployment systems such as Windows Update or SCOM should be relatively straightforward.

Initializing PackageManagement

Once installed, you have to initialize `PackageManagement` by running a command to the `bootstrap` NuGet on the target node. This can either be done on demand when a call to `PackageManagement` is performed, such as `Find-Module` or `Install-Module` cmdlet, or it can be done interactively on the command line, as follows:

```powershell
```powershell
[PS]> Get-PackageProvider -Name NuGet -ForceBootstrap
 NuGet-anycpu.exe is required to continue.
 PowerShellGet requires NuGet-anycpu.exe to interact with NuGet based
galleries. NuGet-anycpu.exe must be available in
 'C:\Program Files\PackageManagement\ProviderAssemblies' or
 'C:\Users\James\AppData\Local\PackageManagement\ProviderAssemblies'. For
more information about NuGet provider, see
 http://OneGet.org/NuGet.html. Do you want PowerShellGet to download NuGet-
anycpu.exe now?
```
```

```
[Y] Yes [N] No [S] Suspend [?] Help (default is "Y"): Y
```

Once bootstrapped, `PackageManagement` will have all it needs to resolve and install packages.

Discover DSC resources in the PowerShell Gallery

Discovering DSC resources in the PowerShell Gallery is a primary use case for the PSGallery and `PackageManagement`, so it is no surprise that it is an easy and smooth task.

You can find all the available DSC resources in the `PSGallery`. While you can use the website to search for and find DSC resources, most of the searching and discovery you perform will be using the `Find-Module` cmdlet. `Find-Module` will work on any `PackageManagement` provider, but here we will focus just on `PSGallery`:

```powershell
[PS]> Find-Module -Includes DscResource
Version Name Repository Description
------- ---- ---------- -----------
0.2.16.6 xJea PSGallery Module with DSC resources for Just Enough Admin
...
1.6.0.0 xWebAdministration PSGallery Module with DSC resources for Web
Administration
3.3.0.0 xPSDesiredStateConfiguration PSGallery The
xPSDesiredStateConfiguration module is a par...
1.2.0 xDatabase PSGallery This module contains 2 resources. xDatabase
allo...
1.3.0 xComputerManagement PSGallery The xComputerManagement module is
originally par...
2.0.0 xWindowsUpdate PSGallery Module with DSC resources for Windows
Update
2.4.0.0 xActiveDirectory PSGallery Module with DSC resources for Active
Directory
```

You can search for a specific DSC resource using its name or wildcards:

```powershell
[PS]> Find-Module -Name xWinEventLog
Version Name Repository Description
------- ---- ---------- -----------
1.0.0.0 xWinEventLog PSGallery Configure Windows Event Logs
[PS]> Find-Module -Name xWin*
Version Name Repository Description
------- ---- ---------- -----------
1.0.0.0 xWindowsEventForwarding PSGallery This module can be used to
manage configuration ...
1.0.0 xWindowsRestore PSGallery This DSC Module includes 2 DSC resources,
```

```
xSyste...
 2.0.0 xWindowsUpdate PSGallery Module with DSC resources for Windows
Update
 1.0.0.0 xWinEventLog PSGallery Configure Windows Event Logs
```

You can also search with a recently added new cmdlet called `Find-DscResource`:

```powershell
[PS]> Find-DscResource -moduleName xWebAdministration
Name Version ModuleName Repository
---- ------- ---------- ----------
 xIisFeatureDelegation 1.7.0.0 xWebAdministration PSGallery
 xIisHandler 1.7.0.0 xWebAdministration PSGallery
 xIisMimeTypeMapping 1.7.0.0 xWebAdministration PSGallery
 xIisModule 1.7.0.0 xWebAdministration PSGallery
 xWebApplication 1.7.0.0 xWebAdministration PSGallery
 xWebAppPool 1.7.0.0 xWebAdministration PSGallery
 xWebAppPoolDefaults 1.7.0.0 xWebAdministration PSGallery
 xWebConfigKeyValue 1.7.0.0 xWebAdministration PSGallery
 xWebsite 1.7.0.0 xWebAdministration PSGallery
 xWebSiteDefaults 1.7.0.0 xWebAdministration PSGallery
 xWebVirtualDirectory 1.7.0.0 xWebAdministration PSGallery
```

Installing DSC resources in the PowerShell Gallery

The cmdlet `Install-Module` is used to install DSC resources from the `PSGallery`. It installs DSC resources to the `$env:ProgramFiles\WindowsPowerShell\Modules` directory by default, which requires administrator privileges:

```powershell
[PS}]> Install-Module -Name xWinEventLog -Verbose
 VERBOSE: The -Repository parameter was not specified. PowerShellGet will
use all of the registered repositories.
 VERBOSE: Getting the provider object for the PackageManagement Provider
'NuGet'.
 VERBOSE: The specified Location is
'https://www.powershellgallery.com/api/v2/' and PackageManagementProvider
is
 'NuGet'.
 VERBOSE: The specified module will be installed in 'C:\Program
Files\WindowsPowerShell\Modules'.
 VERBOSE: The specified Location is 'NuGet' and PackageManagementProvider
is 'NuGet'.
 VERBOSE: Downloading module 'xWinEventLog' with version '1.0.0.0' from the
repository
 'https://www.powershellgallery.com/api/v2/'.
 VERBOSE: NuGet: GET
```

```
https://www.powershellgallery.com/api/v2/Packages(Id='xWinEventLog',Version
='1.0.0.0')
 VERBOSE: NuGet: GET
https://www.powershellgallery.com/api/v2/package/xWinEventLog/1.0.0
 VERBOSE: NuGet: Installing 'xWinEventLog 1.0.0.0'.
 VERBOSE: NuGet: Successfully installed 'xWinEventLog 1.0.0.0'.
 VERBOSE: Module 'xWinEventLog' was installed successfully.
```

You can also pipe `Find-Module` to `Install-Module`:

```powershell
[PS]> Find-Module -Name xWinEventLog | Install-Module
```

By default, `Install-Module` installs the latest version of a DSC resource, so if you are looking for a specific version, you can specify the `RequiredVersion` parameter:

```powershell
[PS]> Install-Module -Name xWinEventLog -RequiredVersion 1.1.0.0
```

You can list the installed DSC resources in two ways:

```
[PS]> Get-DscResource
Implemented As Name Module Properties
-------------- ---- ------ ----------
 Binary File {DestinationPath, Attributes, Checksum, Con...
 PowerShell Archive PSDesiredStateConfiguration {Destination, Path,
Checksum, Credential...}
 PowerShell Environment PSDesiredStateConfiguration {Name, DependsOn,
Ensure, Path...}
 PowerShell Group PSDesiredStateConfiguration {GroupName, Credential,
DependsOn, Descript...
 Binary Log PSDesiredStateConfiguration {Message, DependsOn}
 PowerShell Package PSDesiredStateConfiguration {Name, Path, ProductId,
Arguments...}
```

You can also specify the exact name to check whether a DSC resource is present:

```powershell
[PS]> Get-DscResource -Name xWinEventLog
ImplementedAs Name Module Properties
-------------- ---- ------ ----------
 PowerShell xWinEventLog xWinEventLog {LogName, DependsOn, IsEnabled,
LogMode...}
```

Custom hosting options

At some point, you might want to create your own host for DSC resources. Maybe you'll want to host your own DSC resources for your company, or you might want to maintain a local copy of DSC resources so you don't have to go to the internet every time you provision a machine. Whatever the reason, hosting your own DSC resource repository is a reasonable desire. Unfortunately, there are not many ready-made solutions out there that work without significant effort. Microsoft has said they are working on a solution, but they have not produced one yet.

Local SMB/network share

If you have a file share ready to hold all your DSC resources, you can create a repository that `PackageManagement` will use to resolve and install your DSC resources.

In order to avoid any issues with DSC resources you may have created during the course of the book, we will use the `xWebAdministration` module. You can download it from the Microsoft GitHub repo at `https://github.com/PowerShell/xWebAdministration`. If you already have it present on the test system, remove it. If you are using a copy of `xWebAdministration` you installed from the `PSGallery`, you may have a second subfolder with the module version as its name. Ensure that you point the following commands to that folder name instead of the root `xWebAdministration` one so that the `Publish-Module` cmdlet can properly find the `.psd1` files.

The first step is to register the network share as a repository:

```powershell
[PS]> Register-PSRepository -Name folder -SourceLocation D:\packages\ -
PublishLocation D:\packages\ -Verbose
 VERBOSE: Repository details, Name = 'PSGallery', Location =
'https://www.powershellgallery.com/api/v2/'; IsTrusted = 'False';
IsRegistered = 'True'.
 VERBOSE: Performing the operation "Register Module Repository" on target
"Module Repository 'folder' (D:\packages\) in provider 'PSModule'".
 VERBOSE: The specified PackageManagement provider name 'NuGet'.
 VERBOSE: Successfully registered the repository 'folder' with source
location 'D:\packages\'.
 VERBOSE: Repository details, Name = 'folder', Location = 'D:\packages\';
IsTrusted = 'False'; IsRegistered = 'True'.
```

The next step is to publish your DSC resource package to the folder using the `Publish-Module` cmdlet. One thing to note is that we pass a value to the `NugetApiKey` parameter; that doesn't mean anything. This is because we are pushing to a local folder and not a NuGet server, such as the `PSGallery`. `Publish-Module` expects you to be pushing to a `PSGallery` based repository but will function just the same with a folder:

```powershell
[PS]> Publish-Module -Path 'C:\example\xWebAdministration\' -NugetApiKey
'j' -Repository folder -Verbose
 VERBOSE: Repository details, Name = 'folder', Location = 'D:\packages\';
IsTrusted = 'False';IsRegistered = 'True'.
 VERBOSE: Repository details, Name = 'folder', Location = 'D:\packages\';
IsTrusted = 'False';IsRegistered = 'True'.
 VERBOSE: Module'xWebAdministration' was found in 'C:\Program
Files\WindowsPowerShell\MOdules\xWebAdministration\'.
 VERBOSE: Repository details, Name = 'folder', Location = 'D:\packages\';
IsTrusted = 'False';IsRegistered = 'True'.
 VERBOSE: Repository details, Name = 'folder', Location = 'D:\packages\';
IsTrusted = 'False';IsRegistered = 'True'.
 VERBOSE: Using the specified source names : 'folder'.
 VERBOSE: Getting the provider object for the PackageManagement Provider
'NuGet'.
 VERBOSE: The specified Location is 'D:\packages\' and
PackageManagementProvider is 'NuGet'.
 VERBOSE: Performing the operation "Publish-Module" on target "Version
'1.7.0.0' of module 'xWebAdministration'".
 VERBOSE: Successfully published module 'xWebAdministration' to the module
publish location 'D:\packages\'. Please allow few minutes for
'xWebAdministration' to show up in the search results.
```

Installing the module works just as if you were installing from the `PSGallery`, except you specify which repository you want to install it from:

```powershell
[PS]> Install-module -Name xWebAdministration -Repository folder -Verbose -
Force -RequiredVersion 1.7.0.0
 VERBOSE: Repository details, Name = 'folder', Location = 'D:\packages';
IsTrusted = 'False'; IsRegistered = 'True'.
 VERBOSE: Repository details, Name = 'folder', Location = 'D:\packages';
IsTrusted = 'False'; IsRegistered = 'True'.
 VERBOSE: Using the specified source names : 'folder'.
 VERBOSE: Getting the provider object for the PackageManagement Provider
'NuGet'.
 VERBOSE: The specified Location is 'D:\packages' and
PackageManagementProvider is 'NuGet'.
 VERBOSE: The specified module will be installed in 'C:\Program
Files\WindowsPowerShell\Modules'.
```

```
 VERBOSE: The specified Location is 'NuGet' and PackageManagementProvider
is 'NuGet'.
 VERBOSE: Downloading module xWebAdministration with version '1.7.0.0' from
the repository 'D:\packages'.
 VERBOSE: NuGet: Installing 'xWebAdministration 1.7.0.0'.
 VERBOSE: NuGet: Successfully installed 'xExampleResource 1.7.0.0'.
 VERBOSE: Module 'xWebAdministration' was installed successfully.
```

NuGet IIS

Another solution builds off of the work the NuGet team did for hosting their own packages. Instructions for setting this up are at `http://blogs.msdn.com/b/powershell/archive/` `2014/05/20/setting-up-an-internal-powershellget-repository.aspx`. This is honestly the hardest to set up as it requires you to compile ASP.NET projects and deploy websites yourself. This may be too much work for you to do, or it may be a piece of cake depending on your experience level.

Third-party NuGet servers

There are several NuGet server options that are from the community and also run on non-Windows systems. An open source project called Chocolatey has a good guide on how to use these at `https://github.com/chocolatey/choco/wiki/How-To-Host-Feed#non-windows-hosting`.

Deploying DSC resources

You have learned the many different ways to create DSC resources and ways to host them in your environments, but how do you deploy them to your target nodes? The answer to this depends on how you will be using your DSC configuration scripts in your environment. We will cover this in greater detail in `Chapter 5`, *Pushing DSC Configurations*, and `Chapter 6`, *Pulling DSC Configurations*, but for now, we will touch on it briefly.

Deploying DSC resources in a push DSC configuration deployment

If you are using the **push** model of DSC configuration deployment, you are responsible for deploying all the DSC resources you use to each and every target node yourself before you push a DSC configuration to the target node. If you don't, then the DSC configuration script will fail with an error, complaining that it cannot find the DSC resource. This is because the DSC engine on the target node is not responsible for finding the DSC resource to use.

Deploying DSC resources in a pull DSC configuration deployment

If you are using the **pull** model of DSC configuration deployment, then the distribution of DSC resources is handled by the DSC pull server you configured for your environment. There are specific rules for packaging the DSC resources for distribution by the pull server, and that is covered in detail in Chapter 6, *Pulling DSC Configurations*.

Summary

In this chapter, we covered the DSC resource structure, syntax, and definitions. We covered how to find DSC resources to fit our needs and how to author useful DSC resources if we do not find what we need. We covered the differences between PowerShell V4 and class-based DSC resources and some reasons you will probably want to move toward class-based DSC resources sooner rather than later.

In the next chapter, we will cover the first way to actually execute DSC configuration scripts: the DSC push model.

5

Pushing DSC Configurations

"The past, like the future, is indefinite and exists only as a spectrum of possibilities"
- Stephen Hawking

We have covered everything there is to know about DSC and its internals at this point, but we have not fully explained the different ways DSC configurations actually get to the target nodes. In the first few chapters of the book, you learned that there are two models to DSC: a push and a pull model. In this chapter, we will be covering the push model. We will first define what the push model is and then move on to how to use it with DSC configurations. We'll take an example configuration and apply it to a local target node and a remote target node.

In this chapter, we will cover the following topics:

- Tooling
- Setting things up
- Locally pushing DSC configurations
- Remotely pushing DSC configurations

 Look at `Chapter 7`, *DSC Cross Platform Support*, for information specific to using DSC on Linux and other platforms. This chapter will focus on only Windows platforms.

Tooling

DSC supports applying DSC configurations locally and remotely using the `Start-DSCConfiguration` cmdlet. This cmdlet handles both the copying of the MOF file to the target node and telling DSC to execute the MOF on the target node.

`Start-DSCConfiguration` can be invoked interactively as well as be run in the background. Interactive executions are run as we are watching and are able to show verbose output as each step in the DSC configuration happens. Background executions are PowerShell jobs that do not block your shell so that you can do other things while the job runs. This means you can use this cmdlet to push a DSC configuration and then walk away or continue to use your current PowerShell console session to do other things as it executes on the target node.

All output from the DSC configuration execution is logged by DSC, and the `Start-DSCConfiguration` cmdlet can show this information if configured. By default, it displays only the error and completion information, but it can be configured to yield verbose output using the `Verbose` parameter.

It is important to note that `Start-DSCConfiguration` does not perform the execution itself; the DSC service does this on the target node. This means nothing is tied to you, your shell, or your session. Your current console session could stop or go away and the execution would still run. This allows a *set it and forget it* workflow where you push a configuration and walk away to do other things while it runs and then come back and find the results of the execution ready and waiting for you.

Setting things up

Up until now, you could have gotten away with just looking at the examples in the book without running them or adapting them slightly to work on your desktop or a test VM or server. At this point, it is really helpful to have a test VM that you can create and destroy several times over as you work through the examples. This is especially true when we try executing DSC configurations remotely later in the chapter.

Test environment

There are several approaches you can take when building and using test environments. If you have spare physical machines, you can set up several machines as test servers to run these configurations. This is the easiest way if you have the extra hardware lying around, but it becomes difficult when you want to treat them as disposable machines. Constantly reinstalling the machines will become tedious without imaging software, so keep in mind the time and cost this entails if you go this route.

A far easier route is **Virtual Machines** (**VM**), which are commonplace in today's world. Hyper-V, VMware, and Parallels have options to run VMs on your desktop or laptop. This allows you to have dependable and repeatable tests on known configurations so that you can keep testing your DSC configurations until you are sure they work.

While each of these vendors' software has the functionality to allow you to perform an operation and then *roll back* to a known good state, it is sometimes slow and cumbersome to use these features. They were designed with infrequent use in mind. We are looking for something that can be brought up in minutes just as easily as it can be destroyed. A good tool to look into using for this purpose is Vagrant (https://www.vagrantup.com/). Setting up and using Vagrant is out of the scope of this book, but there are a good many resources out there to get you started. It will make your life a lot easier to use tools such as Vagrant, VMware, or Hyper-V to automate your development environments.

For the purpose of this book, it is not necessary to have these setups specifically, but we will assume that you are at least using a test machine on which you can run these commands time and again while you get used to these operations.

We are going to build two test computers and call them box1 and box2. We will use box1 both as the place where we make the DSC configuration and the place where we execute it from. The second test computer, box2, will be our target node that receives DSC configurations from us so that we can demonstrate remote operations. Because of this, both computers need to be able to access each other on the network, so configure your IP addresses appropriately.

One additional thing we are going to do is add a custom prompt to both boxes so we can easily identify which box we are on. Add this to the PowerShell profile on each box:

```
function prompt { "[$($env:COMPUTERNAME) PS] > " }
```

This will output a prompt that looks like this:

```
[BOX1 PS] >
```

Locally pushing DSC configurations

What do we mean by "*pushing DSC configurations locally?*" When we apply a DSC configuration to the computer we are logged into, we are applying or pushing the DSC configuration onto the computer. We call it *pushing* because we are actively copying the MOF file and triggering an execution on the target node; we are active participants in the whole process. The `Start-DSCConfiguration` cmdlet does the work for us, but we are actively requesting the operations to be performed. This is clear when we contrast this with a DSC pull server. The DSC engine on the target node pulls the DSC configuration when an execution run is scheduled, whereas we push the DSC configuration to the target node when we want to execute it interactively using `Start-DSCConfiguration`.

The `Start-DSCConfiguration` cmdlet syntax we will be using is this:

```
Start-DSCConfiguration [-Path] <System.String> [-Wait] [-Force]
[<CommonParameters>] -CimSession <CimSession[]>
```

It is a modified version of what you would see if you used the `Get-Help` cmdlet because we have omitted extra parameters to better illustrate what we are doing in this chapter. This is significantly simpler than what we will be dealing with when we push DSC configuration files remotely, so it is a good place to start.

`Start-DSCConfiguration` accepts a `-Path` variable where the MOF file will be and a `Boolean` parameter called `-Wait`, along with common parameters such as `Verbose` and `Debug`. The `Wait` parameter is the indication that we want the job to run in front of us and only return when the DSC execution is completed. Any errors during execution will be presented to us during the execution run, but there will be no other information. For this reason, when using `Wait`, it is commonplace to use `Verbose` as well so that the running output from the DSC configuration is presented to you as it happens. We'll be using this combination as we proceed for this very reason, but we may not include all the output text as it can become quite verbose (pun intended).

Setting up the test environment locally

Besides building the test computer, there is not much setup to do in order to run things locally.

Compiling configurations for local target nodes

Our focus in this chapter is on how to push DSC configurations and not how to use DSC configurations, so our example configuration is simple and short. This reduces the amount of code we are working with and the amount of logging we output, which allows us to fit the DSC configurations in our chapter without having pages of printouts.

 At this point, you should be familiar with compiling DSC configuration scripts into MOF files. In this chapter, we make the assumption that you have a good grasp of the DSC configuration block syntax and how to use and author DSC configuration scripts. If you are skipping around or feeling fuzzy about these concepts, refer to these chapters before you continue.

In our example script, we will create a text file on the primary drive with dummy contents. Again, we are purposely not being fancy here in order to focus on how to push DSC configurations and not the DSC configurations themselves:

```
Configuration SetupAllTheThings
{
  Node "localhost"
  {
    File CreateFile
    {
      Ensure          = "Present"
      DestinationPath = "c:\test.txt"
      Contents        = "Wakka"
    }
  }
}

$mofPath = [IO.Path]::Combine($PSScriptRoot, "SetupAllTheThings")
SetupAllTheThings -OutputPath $mofPath
```

Compiling the preceding DSC configuration script gives us a valid MOF file that we can use on the local computer. This should all be straightforward for you by now, and you should see the following results from the compiling of the MOF file:

```
[BOX1 PS] > C:\vagrant\SetupAllTheThings.ps1
    Directory: C:\vagrant\SetupAllTheThings
    Mode                LastWriteTime     Length Name
    ----                -------------     ------ ----
    -----          7/01/2015   3:19 PM      1276 localhost.mof
```

If that doesn't compile correctly, look at your syntax and ensure it's the same as what we have laid out here. It may help if you add the Verbose parameter to our DSC configuration function to see what is going on as the MOF is compiled. If you are still having trouble or want to see even more information, then you can set your $DebugPreference to Continue and receive even more diagnostic information. An example output is as follows:

```
DEBUG:      MSFT_PackageResource: ResourceID = [Package]InstallTheThing
DEBUG:      MSFT_PackageResource: Processing property 'DependsOn' [
DEBUG:      MSFT_PackageResource:    Processing completed 'DependsOn' ]
DEBUG:      MSFT_PackageResource: Processing property 'Ensure' [
DEBUG:      MSFT_PackageResource:    Processing completed 'Ensure' ]
DEBUG:      MSFT_PackageResource: Processing property 'Name' [
DEBUG:      MSFT_PackageResource:       Canonicalized property 'Name' = 'The
Thing'
DEBUG:      MSFT_PackageResource:    Processing completed 'Name' ]
DEBUG:      MSFT_PackageResource: Processing property 'Path' [
DEBUG:      MSFT_PackageResource:   Canonicalized property 'Path' =
'c:\allthethings\thing.msi'
DEBUG:      MSFT_PackageResource:    Processing completed 'Path' ]
DEBUG:      MSFT_PackageResource: Processing property 'ProductId' [
DEBUG:      MSFT_PackageResource:   Canonicalized property 'ProductId' =
'{8f665668-7679-4f53-acde-06cf7eab5d73}'
```

 Sometimes, it's hard to see the exact error in the DSC output, so get used to using PowerShell to inspect the built-in $error array to drill down and find the exact information you need, as shown here:

[BOX1 PS] > $error[0] | Format-List –Property * –Force

If we examine the localhost.mof file, we will see that the file resource laid out applies to a target node named localhost. This means that although we compile this MOF file on the computer we are sitting at, this MOF file can be pushed to any computer, whether locally or remotely, because localhost applies to any computer. If we wanted to restrict which target nodes used specific MOF files, we would need to specify their host names in the Node block. We will cover this when we deal with pushing DSC configurations remotely in a little bit.

Executing configurations for local target nodes

Now that we have the MOF file compiled, we can apply it to our local computer using `Start-DscConfiguration`. We will use the `Verbose`, `Wait`, and `Force` parameters to indicate that we want it to execute interactively and output verbose information to our shell. We use `Force` to tell DSC to apply the MOF file regardless of the current state of the target node (whether it has a pending MOF file or not):

```
[BOX1 PS] > Start-DscConfiguration -Path C:\vagrant\SetupAllTheThings -
Verbose -Wait -Force
VERBOSE: Perform operation 'Invoke CimMethod' with following parameters,
''methodName' =
    SendConfigurationApply,'className' =
MSFT_DSCLocalConfigurationManager,'namespaceName' =
    root/Microsoft/Windows/DesiredStateConfiguration'.
    VERBOSE: An LCM method call arrived from computer BOX1 with user sid
    S-1-5-21-1953236517-242735908-2433092285-500.
VERBOSE: [BOX1]: LCM:  [ Start  Set       ]
VERBOSE: [BOX1]: LCM:  [ Start  Resource  ]  [[File]CreateaFile]
VERBOSE: [BOX1]: LCM:  [ Start  Test      ]  [[File]CreateaFile]
VERBOSE: [BOX1]:                             [[File]CreateaFile] The system
cannot find the file specified.
VERBOSE: [BOX1]:                             [[File]CreateaFile] The related
file/directory is: c:\test.txt.
VERBOSE: [BOX1]: LCM:  [ End    Test      ]  [[File]CreateaFile]  in 0.0320
seconds.
VERBOSE: [BOX1]: LCM:  [ Start  Set       ]  [[File]CreateaFile]
VERBOSE: [BOX1]:                             [[File]CreateaFile] The system
cannot find the file specified.
VERBOSE: [BOX1]:                             [[File]CreateaFile] The related
file/directory is: c:\test.txt.
VERBOSE: [BOX1]: LCM:  [ End    Set       ]  [[File]CreateaFile]  in 0.0000
seconds.
VERBOSE: [BOX1]: LCM:  [ End    Resource  ]  [[File]CreateaFile]
VERBOSE: [BOX1]: LCM:  [ End    Set       ]
VERBOSE: [BOX1]: LCM:  [ End    Set       ]    in  0.0790 seconds.
VERBOSE: Operation 'Invoke CimMethod' complete.
VERBOSE: Time taken for configuration job to complete is 0.16 seconds
[BOX1 PS] >
[BOX1 PS] > Test-Path C:\test.txt
True
```

We get a lot of information back, so let's go over what we see. It initially tells us that it's performing a DSC operation and then tells us about the methods it's using to invoke. This is where we see that the `Start-DSCConfiguration` cmdlet is just a wrapper over the CIM methods that actually execute the DSC functions. You won't need to know these CIM methods for everyday use, but it's interesting to see the inner workings shown here. The next line tells us that all the subsequent lines come from our target node `box1` and were initiated by a user with this SID. It doesn't look too important here as we're running on the same box we've compiled the MOF on, but when we deal with remote pushes, noting which target node had which operations occur on it, it becomes very important. The rest of the lines tell us that the file did not exist and that DSC had to create it. Not so hard, is it?

Remotely pushing DSC configurations

Once you have mastered pushing DSC configuration files locally, you will find that there isn't a lot of difference in pushing them remotely. It follows pretty much the same steps but with the addition of creating a remote session on the target host before pushing. We can either create remote sessions called `CimSessions` ourselves or allow `Start-DSCConfiguration` to create them for us in order to pass information and commands to the remote host.

We would create `CimSessions` ourselves if we wanted to reuse the sessions for multiple attempts, as this would save us time connecting, closing, and reconnecting each time we attempted to push DSC configurations. We would also create `CimSessions` if we had a nonstandard WinRM setup, for example, HTTPS endpoints or different authentication methods (Kerberos or basic authentication, and so on).

You will definitely create your own `CimSessions` in a non-domain or workgroup environment, as the account you are using to issue the `Start-DSCConfiguration` command will be local to the computer you are sitting at and not present on the remote target node. You would also have to configure the authentication methods in order to have local token policies allow remote use of the administrator account. Configuring remote sessions is a huge topic and varies with environments; you should look up the PowerShell documentation for more information about special options when connecting with WinRM and PowerShell remoting. Some places to start are
`http://blogs.technet.com/b/heyscriptingguy/archive/2013/11/29/remoting-week-non -domain-remoting.aspx` and
`http://blogs.msdn.com/b/wmi/archive/2009/07/24/powershell-remoting-between-two- workgroup-machines.aspx`.

Before continuing with this section, it is helpful to know what PowerShell Remoting and PowerShell CimSessions are. These features are used heavily with the remote use of DSC, so having an understanding of how they work will be the key for you to use it effectively. Explaining PSRemoting is outside the scope of this book, but there are several resources online to follow. A good place to start is on the TechNet site: http://blogs.technet.com/b/heyscriptingguy/archive/2014/01/31/co mparing-powershell-pssessions-and-cim-sessions.aspx.

You may not be familiar with CimSessions as much as you are with PSSession, but they both describe remote sessions on a target node. What is important to know for this chapter is that CimSessions cannot execute arbitrary code like a PSSession can; it executes specific CIM methods on a remote target node. Start-DSCConfiguration and other DSC cmdlets are mostly wrappers around CIM methods. This is not a limitation for CimSessions, as working this way takes up fewer system resources on the target node.

You create CimSessions using the New-CimSession cmdlet and storing the result in a variable that you can pass to the Start-DSCConfiguration cmdlet:

```
[PS]> $cred = Get-Credential
[PS]> $session = New-CimSession -ComputerName "foo" -Credential $cred
```

As you can see, the New-CimSession cmdlet accepts a computer name and a PSCredential object. We can also create many CimSessions at the same time by passing an array of computer names, as follows:

```
[PS]> $session = New-CimSession -ComputerName "foo","Bar" -Credential (Get-Credential)
```

Now that we know how to connect to a target node, we can start setting up the environment.

Setting up the test environment remotely

Pushing DSC configurations remotely requires some extra steps. Some of these steps may not be needed in your environment, depending on how you configured it. We will note which case it is as we come to each step.

On `box1`, we run the following commands to allow `PSRemoting` to connect using IP addresses. This is not necessary in a production environment and is only necessary when you are using IP addresses and not short domain names or **fully qualified domain names (FQDN)**. Since the example test environment is using test VMs that have no DNS here, we have to allow IP addresses to be used:

```
[BOX1 PS] >Set-Item WSMan:\localhost\Client\TrustedHosts -Value *
WinRM Security Configuration.
This command modifies the TrustedHosts list for the WinRM client. The
computers in the TrustedHosts list might not be authenticated. The client
might send credential information to these computers. Are you sure that you
want to modify
this list?
[Y] Yes  [N] No  [S] Suspend  [?] Help (default is "Y"): Y
[BOX1 PS] >
```

In `box2`, we run the following commands. Modifying the built-in firewall is only necessary in a test environment to make life easier and is not recommended in a production environment. In a production environment, you would have already allowed rules in your firewall setup for `PSRemoting`, so this should not be necessary. The second command enables `PSRemoting`. DSC doesn't require `PSRemoting` exactly; it requires WinRM to work against remote target nodes. We use the commands to enable `PSRemoting` because these commands configure and start up WinRM for us without any extra effort on our part. Starting with Windows 2012, `PSRemoting` comes enabled by default, so it really is not much of an imposition to expect both to be configured on target nodes:

```
[BOX2 PS] >Set-NetFirewallProfile -All -Enabled False
[BOX2 PS] >Enable-PSRemoting -Force
WinRM is already set up to receive requests on this computer.
WinRM is already set up for remote management on this computer.
```

We can test connections from `box1` to `box2` by creating a `CimSession` using the commands we covered earlier:

```
[BOX1 PS] > $cred = Get-Credential administrator
[BOX1 PS] > $session = New-CimSession -ComputerName "192.168.0.13" -
Credential $cred
[BOX1 PS] > $session
Id           : 1
Name         : CimSession1
InstanceId   : 687de6e6-aa1a-43f6-8419-dadef292efa7
ComputerName : 192.168.0.13
Protocol     : WSMAN
```

If errors occur, then check your network connectivity and permissions. Consult the PowerShell remoting documentation for more information on how to troubleshoot **PSRemoting** connections.

Compiling configurations for remote target nodes

If you remember earlier when we were pushing DSC configurations locally, the state of our test computer (called `box1`) looks like this:

```
[BOX1 PS] > C:\vagrant\SetupAllTheThings.ps1
    Directory: C:\vagrant\SetupAllTheThings
    Mode                LastWriteTime     Length Name
    ----                -------------     ------ ----
    -----            7/01/2015   3:19 PM     1276 localhost.mof
```

We want to apply this same DSC configuration to another computer without actually logging into that computer ourselves. Creating the **CimSession** as we did earlier is not enough. This allows us to connect to the remote host, but we need a way to tell DSC that we want this DSC configuration file to be executed on that target node. If we recall our previous chapters on DSC configurations and DSC configuration data, we know that we can create a configuration data section with the relevant information on our target nodes and not have to change our DSC configuration much at all. We'll add a DSC configuration data hash and add the information for `box1` and `box2` to it now. Then, we'll modify the `Node` block and use the `$AllNodes` variable to pass the node information to the DSC configuration:

```
$data = @{
  AllNodes = @(
    @{ NodeName = 'localhost' },
    @{ NodeName = '192.168.0.13' }
  )
}
Configuration SetupAllTheThings
{
  Node $AllNodes.NodeName
  {
    File CreateFile
    {
      Ensure            = "Present"
      DestinationPath   = "c:\test.txt"
      Contents          = "Wakka"
    }
  }
}
```

```
$mofPath = [IO.Path]::Combine($PSScriptRoot, "SetupAllTheThings")
SetupAllTheThings -ConfiurationData $data -OutputPath $mofPath
```

Compiling this DSC configuration into an MOF file in box1 results in the following output:

```
[BOX1 PS] > C:\vagrant\SetupAllTheThings.ps1
    Directory: C:\vagrant\SetupAllTheThings
    Mode               LastWriteTime     Length Name
    ----               -------------     ------ ----
    -----         8/1/2015   1:44 AM       1234 localhost.mof
    -----         8/1/2015   1:44 AM       1240 192.168.0.13.mof
```

We now have two MOF files: one for the localhost (box1) and now one for 192.168.0.13 (box2). Looking at 192.168.0.13.mof, we see that it has information for box2 inside it. This is the information that Start-DscConfiguration needs in order to determine which target nodes need to be pushed to the DSC configuration. The **CimSessions** give us the transport for the target nodes, but the MOF files give us the destinations.

Executing configurations for remote target nodes

Now that we have MOF files and **CimSessions** and are ready to start pushing DSC configurations to remote target nodes, we use Start-DSCConfiguration just like we did earlier, with the addition of using the **CimSession** parameter and passing the **CimSession** that we created previously to it.

Again, we use **CimSession** here because sometimes, you need special credentials, authentication, or other options in order to connect to remote target nodes. You can omit the creation of a separate **CimSession** here if you wish:

```
[BOX1 PS] > Start-DscConfiguration -Path C:\vagrant\SetupAllTheThings -
Verbose -Wait -Force -CimSession $session
VERBOSE: Perform operation 'Invoke CimMethod' with following parameters,
''methodName' =
 SendConfigurationApply,'className' =
MSFT_DSCLocalConfigurationManager,'namespaceName' =
 root/Microsoft/Windows/DesiredStateConfiguration'.
 VERBOSE: Perform operation 'Invoke CimMethod' with following parameters,
''methodName' =
 SendConfigurationApply,'className' =
MSFT_DSCLocalConfigurationManager,'namespaceName' =
 root/Microsoft/Windows/DesiredStateConfiguration'.
VERBOSE: An LCM method call arrived from computer BOX1 with user sid
S-1-5-21-1953236517-242735908-2433092285-500.
 VERBOSE: An LCM method call arrived from computer BOX1 with user sid
S-1-5-21-1953236517-242735908-2433092285-500.
```

```
VERBOSE: [BOX2]: LCM: [ Start Set ]
VERBOSE: [BOX1]: LCM: [ Start Set ]
VERBOSE: [BOX2]: LCM: [ Start Resource ] [[File]CreateaFile]
VERBOSE: [BOX2]: LCM: [ Start Test ] [[File]CreateaFile]
VERBOSE: [BOX2]: [[File]CreateaFile] The system cannot find the file
specified.
VERBOSE: [BOX2]: [[File]CreateaFile] The related file/directory is:
c:\test.txt.
VERBOSE: [BOX2]: LCM: [ End Test ] [[File]CreateaFile] in 0.0000 seconds.
VERBOSE: [BOX2]: LCM: [ Start Set ] [[File]CreateaFile]
VERBOSE: [BOX2]: [[File]CreateaFile] The system cannot find the file
specified.
VERBOSE: [BOX2]: [[File]CreateaFile] The related file/directory is:
c:\test.txt.
VERBOSE: [BOX2]: LCM: [ End Set ] [[File]CreateaFile] in 0.0000 seconds.
VERBOSE: [BOX2]: LCM: [ End Resource ] [[File]CreateaFile]
VERBOSE: [BOX2]: LCM: [ End Set ]
VERBOSE: [BOX2]: LCM: [ End Set ] in 0.0000 seconds.
VERBOSE: Operation 'Invoke CimMethod' complete.
VERBOSE: [BOX1]: LCM: [ Start Resource ] [[File]CreateaFile]
VERBOSE: [BOX1]: LCM: [ Start Test ] [[File]CreateaFile]
VERBOSE: [BOX1]: [[File]CreateaFile] The destination object was found and
no action is
required.
VERBOSE: [BOX1]: LCM: [ End Test ] [[File]CreateaFile] in 0.0160 seconds.
VERBOSE: [BOX1]: LCM: [ Skip Set ] [[File]CreateaFile]
VERBOSE: [BOX1]: LCM: [ End Resource ] [[File]CreateaFile]
VERBOSE: [BOX1]: LCM: [ End Set ]
VERBOSE: [BOX1]: LCM: [ End Set ] in 0.0630 seconds.
VERBOSE: Operation 'Invoke CimMethod' complete.
VERBOSE: Time taken for configuration job to complete is 0.086 seconds
[BOX1 PS] >
```

If all went well, you should see the preceding output on your test system. In the output, note that both box2 and box1 had DSC configurations applied to them. You can also see that we have more output for box2 than we have for box1. That is because the file was not present in box2, while it was present in box1. This is a great example of the benefit of CM products such as DSC; it detected that the file was already present in box1 and did not need to touch it while noticing that it was not present in box2 as well as creating it. Both actions were easily discovered in the log.

Also, note that we get the same format logging as we do when pushing DSC configurations locally even though we are operating on remote target nodes. Each log has the node that it is coming from, so it is easy to see which ones are for which hosts. This is useful for our `Verbose` messages but even more useful for any `ErrorMessages` that come from our executions. If we received an error during execution, it would look like this:

```
[BOX1 PS] > $error[0] | fl * -for
    writeErrorStream       : True
    PSMessageDetails       :
    OriginInfo             : REMOTE-TEST-COMPUTER
    Exception              :
Microsoft.Management.Infrastructure.CimException: A configuration is
    ...
```

The `OriginInfo` property tells us which target node is sending us the error information. Of course, DSC logs all this information on the remote host, but it is very useful to receive it interactively as you test and develop your DSC configurations.

Something that we glossed over is that we pointed `Start-DSCConfiguration` to a folder containing more than one MOF file and it executed each MOF file on the respective target nodes with the correct credentials. How did it know that we needed to do that? This is a potentially powerful scenario.

Since `Start-DSCConfiguration` uses WinRM as the transport mechanism, it inherits all the power and flexibility of the command structures provided by WinRM. One of these is the ability to connect to many target nodes and execute a command at the same time. While we may have seen the output from `box1` and `box2` sequentially, the DSC execution jobs were performed in parallel or on both machines at once. The amount of work done in the DSC configuration file for each target node will determine how long the executions take on each node. Note that `box2` finished earlier because it had less to do than `box1`. It only seemed like each target node was operated on sequentially because we used the `Wait` parameter, which indicated to `Start-DSCConfiguration` to only return control to the console session when all jobs had completed. You can imagine the usefulness when you can apply this to hundreds of machines at the same time.

Things you must consider when pushing DSC configurations

Our example DSC configuration is pretty simple even if it worked well to showcase how to push DSC configurations. When DSC configurations become more complex, there are things you must take into consideration.

Up until now, we have been configuring settings or enabling software with DSC Resources that were already present on the target host. What if we tried to use text files and MSIs that were not present on the target node? In all our examples, we haven't had to actually do any work to get the files we want onto our target nodes. And herein lies the main problem with pushing DSC configurations. Nothing is done for us; we have to copy everything and ensure everything is present and accessible on the target nodes. So, what do we have to do for ourselves when pushing DSC configurations?

When pushing DSC configurations, DSC does not copy DSC Resources for you. While you may be annoyed by this, it makes sense when you think about it. DSC Resources can be placed in several places, and there isn't a file transfer mechanism that can be used to put them there without involving the user to make a choice or provide credentials. You might also be wondering why we need to copy the DSC modules if we have already compiled the MOF locally. The MOF compilation process produces the manifest that DSC uses to list the things to do on the target node and the DSC Resource holds the code that makes the decisions and actions to bring the system to the desired state, so it has to be present on the target node for it to be executed.

The only way to solve this is to copy the DSC Resources to the target nodes yourself when pushing DSC configurations. If you are thinking about using DSC to do this, that's good inventive thinking, but this is not that easy a problem to solve using DSC. It's a chicken and egg scenario. DSC can't do this for you because it uses the DSC Resources present on the machine to validate that it can execute the incoming DSC configuration you are pushing to it. It parses the MOF before it executes it and tries to find out whether all the required DSC Resources are present on the host. If they aren't present, then it exits with an error.

When copying DSC Resources, you will have to deal with the normal file copying problems related to which transfer method should be used (network or SMB shares, credentials, and so on). If you are copying new DSC Resources, then you may have to deal with different versions. Each DSC Resource comes with version information in its manifest file, but it may include or remove files at its own discretion. A blind file copy will not know how to remove files or deal with file renames, among other possible version scenarios. Using `PackageManagement` (as described in `Chapter 4`, *DSC Resources*) or a file-sync tool will help alleviate this issue somewhat, but at the same time, it introduces steps you have to perform on the remote target nodes before you can push DSC configurations to them. This means setup steps that you have to either script or manually follow each time, determine drift yourself each time, and so on. Dealing with this via scripting (deleting if present, reading version files, and so on) adds more complexity to your deployments and makes you do all the work of detecting drift when you started out this journey wanting DSC to do this for you.

This is somewhat alleviated in DSC V5, where different DSC Resource versions can coexist side by side. Details of how this works are still considered experimental, so whether this will help in pushing DSC configurations or only help pull server scenarios remains to be seen.

The only way to cheat and accomplish this using DSC is to have two separate DSC configuration script files. One copies the DSC Resources, and the other contains the real manifest, but the same problems discussed earlier apply here. In WMF 5, a potential solution to this problem exists. You can use a DSC pull server to distribute DSC Resources while still pushing DSC configurations directly to the target nodes.

With all these problems, it is evident that this is not meant to be a scalable long-term operation for you to perform yourself on thousands of hosts and that a pull server was meant to handle this for you.

Summary

And there you have it: pushing DSC configurations! We have covered how to push them locally and how to use them remotely for both one machine and many. We looked at how to push DSC configurations sequentially and all at once. We also covered the potential drawbacks to the push model and the steps you must take in pushing DSC configurations that you do not have to with DSC pull servers.

In the next chapter, we will cover how to set up DSC pull servers and how to use DSC configurations with them.

6
Pulling DSC Configurations

If you want to make an apple pie from scratch, you must first create the universe.
- Carl Sagan

In `Chapter 5`, *Pushing DSC Configurations*, we covered how to push a DSC configuration to a target node using `Start-DscConfiguration`. This method required a lot of steps to be performed each time you provisioned a new target node as well as a few repetitive steps each time you pushed a new DSC configuration to it. Some of it could be scripted away, but it required extra work out of you to accomplish the automation. A **DSC pull server** provides features that remove the responsibility of automating these steps away from you and performs them itself, saving both time and effort. Through the course of this chapter, we will cover the ways in which DSC pull servers will help you in managing the configuration of your target nodes as well as reducing the amount of work you have to perform.

In this chapter, we will cover the following topics:

- Creating DSC pull servers
- Validating a DSC pull server installation
- Registering target nodes with a DSC pull server
- Pulling DSC configurations with a DSC pull server
- DSC pull server and target node status

Creating DSC pull servers

We covered how to install DSC pull servers briefly in Chapter 2, *DSC Architecture*, by showing an example DSC configuration script and listing several steps to configure the server afterward. If we covered it there, why do we need to devote a chapter to it here? Well, for one, we skipped a lot of detail about how to actually use that DSC configuration. We dived right into an example DSC configuration script, but you couldn't actually use it then because we hadn't yet gotten to Chapter 5, *Pushing DSC Configurations*, where you learned how to push DSC configurations. Installing the first DSC pull server with DSC is like the chicken and egg problem; you want to use DSC pull servers to deploy DSC configurations and handle all the deployment processes for you, but you need to first push a DSC configuration to install the DSC pull server. It will require some one-time setup work, but the initial effort will pay dividends as time goes on and you continue to use the DSC pull server.

If there are extra steps or other problems with installing DSC servers automatically using DSC, why bother? You could, in theory, install a DSC pull server yourself by hand if you wanted to, but it is clearly not an option Microsoft or anyone who uses DSC expects you to take. There are no instructions out there to tell you the steps to do that by hand, and the configuration of the components used by the DSC pull server is not documented for you to reproduce. It would take a lot of time and effort for you to accomplish this, with no substantial benefit to you. There are many complex parts to a DSC pull server that aren't Microsoft DSC-software-specific, so there isn't an MSI or package to distribute to you. As we covered earlier, some components are already present on the target server (IIS, DSC feature, and so on) and others need copying and configuration (IIS website files and OData endpoint configurations). It is a complex set of software that acts together to present one whole or system.

Another reason for devoting a whole chapter to DSC pull servers is that we did not cover the new features of a WMF 5 pull server and how they affect your deployment choices. In WMF 5, the PowerShell team added new target node registration methods as well as a new feature for DSC configurations, called partial configurations. We'll address these new features and changes throughout the course of this chapter.

While we go through each step here with code examples, there are complete working examples with a Vagrant environment in the downloadable source code online. It is a good reference if you want to see the entirety of the examples working together.

DSC pull server setup considerations

There are some considerations to decide on before you start installing DSC pull servers. Making these decisions now will not only allow you to install the DSC pull server successfully the first time, but it will also ensure that the pull server continues to operate correctly in your environment as time goes on.

We said earlier that you will be doing most of the work to install a DSC pull server yourself. While this is true, it doesn't mean you can't script most of the tasks. We are going to use the approach of putting all the steps in individual scripts and then wrapping them all in a root invocation script. We do this because this is a test environment and we will be generating SSL certs and DSC pull server endpoint URLs on demand, in comparison to a production environment, where you will have a known SSL certificate and endpoint URL to deal with. We will start by addressing each step in the process and then showing the completed "root" script. This will make more sense as we move on, so bear with us.

DSC pull server type

A DSC pull server can be installed either as an HTTP pull server or an SMB pull server. You must choose which type to use before installing your DSC pull server as it determines how the target nodes communicate with the DSC pull server and how it functions internally.

An SMB pull server is very easy to get running as it requires just a properly set up file share to function. In simple network topology environments or ones with existing file shares, it may be easier to use an SMB DSC pull server. In more complicated network topology environments, accessing file shares with complicated permission rules across firewalls or multi-domain AD forests is difficult to get right. SMB pull servers also introduce two points of contact for a target node to work: the DSC pull server itself and the server where the file share is hosted. All target nodes must be able to reach the file share server, something that may be harder to accomplish for a file server than a single purpose DSC pull server.

An HTTP pull server, in comparison, requires more initial effort to get working but may be easier to use in the long term. In the short term, it requires you to set up an HTTP endpoint, which means IIS and dependent services need to be installed and configured correctly. If you set up a website, you're going to want to use HTTPS and SSL certificates. Depending on the location from which you get your SSL certificate, this might add extra work for you to procure and deploy (we will cover these steps in a moment). While it may require more initial effort, an HTTPS endpoint is easier to access. There's no dependency on permission rules or AD forests. In complicated network environments, getting one port allowed on multiple firewalls is much easier than allowing the SMB traffic through.

Considerations such as these largely depend on your environment, so evaluate your options carefully before proceeding.

The Windows management framework version

Since the release of the first edition of this book, both WMF 5.0 and WMF 5.1 have been released and stabilized and WMF 4.0 has been largely deprecated. While you can still install a DSC pull server in WMF 4.0 manually, the tooling we described in the first edition moved forward and stopped supporting 4.0 directly. This is largely because of the new features and settings WMF 5.0 and 5.1 make it hard to support the older 4.0 limited set. This doesn't mean your entire fleet has to be WMF 5.0 or 5.1 just yet; it just means if you are starting out, you should start with a WMF 5.1 DSC pull server instead of a WMF 4.0 one and your clients can be any version from WMF 4.0 to 5.1.

 In the first edition of this book, there were examples and tooling to install and configure a WMF 4.0 DSC pull server, which we have removed from the second edition to make way for the new features WMF 5 and WMF 5.1 introduced. If you still need to support the installation and configuration of WMF 4.0 DSC pull servers, you can either reference the first edition of this book or consult the accompanied source code for this book, which still has a folder for the WMF 4.0 files.

Initial setup tasks

Before we can actually install the DSC pull server, there are some setup tasks you have to perform. These tasks have to be performed only by you (whether manually or through a script) for the first DSC pull server you deploy, and they can be added to your DSC deployments as time goes on. Again, we reference the chicken and the egg problem; naturally, some of this requires us to do some work until we have something set up to do the work for us.

Installing required DSC resources

Whether you are compiling your DSC configuration to an MOF file on your desktop or on the DSC pull server itself, you need to have the xPSDesiredStateConfiguration module that contains the xDscWebService DSC resource in $env:PSModulePath.

You can use the built-in `PackageManagement` module to download
`xPSDesiredStateConfiguration`, clone `xPSDesiredStateConfiguration` directly
from `https://github.com/PowerShell/xPSDesiredStateConfiguration` using Git, or
download it in a ZIP file from the `GitHub` website:

For more information on the sources of DSC resources, refer to `Chapter 4`,
DSC Resources.

To use the built-in `PackageManagement` cmdlets to download and install the DSC resource
to the correct place automatically (note the backticks that allow the multi-line command),
take a look at this:

```
Install-Package -Name 'xPSDesiredStateConfiguration' `
                -RequiredVersion 6.4.0.0 `
                -Force
```

Note that we specified the version in the code example. We did this to show what version we were working with when the book was written so that you know which version to use when running examples. You may use a newer version in production than the one specified here, as it is bound to change as time moves on.

In our downloadable example code, we also download and install the `xWebAdministration` DSC resource as we use this in our example DSC configuration that we will be pushing to the target nodes (note the backticks that allow the multi-line command):

```
Install-Package -Name 'xWebAdministration' `
                -RequiredVersion 1.18.0.0 `
                -Force
```

If you are going to use the SMB DSC pull server, then you must also download the `xSmbShare` DSC resource in order to automatically create SMB shares:

```
Install-Package -Name 'xSmbShare' `
                -RequiredVersion 2.0.0.0 `
                -Force
```

In the first edition of this book, we went through a lot of hoops in order to package the DSC resources we want the DSC pull server to deploy for us. Fortunately, in the time that has elapsed, the tooling has caught up and we no longer need the custom PowerShell scripts the author wrote to do this. We can now use the `DSCPullServerSetup` module provided in the `xPSDesiredStateConfiguration` DSC resource repository: `https://github.com/PowerShell/xPSDesiredStateConfiguration/tree/dev/DSCPullServerSetup`. As we're about to see later on, we can point the new tooling at the folder we downloaded the DSC Resources to using `PackageManagement` (**Install-Module**), and it will discover and package the correct folders for us.

The reason this is a welcome change is that the folder structure downloaded by `Install-Module` supports the side-by-side installation mechanics in WMF 5, which means it contains a subfolder named with the version number:

```
[PS]> ls $env:ProgramFiles\WindowsPowerShell\Modules\xWebAdministration

    Directory: C:\Program Files\WindowsPowerShell\Modules\xWebAdministration

Mode          LastWriteTime     Length Name
----          -------------     ------ ----
d-----  9/17/2015 1:49 PM              1.18.0.0

[PS]> ls
$env:ProgramFiles\WindowsPowerShell\Modules\xWebAdministration\1.18.0.0
```

```
 Directory: C:\Program
Files\WindowsPowerShell\Modules\xWebAdministration\1.18.0.0

Mode         LastWriteTime  Length Name
----         -------------  ------ ----
d-----  9/17/2015 1:49 PM          DSCResources
-a----  9/17/2015 1:49 PM    1473 xWebAdministration.psd1
```

The DSC pull server doesn't recognize that format and so we would have had to manually account for that if not for the new tooling. Thanks to the `Publish-DSCModuleAndMof` function in the `DSCPullServerSetup` module, we can skip packaging the DSC resources now and put it as part of our deployment process later on in this chapter when we compile and deploy the MOFs to the DSC pull server. This simplifies your steps and makes things altogether easier and we'll get to that soon; first, however, there is one more pre-installation step to explain.

SSL certificates

When installing an HTTPS DSC pull server, you will need to have an SSL certificate. You can use any valid non-expired SSL certificate that is trusted by the server you are installing the DSC pull server on and any target nodes that will communicate with it. It can be a self-signed certificate, an AD domain certificate, or an online registrar certificate. The only limitation is that it must be trusted on each target node and pull server you deploy.

> If you chose to use an SMB pull server, then you might think you can skip this step. However, you can only skip using SSL certificates if you do not use SSL to encrypt any credentials you might have used inside your DSC configuration blocks.

In production, you'll likely be using an AD domain certificate or an online registrar certificate as those afford the easiest deployment scenarios for long-term use. To use either of these instead of the self-signed certificates we will be using in the following examples, use the thumbprint for the certificate that is trusted by all of the nodes.

Since we will be using a self-signed certificate in our following examples, we need to create an SSL certificate and install it on both the DSC pull server and the target nodes.

> This step is not needed if you are not using self-signed certificates

The following code uses the built-in PowerShell cmdlets on Windows 2012 R2 to create a self-signed SSL certificate and install it on both the `Root` and my trusted `LocalMachine` cert stores. It also exports the certificate to a file so it can be copied to and installed on the target nodes:

```
$CertPath = 'C:\vagrant\servercert.cer'

$cert = Get-ChildItem -Path Cert:\LocalMachine\My\ | ? { $_.Subject -eq
'CN=dsc-box1' }

if($cert.Count -eq 0){
  $cert = New-SelfSignedCertificate `
              -DnsName 'dsc-box1' `
              -CertStoreLocation cert:\LocalMachine\My
}

Export-Certificate -Cert "Cert:\LocalMachine\My\$($cert.ThumbPrint)" `
    -FilePath $CertPath

Import-Certificate -FilePath $CertPath `
        -CertStoreLocation Cert:\LocalMachine\Root
```

It is advised that you provide a resolvable name for the `DnsName` parameter for `New-SelfSignedCertficate` to create the self-signed certificate. The next step is to install the self-signed certificate on our target node. In our downloadable code examples, we use a common shared folder and PowerShell remoting to install the certificate, but feel free to use whichever method suits your environment:

```
Import-Certificate `
    -FilePath "C:\vagrant\servercert.cer" `
    -CertStoreLocation 'Cert:\LocalMachine\Root'
```

We are using self-signed certificates here only because we are using local test machines not joined to an AD domain. Self-signed certificates are harder to use than AD domain certificates; they are somewhat less secure and require you to install them on all machines in order for them to work. In your production environment, you will most likely use an AD domain certificate or another SSL certificate from a trusted vendor that all of your target nodes trust.

If you are having trouble creating the certificate using the previous code or you can't use the built-in PowerShell cmdlets, a good place to start for more information is https://msdn.microsoft.com/en-us/library/bfsktky3(v=vs.110).aspx.

SMB share creation

You can create SMB shares for use with DSC pull servers either inside the DSC configuration script using the xSMBShare DSC resource, ahead of time using native Windows tooling or PowerShell cmdlets, or with existing SMB shares that you already have.

 If you choose to use an HTTPS DSC pull server, you can skip this step.

Since the release of the first edition of this book, the documentation for setting up SMB shares has greatly improved, and you can create and provision the shares inside the DSC configuration script itself, just like the HTTPS SSL certificates. We'll look at how to do this in the SMB DSC pull server example.

Preparing DSC resources for pull server distribution

We covered how to prepare DSC resources for a DSC pull server deployment briefly in Chapter 2, *DSC Architecture*. To review what you have learned, here are the steps:

1. Compress the DSC resource module to a single archive file.
2. Version the name of the archive file.
3. Copy the archive file to the DSC pull server.
4. Create a checksum file for the archive file.

By compressing the DSC resource module folders into archive files, we save space on the DSC pull server and save time and bandwidth in transmitting them to the target nodes. We version the file names so that DSC can determine which DSC resource to use for a given target node. This allows many different versions of the same DSC resource to exist on the DSC pull server and handle the potentially many versions that are deployed in different DSC configuration scripts.

The manual actions we covered to accomplish the preceding steps in Chapter 2, *DSC Architecture*, are fine if we do this infrequently, but since this is something we will be performing every time there is a new version of a DSC resource or we use a new DSC Resource altogether, these actions should be automated to reduce errors and increase our deployment speed.

Since the publication of the first edition of this book, Microsoft has released several tools to help with DSC deployments. One of those is aimed at automating packaging and deploying DSC resources to a DSC pull server, and it is located at `https://github.com/PowerShell/xPSDesiredStateConfiguration/tree/dev/DSCPullServerSetup`. In the first edition, I laid out several functions that accomplished the same purpose as what Microsoft released, but they are not needed anymore. If you want to see the source of the original functions, they are still available to download on the companion website for this book on the Packt website. In this edition, we will cover this using the Microsoft-provided functions to accomplish the task of packaging up and deploying our example DSC resources.

In the first edition of this book, we handled compressing the DSC resources in the pre-setup tasks and compiling our DSC configuration and deploying both at the end of the tasks. With the advent of `Publish-DSCModuleAndMOF`, we can now employ both as part of our deployment process and not have to split tasks and keep things in sync ourselves. We will cover this using `Publish-DSCModuleAndMOF` in the Deploying DSC configurations section of this chapter; however, for now, here is an example:

```
$moduleList = @("xWebAdministration", "xPSDesiredStateConfiguration")
Publish-DSCModuleAndMOF -Source C:\LocalDepot -ModuleNameList $moduleList
```

Miscellaneous tasks

You may be required to perform additional tasks in order for your DSC pull server to function. In your production environment, you will most likely add firewall port accept rules for the ports you choose to run the DSC pull server on and have DNS set up in your environment. Read through our instructions here to decide if there are more steps for your particular environment.

In our downloadable code example, we disable the firewall to allow network communication on the HTTP ports we use and add IP addresses to the host file in order to allow name resolution between the two hosts. This is entirely because we are using a non-domain joined workgroup test machine, so name resolution is not available and we don't need to worry about blocking ports.

Creating an SMB DSC pull server

As we covered in the beginning of this chapter, here and in the next section, we will see that creating an SMB DSC pull server is much easier than an HTTPS DSC pull server. This is because there are far fewer moving parts to an SMB share and fewer decisions that need to be made. The core set of decisions you need to account for is the service account you will grant full access to the share, the account you will give read access to the share, and the location of the share. In the following example, we use the administrator account for full access, but in production, you'll most likely use a dedicated service account created for this purpose.

The account for read access needs to be the computer account for the target node, as it needs to be able to read the DSC configuration MOFs placed in the share. You can add the computer name, as follows:

```
ReadAccess = 'DomainName\Target-Node-Name$'
```

This will quickly become awkward to keep up to date for large amounts of large nodes. If you are in an AD environment, then you can add the name for the group of all domain joined computers as follows:

```
ReadAcces = 'DomainName\Domain Computers'
```

However you choose to give permission, the following DSC configuration script will provision the SMB DSC pull server for you:

```
configuration SMBDSCPullServer
{
  Import-DSCResource -ModuleName PSDesiredStateConfiguration
  Import-DSCResource -ModuleName xSmbShare
  Import-DSCResource -ModuleName xNtfsAccessControl

  Node $AllNodes.Where({ $_.Roles -contains 'PullServer'}).NodeName
  {
    File SmbShareFolder {
      DestinationPath = $Node.SmbSharePath
      Type = 'Directory'
      Ensure = 'Present'
    }
    xSMBShare CreateSmbShare {
      Name = 'DscSmbShare'
      Path = $Node.SmbSharePath
      FullAccess = $Node.SmbAccountNameFullAccess
      ReadAccess = $Node.SmbAccountNameReadAccess
      FolderEnumerationMode = 'AccessBased'
      Ensure = 'Present'
```

```
            DependsOn = '[File]SmbShareFolder'
        }
    cNtfsPermissionEntry SmbSharePermission {
        Ensure = 'Present'
        Path = '$Node.SmbSharePath
        Principal = $Node.SmbAccountNameReadAccess
        AccessControlInformation = @(
            cNtfsAccessControlInformation{
                AccessControlType = 'Allow'
                FileSystemRights = 'ReadAndExecute'
                Inheritance = 'ThisFolderSubfoldersAndFiles'
                NoPropagateInherit = $false
            }
        )
        DependsOn = '[File]SmbShareFolder'
        }
    }
}
```

All of this looks remarkably similar to any DSC configuration script we have done so far. As we keep seeing with DSC, this is explicitly on purpose. These standard ways of expressing the state of a target node allow you to apply the knowledge you gained from deploying one piece of software or system to any piece of software or system. There are a few other ways to assign permissions using DSC Resources, and you can choose the DSC Resource or method that works in your environment.

Keeping with the theme of separating our configuration data from our execution script, we have saved the configuration data in a separate file:

```
$configData = @{
    AllNodes = @(
        @{
            NodeName = "*"
            RefreshMode = "PULL"
            ConfigurationMode = "ApplyAndAutocorrect"
            AllowModuleOverwrite = $true
            RebootNodeIfNeeded = $true
        },
        @{
            NodeName = 'dsc-box1'
            Roles = @('PullServer')
            SmbSharePath = 'C:\DscSmbShare'
            SmbAccountNameFullAccess = 'Administrator'
            SmbAccountNameReadAccess = 'myDomain\Contoso-Server$'
        },
        @{
            NodeName = 'dsc-box2'
```

```
        Roles = @('Target')
        ConfigurationId = 'c19fbe22-b664-4a8a-a2a1-477f16ce9659'
        WebSiteFolder = 'C:\testsite'
        IndexFile = 'C:\testsite\index.html'
        WebSiteName = 'TestSite'
        WebContentText = '<h1>Hello World</h1>'
        WebProtocol = 'HTTP'
        Port = '80'
    }
  );
}
return $configData
```

Running this example is as simple as the following command:

```
$dataScript = ([IO.Path]::Combine($PSScriptRoot, 'smb_config_data.ps1'))
$configData = &$dataScript
$pullServerMOfDir = ([IO.Path]::Combine($PSScriptRoot, 'SMBPullServer'))

c:\vagrant\smb_pull_server.ps1 -OutputPath $pullServerMOfDir `
                               -ConfigData $configData `
Start-DscConfiguration -Path $pullServerMOfDir -Wait -Verbose -Force
```

Creating an HTTPS DSC pull server

We are going to follow the same DSC configuration script we used in Chapter 2, *DSC Architecture*, here in order to set up our HTTPS DSC pull server, with the addition of ensuring that HTTPS and SSL are set up and configured. Note that we have to place the certificate thumbprint in the appropriate property for the PullServer endpoint. This will set up the IIS website with the correct SSL cert. Another decision that we have to make is where to keep the DSC resources and where to store the DSC service configuration. For the most part, you will follow the standard locations (as we do next) unless you have customized drive and partition setups. The final choice you have to make is what port to host these endpoints on. We have used the default suggested ports here, but you can choose which ones to use in your environment. This is especially helpful if there are other services running on the server you decide to install the DSC pull server on.

The result of these decisions is the following DSC configuration script:

```
configuration HTTPSDSCPullServer
{
  Import-DSCResource -ModuleName PSDesiredStateConfiguration
  Import-DSCResource -ModuleName xPSDesiredStateConfiguration

  Node $AllNodes.Where({ $_.Roles -contains 'PullServer'}).NodeName
```

```
  {
    WindowsFeature DSCServiceFeature
    {
      Ensure = "Present"
      Name = "DSC-Service"
    }
    xDscWebService PSDSCPullServer
    {
      Ensure = "Present"
      State = "Started"
      EndpointName = $Node.PullServerEndpointName
      Port = $Node.PullServerPort
      AcceptSelfSignedCertificates = $Node.AcceptSelfSignedCertificates
      UseSecurityBestPractices = $Node.UseSecurityBestPractices
      PhysicalPath = $Node.PullServerPhysicalPath
      ModulePath = $Node.ModulePath
      ConfigurationPath = $Node.ConfigurationPath
      RegistrationKeyPath = $Node.RegistrationKeyPath
      CertificateThumbPrint = $certificateThumbPrint
      DependsOn = "[WindowsFeature]DSCServiceFeature"
    }
    File RegistrationKeyFile
    {
      Ensure = 'Present'
      Type = 'File'
      DestinationPath = $Node.RegistrationKeyPath
      Contents = $Node.RegistrationKey
    }
  }
}
```

 Note that we will be explaining RegistrationKeys and ConfiguratioNames later in this chapter, so if these are new terms to you, don't worry; we'll get to it!

One thing to note is that we copy the archived DSC resources as we did in the initial steps at the beginning of this chapter from a deployment directory to the DSC pull server module directory. You can include this step to keep your DSC pull server distribution up to date with new module versions.

Keeping with the theme of separating our configuration data from our execution script, we have saved the configuration data in a separate file, but we haven't made it a `.psd1` file. We used this approach because we did not know the certificate thumbprint that would be generated using the scripts we are about to show that compile the DSC configuration script, so we make it a `.ps1` file so we can execute some code to get the certificate thumbprint:

```
$cert = Get-ChildItem -Path Cert:\LocalMachine\Root\ | ? { $_.Subject -eq
'CN=dsc-box1' }
$configData = @{
  AllNodes = @(
    @{
        NodeName = "*"
        PullServerURL = "https://dsc-box1:8080/PSDSCPullServer.svc"
        CertificateID = "$($cert.ThumbPrint)"
        RefreshMode = "PULL"
        ConfigurationMode = "ApplyAndAutocorrect"
        AllowModuleOverwrite = $true
        RebootNodeIfNeeded = $true
    },
    @{
        NodeName = 'dsc-box1'
        Roles = @('PullServer')
        AcceptSelfSignedCertificates = $true
        UseSecurityBestPractices = $true
        CertificateThumbPrint = "$($cert.ThumbPrint)"
        ModulePath =
"$env:PROGRAMFILES\WindowsPowerShell\DscService\Modules"
        ConfigurationPath =
"$env:PROGRAMFILES\WindowsPowerShell\DscService\Configuration"
        PullServerEndpointName = 'PSDSCPullServer'
        PullServerPhysicalPath = "$env:SystemDrive\inetpub\PSDSCPullServer"
        PullServerPort = 8080
    },
    @{
        NodeName        = 'dsc-box2'
        Roles           = @('Target')
        ConfigurationId = 'c19fbe22-b664-4a8a-a2a1-477f16ce9659'
        WebSiteFolder   = 'C:\testsite'
        IndexFile       = 'C:\testsite\index.html'
        WebSiteName     = 'TestSite'
        WebContentText  = '<h1>Hello World</h1>'
        WebProtocol     = 'HTTP'
        Port            = '80'
    }
  );
}
return $configData
```

You might not use this approach in your production environment as the certificate thumbprint and other details will be determined beforehand and not generated at runtime like this. You could choose to use this approach in production for a fully automated script if you have to make several decisions on what data to generate for each of your DSC pull servers.

Since we are setting up the DSC pull server, we can't expect to have it pull the DSC configuration, so we will push it using the knowledge we gained from Chapter 5, *Pushing DSC Configurations*. We are running it locally on the DSC pull server, but as we saw in the previous chapter, you can push DSC configurations remotely, so this will work as well remotely as it does here locally:

```
$dataScript = ([IO.Path]::Combine($PSScriptRoot, 'https_config_data.ps1'))
$configData = &$dataScript
$pullServerMOFDir = ([IO.Path]::Combine($PSScriptRoot, 'HTTPSPullServer'))
c:\vagrant\https_pull_server.ps1 -OutputPath $pullServerMOFDir -ConfigData $configData
Start-DscConfiguration -Path $pullServerMOFDir -Wait -Verbose -Force
```

We used this approach so that we invoke code to find the thumbprint at runtime to compile the MOF file and install the DSC pull server. The preceding code finds the configuration data script and executes it to return the configuration data hash we need to compile the MOF in the `https_pull_server.ps1` script. It then installs the DSC pull server using `Start-DscConfiguration`:

```
[PS]> C:\vagrant\02_install_pull_server.ps1
    Directory: C:\vagrant\book\ch06\WMF4PullServer
Mode                 LastWriteTime         Length Name
----                 -------------         ------ ----
-----          9/19/2015    9:24 AM          4918 dsc-box1.mof
VERBOSE: Perform operation 'Invoke CimMethod' with following parameters,
''methodName' =
    SendConfigurationApply,'className' =
MSFT_DSCLocalConfigurationManager,'namespaceName' =
    root/Microsoft/Windows/DesiredStateConfiguration'.
    VERBOSE: An LCM method call arrived from computer DSC-BOX1 with user
sid
    S-1-5-21-2584411961-1507261911-1533134791-1001.
VERBOSE: [DSC-BOX1]: LCM:  [ Start  Set      ]
VERBOSE: [DSC-BOX1]: LCM:  [ Start  Resource ]
[[WindowsFeature]DSCServiceFeature]
VERBOSE: [DSC-BOX1]: LCM:  [ Start  Test     ]
[[WindowsFeature]DSCServiceFeature]
VERBOSE: [DSC-BOX1]:                                   [[WindowsFeature]
<# ... #>
VERBOSE: [DSC-BOX1]:                                   [[File]CopyPackagedModules]
```

```
Copying file
    c:\Modules\xWebAdministration_1.7.0.0.zip to
C:\ProgramFiles\WindowsPowerShell\DscService\Modules\xWebAdministration_1.7
.0.0.zip.
VERBOSE: [DSC-BOX1]:                              [[File]CopyPackagedModules]
Copying file
    c:\Modules\xWebAdministration_1.7.0.0.zip.checksum to
C:\ProgramFiles\WindowsPowerShell\DscService\Modules\xWebAdministration_1.7
.0.0.zip.checksum.
VERBOSE: [DSC-BOX1]: LCM:    [ End     Set      ]  [[File]CopyPackagedModules]
in 0.0160 seconds.
VERBOSE: [DSC-BOX1]: LCM:    [ End     Resource ]  [[File]CopyPackagedModules]
VERBOSE: [DSC-BOX1]: LCM:    [ End     Set      ]   in  1.2105 seconds.
VERBOSE: Operation 'Invoke CimMethod' complete.
VERBOSE: Time taken for configuration job to complete is 1.208 seconds
```

DSC pull server and registration keys

Installing and configuring a WMF 5 DSC pull server is much the same as a WMF 4 DSC pull server, with one major exception: the registration key feature. In WMF 5, the PowerShell team has added the ability to register a target node using pre-shared unique keys called `RegistrationKeys` that are easier to track than the `ConfigurationId` GUID concept in WMF 4. We will go into further detail about registration keys in the DSC configuration example section next.

> We will review what `RegistrationKeys` refers to and how it's used in registering a node with a WMF 5 DSC pull server section later on.

You can choose to continue using `ConfigurationIds` to register your target nodes in WMF 5. If you choose to do that, you can reuse the WMF 4 DSC configuration script without modification in WMF 5. If you choose to use the `RegistrationKeys` feature, you will modify your DSC configuration script, as follows:

```
configuration HTTPSDSCPullServer
{
  Import-DSCResource -ModuleName PSDesiredStateConfiguration
  Import-DSCResource -ModuleName xPSDesiredStateConfiguration

  Node $AllNodes.Where({ $_.Roles -contains 'PullServer'}).NodeName
  {
    WindowsFeature DSCServiceFeature
    {
```

```
        Ensure = "Present"
        Name = "DSC-Service"
    }
    File RegistrationKeyFile
    {
        Ensure = 'Present'
        Type = 'File'
        DestinationPath =
"$env:ProgramFiles\WindowsPowerShell\DscService\RegistrationKeys.txt"
        Contents = $RegistrationKey
    }
    xDscWebService PSDSCPullServer
    {
        Ensure = "Present"
        State = "Started"
        EndpointName = "PSDSCPullServer"
        Port = 8080
        AcceptSelfSignedCertificates = $true
        UseSecurityBestPractices = $true
        PhysicalPath = "$env:SystemDrive\inetpub\PSDSCPullServer"
        ModulePath = "$env:PROGRAMFILES\WindowsPowerShell\DscService\Modules"
        ConfigurationPath =
"$env:PROGRAMFILES\WindowsPowerShell\DscService\Configuration"
        RegistrationKeyPath =
"$env:PROGRAMFILES\WindowsPowerShell\DscService"
        CertificateThumbPrint = $certificateThumbPrint
        DependsOn = "[WindowsFeature]DSCServiceFeature"
    }
  }
}
```

We have added a file DSC resource statement to create the `RegistrationKey` file and populate it with `RegistrationKey` we have chosen, and we've also added `RegistrationKeyPath` to the pull server `xDscWebService` DSC resource statement.

We update our DSC configuration data script with the following data. There's no need to put the same configuration data script again, so we are just listing the relevant node hash:

```
# TODO add node hash
```

We use the same approach as the one used in the WMF 4 example to install the WMF 5 DSC pull server. All you have to do is change the filenames, and you are good to go. The script has some hardcoded values and looks a little clunky and is very repetitive, but remember that this is only needed to get the first DSC pull server installed. Once the DSC pull server is up and running, installing other DSC pull servers or maintaining the configuration of the existing one is easy using DSC:

```
$dataScript = ([IO.Path]::Combine($PSScriptRoot, 'https_config_data.ps1'))
$configData = &$dataScript
$pullServerMOFDir = ([IO.Path]::Combine($PSScriptRoot, 'HTTPSPullServer'))
c:\vagrant\https_pull_server.ps1 -OutputPath $pullServerMOFDir -ConfigData
$configData
Start-DscConfiguration -Path $pullServerMOFDir -Wait -Verbose -Force
```

Executing it shows similar output to the WMF 4 installation:

```
[PS]> C:\vagrant\02_install_pull_server.ps1
        Directory: C:\vagrant\HTTPSPullServer
    Mode                LastWriteTime              Length Name
    ----                -------------              ------ ----
    ------          9/19/2015   7:57 AM              7276 dsc-box1.mof
VERBOSE: Perform operation 'Invoke CimMethod' with following parameters,
''methodName' =
    SendConfigurationApply,'className' =
MSFT_DSCLocalConfigurationManager,'namespaceName' =
    root/Microsoft/Windows/DesiredStateConfiguration'.
VERBOSE: An LCM method call arrived from computer DSC-BOX1 with user sid
    S-1-5-21-2584411961-1507261911-1533134791-1001.
VERBOSE: [DSC-BOX1]: LCM:  [ Start  Set      ]
    <#  ... #>
VERBOSE: [DSC-BOX1]: LCM:  [ End    Set      ]  [[File]CopyPackagedModules]
in 0.0000 seconds.
VERBOSE: [DSC-BOX1]: LCM:  [ End    Resource ]  [[File]CopyPackagedModules]
VERBOSE: [DSC-BOX1]: LCM:  [ End    Set      ]
VERBOSE: [DSC-BOX1]: LCM:  [ End    Set      ]    in  50.6250 seconds.
VERBOSE: Operation 'Invoke CimMethod' complete.
VERBOSE: Time taken for configuration job to complete is 51.139 seconds
```

Validating a DSC pull server install

We can test that the pull server endpoint is available by navigating to its endpoint using a web browser or the command line.

Testing using a web browser

On the target node where we installed the DSC pull server, enter
`https://localhost:8080/PSDSCPullServer.svc/$metadata` in your web browser
and check to see whether it loads.

Replace `localhost` with the name of the target node if you are running this on a machine
other than the pull server:

If you see the preceding XML, then your pull server endpoint is up and running. Note that
we get an SSL certificate warning because we are using a self-signed certificate. You would
not see this using a real SSL certificate.

Testing using the command line

We can do the same test from the command line using the PowerShell cmdlet `Invoke-RestMethod`. This produces the same output but can be scripted for monitoring or other purposes:

```
[PS]> Invoke-RestMethod -Uri
'https://localhost:8080/PSDSCPullServer.svc/$metadata'
```

The output obtained is as follows:

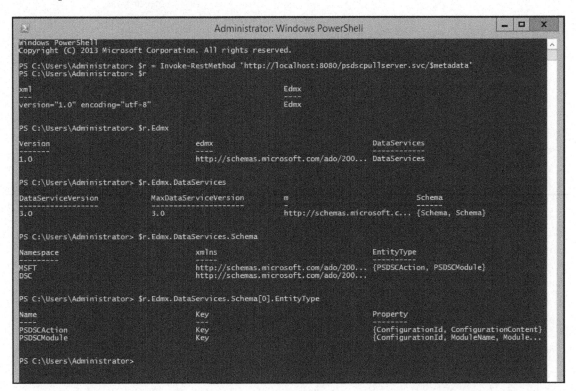

Registering target nodes with a DSC pull server

Now that the DSC pull server is set up and verified as working, we can address telling the target nodes where the DSC pull server is. We do this by configuring the LCM with the endpoint information for the DSC pull server; there isn't a self-discovery method to use.

Registering a target node using a configuration ID

Note how this is a similar DSC configuration script to any we have used so far until we get to the `LocalConfigurationManager` keyword. We use this keyword to configure the local LCM to operate how we want it to:

```
Configuration ConfigurationIDTargetNodeLCM
{
  Node $AllNodes.Where({ $_.Roles -contains 'Target'}).NodeName
  {
    LocalConfigurationManager
    {
      ConfigurationId     = $Node.ConfigurationId
      RefreshMode         = $Node.RefreshMode
      ConfigurationMode   = $Node.ConfigurationMode
      DownloadManagerName = 'WebDownloadManager'
      DownloadManagerCustomData = @{
        ServerURL     = $Node.ConfigurationServerURL
        CertificateID = $Node.CertificateID
      }
    }
  }
}
```

We use the same configuration data script that we used to create the DSC pull server here, but you can choose to have different data files or keep the same. We'll invoke this just like we did with the DSC pull server using a wrapper script, as shown here:

```
$outputPath = ([IO.Path]::Combine($PSScriptRoot, 'WMF4TargetNodeLCM'))
$dataScript = ([IO.Path]::Combine($PSScriptRoot, 'wmf4_config_data.ps1'))
$configData = &$dataScript
C:\vagrant\configurationid_target_node.ps1 -configdata $configData `
                                           -output $outputPath
Set-DscLocalConfigurationManager -Path $outputPath -Verbose
```

This step only needs to be done once per target node; after this, the DSC pull server can handle any changes you might need to make.

When we want to apply these settings to the LCM, we use the `Set-DscLocalConfigurationManager` cmdlet. This cmdlet behaves like `Start-DscConfiguration` in that it can operate both locally and remotely and can operate on as many machines as desired at the same time:

```
[PS]> C:\vagrant\03_install_target_node.ps1
        Directory: C:\vagrant\book\ch06\WMF4TargetNodeLCM
    Mode                LastWriteTime     Length Name
    ----                -------------     ------ ----
    -----            9/19/2015   9:27 AM       1840 dsc-box2.meta.mof
VERBOSE: Performing the operation "Start-DscConfiguration:
SendMetaConfigurationApply" on target
    "MSFT_DSCLocalConfigurationManager".
    VERBOSE: Perform operation 'Invoke CimMethod' with following
parameters, ''methodName' =
    SendMetaConfigurationApply,'className' =
MSFT_DSCLocalConfigurationManager,'namespaceName' =
    root/Microsoft/Windows/DesiredStateConfiguration'.
VERBOSE: An LCM method call arrived from computer DSC-BOX1 with user sid
    S-1-5-21-2584411961-1507261911-1533134791-1001.
VERBOSE: [DSC-BOX2]: LCM:  [ Start  Set        ]
VERBOSE: [DSC-BOX2]: LCM:  [ Start  Resource ]  [MSFT_DSCMetaConfiguration]
VERBOSE: [DSC-BOX2]: LCM:  [ Start  Set      ]  [MSFT_DSCMetaConfiguration]
VERBOSE: [DSC-BOX2]: LCM:  [ End    Set      ]  [MSFT_DSCMetaConfiguration]
in 0.0400 seconds.
VERBOSE: [DSC-BOX2]: LCM:  [ End    Resource ]  [MSFT_DSCMetaConfiguration]
VERBOSE: [DSC-BOX2]: LCM:  [ End    Set      ]   in  0.0922 seconds.
VERBOSE: Operation 'Invoke CimMethod' complete.
VERBOSE: Set-DscLocalConfigurationManager finished in 0.146 seconds.
```

Registering a target node using RegistrationKey

The PowerShell team improved the LCM configuration authoring story in WMF 5 by introducing new DSC resource statement blocks that address all the configuration points needed. Instead of one large `LocalConfigurationManager` block, there are now three blocks to use: `Settings`, `ConfigurationRepositoryWeb`, and `ReportServerWeb`. While named differently, these blocks contain all the same pieces of information as before, just arranged together logically.

The last new addition is the `DscLocalConfigurationManger` attribute, which restricts our DSC configuration script to contain only information for configuring the LCM.

If you are using the version of WMF 5 that was released in the first Windows 10 RTM builds, then you might have trouble authoring the following configuration in the PowerShell ISE. In our testing, this version of WMF 5 does not recognize following the RegistrationKey properties. This error does not happen in the latest WMF 5.1 release at the time of writing this.

Our updated LCM configuration script is as follows:

```
[DscLocalConfigurationManager()]
Configuration WMF5TargetNodeLCM
{
  Node $AllNodes.Where({ $_.Roles -contains 'Target'}).NodeName
  {
    Settings
    {
        RefreshMode          = $Node.RefreshMode
        ConfigurationMode    = $Node.ConfigurationMode
        CertificateID        = $Node.CertificateID
        RebootNodeIfNeeded   = $Node.RebootNodeIfNeeded
        AllowModuleOverwrite = $Node.AllowModuleOverwrite
    }
    ConfigurationRepositoryWeb ConfigurationManager
    {
        ServerURL         = $Node.PullServerURL
        RegistrationKey   = $Node.RegistrationKey
        CertificateID     = $Node.CertificateID
        ConfigurationNames = @('ExampleConfiguration')
    }
    ReportServerWeb ReportManager
    {
        ServerURL              = $Node.PullServerURL
        RegistrationKey        = $Node.RegistrationKey
        CertificateID          = $Node.CertificateID
        AllowUnsecureConnection = $true
    }
  }
}
```

The Settings DSC resource holds the expected set of parameters that we saw in the WMF 4 version we just reviewed. The old LocalConfigurationManager block still works and is left in for backward compatibility, but you should move toward using the settings block as you migrate to WMF 5.

Since we set up our pull server to use HTTPS, we have to use the
`ConfigurationRepositoryWeb` DSC resource to set the pull server address, registration
key, and certificate thumbprint. Notice the `RegistrationKey` property, where we pass
`RegistrationKey` that we generated when we installed the DSC pull server. These values
have to match, or the node will not be authorized to use the DSC pull server.

We use a similar approach to how we installed the WMF 5 DSC pull server and use a
wrapper script to invoke the configuration data script and compile the MOF, passing it to
the `Set-DscLocalConfigurationManger` cmdlet to install. Remember that this step
needs to be done only once per target node; after this, the DSC pull server can handle any
changes you might need to make:

```
$outputPath = ([IO.Path]::Combine($PSScriptRoot, 'WMF5TargetNodeLCM'))
$dataScript = ([IO.Path]::Combine($PSScriptRoot, 'wmf5_config_data.ps1'))
$configData = &$dataScript
C:\vagrant\wmf5_target_node.ps1 –configdata $configData –output $outputPath
Set-DscLocalConfigurationManager -Path $outputPath -Verbose
```

The output looks just as we would expect at this point:

```
[PS]> C:\vagrant\book\ch06\wmf5_03_install_target_node.ps1
        Directory: C:\vagrant\book\ch06\WMF5TargetNodeLCM
    Mode                LastWriteTime         Length Name
    ----                -------------         ------ ----
    ------         9/19/2015   8:54 AM           3528 dsc-box2.meta.mof
VERBOSE: Performing the operation "Start-DscConfiguration:
SendMetaConfigurationApply" on target
    "MSFT_DSCLocalConfigurationManager".
VERBOSE: Perform operation 'Invoke CimMethod' with following parameters,
''methodName' =
    SendMetaConfigurationApply,'className' =
MSFT_DSCLocalConfigurationManager,'namespaceName' =
    root/Microsoft/Windows/DesiredStateConfiguration'.
VERBOSE: An LCM method call arrived from computer DSC-BOX1 with user sid
    S-1-5-21-2584411961-1507261911-1533134791-1001.
VERBOSE: [DSC-BOX2]: LCM:  [ Start  Set       ]
VERBOSE: [DSC-BOX2]: LCM:  [ Start  Resource ] [MSFT_DSCMetaConfiguration]
VERBOSE: [DSC-BOX2]: LCM:  [ Start  Set       ] [MSFT_DSCMetaConfiguration]
VERBOSE: [DSC-BOX2]: LCM:  [ End    Set       ] [MSFT_DSCMetaConfiguration]
in 0.0320 seconds.
VERBOSE: [DSC-BOX2]: LCM:  [ End    Resource ] [MSFT_DSCMetaConfiguration]
VERBOSE: [DSC-BOX2]: LCM:  [ End    Set       ]
VERBOSE: Operation 'Invoke CimMethod' complete.
VERBOSE: Set-DscLocalConfigurationManager finished in 2.899 seconds.
```

Pulling DSC configurations with a DSC pull server

We briefly covered compiling DSC configurations for use on a pull server in Chapter 2, *DSC Architecture*, and we will build on that introduction here. We are going to use the following example DSC configuration with our DSC pull server. It's not fancy and it doesn't do a whole lot, but it is great at showing how DSC pull servers do the work for us:

```
Configuration SetupTheSite
{
  Import-DscResource -Module PSDesiredStateConfiguration
  Import-DscResource -Module xWebAdministration
  Node $AllNodes.Where({ $_.Roles -contains 'Target'}).NodeName
  {
    WindowsFeature IIS
    {
      Ensure = 'Present'
      Name   = 'Web-Server'
    }
    <#..#>
    xWebsite NewWebsite
    {
      Ensure       = 'Present'
      State        = 'Started'
      Name         = $Node.WebSiteName
      PhysicalPath = $Node.WebSiteFolder
      BindingInfo  = MSFT_xWebBindingInformation{
        Protocol = 'HTTP'
        Port     = '80'
      }
      DependsOn = '[File]WebContent'
    }
  }
}
```

It uses the xWebSite and xWebApplication DSC resources from the xWebAdministration module to install a simple website on our target node. This allows us to showcase the DSC pull server distributing the MOF to the target nodes and distributing the xWebAdministrion module to all the target nodes as well. For these reasons, the following example DSC configuration is cut for length, so download the example book code to see the entire thing.

Compiling DSC configurations using ConfigurationIDs

To register target nodes with the DSC pull server, we assign `ConfigurationIDs` to each target node's LCM and then name the MOF file with the same `ConfigurationID`. We already registered the `ConfigurationID` with the target node by setting it in the LCM configuration block earlier in the chapter. We now have to rename the MOF file with the `ConfigurationID` and place it in the DSC pull server directory:

```
$outputPath = ([IO.Path]::Combine($PSScriptRoot, 'SetupTheSite'))
$dataScript = ([IO.Path]::Combine($PSScriptRoot, 'https_config_data.ps1'))
$configData = &$dataScript
c:\vagrant\book\ch06\example_configuration.ps1 -outputPath $outputPath -
configData $configData | Out-Null
Rename-Item -Path (Join-Path $($outputPath) 'dsc-box2.mof') `
        -NewName 'c19fbe22-b664-4a8a-a2a1-477f16ce9659.mof'
```

In your production scripts, you could place the `ConfigurationID` in the `NodeName` field instead of the name of the node. This will cause the resulting MOF file to be automatically named with the `ConfigurationID`. We chose not to do this in the example in order to have the least number of changes in the data file in the examples.

Compiling DSC configurations using RegistrationKeys

When making the MOF files for DSC pull servers that use `RegistrationKeys`, you do not name the MOF file with the `ConfigurationID` of the target node, as there is no `ConfigurationID` assigned to the target node. Instead, the target node has the same `RegistrationKey` configured in its LCM that the DSC pull server has. This allows us to name the MOF files with descriptive human readable names as well as use DSC partial configurations.

The example code that follows is relatively naïve since it only handles the one MOF file we are compiling. In production, you would have this part of a release process where you compiled and renamed the MOF according to the naming scheme you chose. Here, we're using `ExampleConfiguration`, but the reason for the name is to name it with some relation to the purpose of the DSC configuration:

```
$outputPath = ([IO.Path]::Combine($PSScriptRoot, 'SetupTheSite'))
$dataScript = ([IO.Path]::Combine($PSScriptRoot, 'wmf5_config_data.ps1'))
$configData = &$dataScript
```

```
c:\vagrant\example_configuration.ps1 -outputPath $outputPath -configData
$configData | Out-Null
if(Test-Path (Join-Path $($outputPath) 'ExampleConfiguration.mof')){
  rm (Join-Path $($outputPath) 'ExampleConfiguration.mof')
}
Rename-Item -Path (Join-Path $($outputPath) 'dsc-box2.mof') -NewName
'ExampleConfiguration.mof'
```

The result of running this script renames `dsc-box2.mof` to
`ExampleConfiguration.mof`.

Deploying DSC Configurations to the DSC pull server

Whether you use `ConfigurationID` or `RegistrationKey` with your DSC configurations,
the compiled MOF files need to be physically put on the DSC pull server in order for the
target nodes to pull them. In addition, any DSC resources you use that are not built into the
installation of DSC will need to be packaged up to be distributed to the DSC pull server.

The manual actions we covered to accomplish these steps in `Chapter 2`, *DSC Architecture*,
are fine if we do this infrequently, but since this is something we will be performing every
time there is a new MOF, a new version of a DSC resource or we use a new DSC resource
altogether, these actions should be automated to reduce errors and increase our deployment
speed.

In the first edition, I laid out several functions that accomplished the same purpose as those
that Microsoft released, but they are not needed anymore. Since the publication of the first
edition of this book, Microsoft has released several tools to help with DSC deployments.
One of those is aimed at automating packaging and deploying DSC resources to a DSC pull
server, and it is located at `https://github.com/PowerShell/`
`xPSDesiredStateConfiguration/tree/dev/DSCPullServerSetup`.

If you want to see the source of the original functions, they are still
available to download on the companion website for this book on the
Packt website. In this edition, we will cover how to use the Microsoft-
provided functions to accomplish the task of packaging and deploying our
example MOF files and DSC resources.

On your DSC pull server, open a PowerShell prompt and then run the following commands:

```
[PS]> Import-Module -Name
"$($env:ProgramFiles)\WindowsPowerShell\Modules\DSCPullServerSetup\PublishM
odulesAndMofsToPullServer.psm1"
```

> We have to download the source for DSCPullServerSetup from the PowerShell repository on GitHub because Microsoft hasn't published it to PowerShellGallery. We also have to manually import the module because it does not have a PowerShell manifest file (.psd1) so the PowerShell module auto-loading does not work.
> You could have also used the copy you installed using Install-Module in $env:ProgramFiles\WindowsPowerShell\Modules\xPSDesiredSta teConfiguration\DSCPullServerSetup instead of cloning this using Git.

In using the PowerShell modules from DSCPullServerSetup, we can package the compiled MOFs from our DSC configurations as well as the DSC resources in one command:

```
$moduleList = @("xWebAdministration", "xPSDesiredStateConfiguration")
Publish-DSCModuleAndMOF -Source C:\vagrant\SetupTheSite -ModuleNameList
$moduleList -Verbose
VERBOSE: Performing the operation "Copy File" on target "Item:
C:\vagrant\SetupTheSite\ExampleConfiguration.mof Destination:
C:\vagrant\temp\ExampleConfiguration.mof".
VERBOSE: Populating RepositorySourceLocation property for module
xWebAdministration.
VERBOSE: Preparing to compress...
VERBOSE: Performing the operation "Compress-Archive" on target "
C:\Program
Files\WindowsPowerShell\Modules\xWebAdministration\1.18.0.0\DSCResources
<# #>
VERBOSE: Adding 'C:\Program
Files\WindowsPowerShell\Modules\xWebAdministration\1.18.0.0\DSCResources\He
lper.psm1'.
<# #>
VERBOSE: Adding 'C:\Program
Files\WindowsPowerShell\Modules\xPSDesiredStateConfiguration\6.4.0.0\xPSDes
iredStateConfiguration.psd1'.
<# #>
VERBOSE: Performing the operation "Copy File" on target "Item:
C:\vagrant\temp\xPSDesiredStateConfiguration_6.4.0.0.zip Destination:
C:\Program
```

```
Files\WindowsPowerShell\DscService\Modules\xPSDesiredStateConfiguration_6.4
.0.0.zip".
<# #>
C:\vagrant\temp\ExampleConfiguration.mof.checksum Destination: C:\Program
Files\WindowsPowerShell\DscService\Configuration\ExampleConfiguration.mof.c
hecksum".
Directory: C:\Program Files\WindowsPowerShell\DscService\Modules
Mode LastWriteTime Length Name
---- ------------- ------ ----
-a---- 8/9/2017 4:13 PM 398103 xPSDesiredStateConfiguration_6.4.0.0.zip
-a---- 8/9/2017 4:13 PM 64
xPSDesiredStateConfiguration_6.4.0.0.zip.checksum
-a---- 8/9/2017 4:13 PM 150316 xWebAdministration_1.18.0.0.zip
-a---- 8/9/2017 4:13 PM 64 xWebAdministration_1.18.0.0.zip.checksum
Directory: C:\Program Files\WindowsPowerShell\DscService\Configuration
Mode LastWriteTime Length Name
---- ------------- ------ ----
-a---- 8/9/2017 4:13 PM 6522 ExampleConfiguration.mof
-a---- 8/9/2017 4:13 PM 64 ExampleConfiguration.mof.checksum
```

As you can see, all of the MOF files and DSC resources are packaged and copied to the correct folder locations on the DSC pull server. It took the MOF files from `C:\LocalDepot` and ran `New-CheckSum` on them and then copied them to `$env:PROGRAMFILES\WindowsPowerShell\DscService\Configuration`. Then, it found the DSC resources we specified and zipped them up and copied them to `$env:PROGRAMFILES\WindowsPowerShell\DscService\Modules`

`Publish-DSCModuleAndMof` is a wrapper function over `Publish-ModuleToPullServer` and `Publish-MOFToPullServer`, which uses a lot of *magic* to make the process easy in that it uses a lot of default configuration in order to ask minimal questions. If your environment does not conform to the defaults it assumes, you can use the other functions to change locations for the pushed MOF and DSC resource packages:

```
Publish-ModuleToPullServer [-Name] <Object> [-ModuleBase] <Object> [-
Version] <Object> [-PullServerWebConfig
<Object>] [-OutputFolderPath <Object>] [<CommonParameters>]
```

```
Publish-MOFToPullServer [-FullName] <Object> [-PullServerWebConfig
<Object>] [<CommonParameters>]
```

These functions provide parameters that allow you specify the locations of the DSC pull server config files as well metadata such as module names and versions. Use as you see fit.

Note that this works only for HTTPS DSC pull servers, and the PowerShell module does not take into account SMB servers.

DSC pull server and target node status

At this point, we have a functioning DSC pull server, a fully configured and registered target node, and an example DSC configuration waiting to be applied to it. How do we confirm it worked? How do we know it tried at all? There are several ways of accomplishing this.

Checking the current LCM configuration status

First off, it is very easy to find out when a DSC configuration script will be applied to a given target node, and by now, you can guess where to look. You configured this information when you set up the target node to talk to the DSC pull server using `Set-DscLocalConfigurationManager`, and you can use `Get-DscLocalConfigurationManager` to view it. `RefreshFrequencyMins` controls how often to check with the DSC pull server if there is a new DSC configuration to apply and `ConfigurationModeFrequencyMins` controls how often DSC checks the target node if the current state has drifted from what is expected:

```
[PS] Get-DscLocalConfigurationManager |
        Select
RefreshFrequencyMins,RefreshMode,ConfigurationModeFrequencyMins
ConfigurationModeFrequencyMins : 15
RefreshFrequencyMins           : 30
RefreshMode                    : PULL
```

The default value for `ConfigurationModeFrequencyMins` is 15, and that is also the lowest it can be set to. If you are wondering why you can't set it any lower, consider that DSC has to check the current state and then correct it and report on it, all between scheduled runs. 15 minutes is more than enough time for this to happen while allowing additional time if things are going slowly or a particularly long DSC configuration is being applied. If this is still bothering you, remember that DSC and other CM products do not guarantee immediate consistency; they guarantee eventual consistency.

At a scale of thousands of nodes, all CM products operate this way to ensure performant response and timely execution. The default value for RefreshFrequencyMins is 30, and the same logic applies to checking for new DSC configurations. You do not want thousands of target nodes contacting your DSC pull server every minute for changes; otherwise, you will overload even the beefiest of servers.

In WMF 5, you can use Get-DscLocalConfigurationManager to get information about its new properties:

```
[PS]> Get-DscLocalConfigurationManager
ActionAfterReboot               : ContinueConfiguration
AgentId                         : D73A1F3E-542D-11E5-80C2-0800279ED44B
AllowModuleOverWrite            : True
CertificateID                   : 32A4F6CC5A79D5EF2D4DEC6454E9CF20A316F3DB
ConfigurationDownloadManagers   :
{[ConfigurationRepositoryWeb]ConfigurationManager}
ConfigurationID                 :
ConfigurationMode               : ApplyAndAutoCorrect
ConfigurationModeFrequencyMins  : 60
Credential                      :
DebugMode                       : {NONE}
DownloadManagerCustomData       :
DownloadManagerName             :
LCMCompatibleVersions           : {1.0, 2.0}
LCMState                        : Idle
LCMStateDetail                  :
LCMVersion                      : 2.0
StatusRetentionTimeInDays       : 10
PartialConfigurations           :
RebootNodeIfNeeded              : True
RefreshFrequencyMins            : 30
RefreshMode                     : Pull
ReportManagers                  : {}
ResourceModuleManagers          : {}
PSComputerName                  :
```

So, we now know how to find out how often DSC will check to see whether there are new DSC configurations to apply and whether or not it has to apply one to the target node.

Triggering a DSC configuration to run on a target node

While one of the best features of DSC is the automatic scheduling mechanisms that maintain and monitor the state of the target nodes, sometimes, waiting for the next scheduled run is inconvenient. You may be testing a new DSC configuration or simply trying to troubleshoot an existing one and want another execution to happen while you are there to see the results. Depending on the WMF version installed on your target node, there are a couple of options you can use.

Triggering a WMF 4 target node

There is no built-in cmdlet or script that you can use to trigger a DSC pull server run on a target node. You can circumvent this using an artifact of the scheduling system that WMF 4 DSC uses to ensure that the state of your target node is in compliance. DSC has two scheduled tasks that periodically monitor the state of the target node; the one we are interested in is called the **consistency** check. Triggering this scheduled task will make the LCM perform the normal routines (contacting the DSC pull server for a new MOF, determining whether all dependent resources are there, and so on) and run our DSC configuration. We can do this using PowerShell by issuing the following command line:

```
[PS]> Start-ScheduledTask -TaskName consistency `
        -TaskPath (Get-ScheduledTask -TaskName consistency).TaskPath
```

You can also do this using the normal `ScheduledTask` management control panel.

Triggering a WMF 5 target node

It is much easier to trigger a DSC configuration on a WMF 5 target node, as the PowerShell team has provided a new cmdlet to handle this scenario: `Update-DscConfiguration`, as shown:

```
[PS]> Update-DscConfiguration -Verbose -Wait
VERBOSE: Perform operation 'Invoke CimMethod' with following parameters,
''methodName' = PerformRequiredConfigurationChecks,'className' =
MSFT_DSCLocalConfigurationManager,'namespaceName' =
root/Microsoft/Windows/DesiredStateConfiguration'.
VERBOSE: An LCM method call arrived from computer DSC-BOX2 with user sid
S-1-5-21-2584411961-1507261911-1533134791-1001.
VERBOSE: [DSC-BOX2]: [] Executing Get-Action with configuration 's
checksum: .
VERBOSE: [DSC-BOX2]: [] Executing Get-Action with configuration 's checksum
```

```
returned result status: GetConfiguration.
VERBOSE: [DSC-BOX2]: [] Checksum is different. LCM will execute
GetConfiguration to pull configuration.
VERBOSE: [DSC-BOX2]: [] Executing GetConfiguration succeed. Configuration
is pulled from server.
VERBOSE: [DSC-BOX2]: [] Applying the new configuration(s) pulled.
<#
#...
#>
VERBOSE: Time taken for configuration job to complete is 64.748 seconds
```

As you can see, it works similarly to Start-DscConfiguration in that it has DSC immediately execute a DSC configuration, but with a key difference. Update-DscConfiguration will not put the MOF file on the target node itself. It only triggers the LCM on the target node to ask the DSC pull server whether it has the latest MOF, and then the LCM executes it.

Using DSC logging to check on the status

The method of using Get-DscConfiguration to check whether the target node status works well if you have direct contact to the target nodes. If you provide multiple CimSessions to operate on, you can even get the status of many computers at one time. However, this doesn't work as well if you want to look at the historical logging of execution runs on target nodes.

DSC logging is the next step in how to get information on the status of DSC applying the DSC configurations. We can use the Get-xDscOperation function from the xDscDiagnostics module we covered earlier in the book in *Chapter 3 Debugging and troubleshooting configuration script files* section. We can use the output from AllEvents to see the logs of the executions that DSC performs. The default sort order shows the most recent first, so we will look at the second in the list to see the first operation DSC performed:

```
[PS]> (get-xdscoperation)[1].AllEvents | fl
TimeCreated : 8/01/2015 4:17:52 PM
Message     : Configuration is sent from computer NULL by user sid
S-1-5-18.
EventType   : OPERATIONAL
TimeCreated : 8/01/2015 4:17:57 PM
Message     : Attempting to get the action from pull server using
Download Manager WebDownloadManager. Configuration
              Id is 07f528b9-0f22-4029-a3a7-b836f8843d3d. Checksum is .
Compliance status is false.
EventType   : OPERATIONAL
TimeCreated : 8/01/2015 4:17:57 PM
```

```
    Message       : WebDownloadManager for configuration 07f528b9-0f22-4029-
a3a7-b836f8843d3d Do-DscAction command with
                  server url: http://192.168.0.12:8080/PSDSCPullServer.svc.
    EventType     : OPERATIONAL
    TimeCreated   : 8/01/2015 4:17:57 PM
    Message       : WebDownloadManager for configuration 07f528b9-0f22-4029-
a3a7-b836f8843d3d Do-DscAction command, GET Url:
PSDSCPullServer.svc/Action(ConfigurationId='07f528b9-0f22-4029-a3a7-
b836f8843d3d')/GetAction.
    EventType     : OPERATIONAL
    TimeCreated   : 8/01/2015 4:17:59 PM
    Message       : Successfully got the action GetConfiguration from pull
server using Download Manager WebDownloadManager.
    EventType     : OPERATIONAL
    TimeCreated   : 8/01/2015 4:17:59 PM
    Message       : WebDownloadManager for configuration 07f528b9-0f22-4029-
a3a7-b836f8843d3d Do-DscAction command, GET call
                  result: GetConfiguration.
    EventType     : OPERATIONAL
```

So far, so good; we see that the target node contacted the DSC pull server and received instructions on what to do next. The target node will now attempt to pull the DSC configuration from the DSC pull server:

```
    TimeCreated   : 8/01/2015 4:17:59 PM
    Message       : Attempting to get the configuration from pull server
using Download Manager
                  WebDownloadManager.Configuration Id is
07f528b9-0f22-4029-a3a7-b836f8843d3d.
    EventType     : OPERATIONAL
    TimeCreated   : 8/01/2015 4:17:59 PM
    Message       : WebDownloadManager for configuration 07f528b9-0f22-4029-
a3a7-b836f8843d3d Get-DscDocument command, GET
                  Url:
PSDSCPullServer.svc/Action(ConfigurationId='07f528b9-0f22-4029-a3a7-
b836f8843d3d')/ConfigurationContent.
    EventType     : OPERATIONAL
    TimeCreated   : 8/01/2015 4:17:59 PM
    Message       : WebDownloadManager for configuration 07f528b9-0f22-4029-
a3a7-b836f8843d3d Get-DscDocument command, File
                  save result:
C:\Windows\TEMP\635756842794223943\localhost.mof.checksum.
    EventType     : OPERATIONAL
    TimeCreated   : 8/01/2015 4:17:59 PM
    Message       : The checksum validation for configuration
C:\Windows\TEMP\\635756842794223943\localhost.mof completed
                  with status code 0.
    EventType     : OPERATIONAL
```

These logs show that the target node successfully downloaded the DSC configuration (the MOF file) from the DSC pull server and verify that the checksum matched what the DSC pull server had:

```
        TimeCreated : 8/01/2015 4:17:59 PM
        Message     : Skipping pulling module PSDesiredStateConfiguration with
version 1.0 as it already exists in this
                      location
C:\Windows\system32\WindowsPowerShell\v1.0\Modules\PSDesiredStateConfigurat
ion\PSDesiredStateCon
                      figuration.psd1.
        EventType   : OPERATIONAL
        TimeCreated : 8/01/2015 4:17:59 PM
        Message     : Attempting to get the modules from pull server using
Download Manager WebDownloadManager. Configuration
                      Id is 07f528b9-0f22-4029-a3a7-b836f8843d3d. Modules are
(xWebAdministration,1.7.0.0).
        EventType   : OPERATIONAL
```

Note that DSC determined that the PSDesiredStateConfiguration and xWebAdministration DSC resources were needed for this MOF file to be executed, so it checked the target node for their presence. It found that the version of PSDesiredStateConfiguration present on the target node matched the version specified in the MOF file, so it did not have to download a new one, but the xWebAdministration DSC resource was not present at all, so it needed to download it:

```
        TimeCreated : 8/01/2015 4:17:59 PM
        Message     : WebDownloadManager Get-DscModule command, module
xWebAdministration, GET Url: PSDSCPullServer.svc/Module(
                      ConfigurationId='07f528b9-0f22-4029-a3a7-
b836f8843d3d',ModuleName='xWebAdministration',ModuleVersion='1.7
                      .0.0')/ModuleContent.
        EventType   : OPERATIONAL
        TimeCreated : 8/01/2015 4:17:59 PM
        Message     : Attempting to get the modules
{(xWebAdministration,1.7.0.0)} from pull server with Server Url
                      http://192.168.0.12:8080/PSDSCPullServer.svc using Web
Download Manager.
        EventType   : OPERATIONAL
        TimeCreated : 8/01/2015 4:17:59 PM
        Message     : WebDownloadManager Get-DscModule command, module
xWebAdministration, File save result:
C:\Windows\TEMP\635756842794223943\xWebAdministration_1.7.0.0.zip.checksum.
        EventType   : OPERATIONAL
        TimeCreated : 8/01/2015 4:17:59 PM
        Message     : WebDownloadManager Get-DscModule command, module
xWebAdministration, File save result:
```

```
C:\Windows\TEMP\635756842794223943\xWebAdministration_1.7.0.0.zip.
    EventType    : OPERATIONAL
    TimeCreated  : 8/01/2015 4:17:59 PM
    Message      : The modules (xWebAdministration,1.7.0.0) were downloaded
to the location
                   C:\Windows\TEMP\\635756842794223943.
    EventType    : OPERATIONAL
    TimeCreated  : 8/01/2015 4:17:59 PM
    Message      : The checksum validation for module xWebAdministration
completed with status code 0.
    EventType    : OPERATIONAL
    TimeCreated  : 8/01/2015 4:18:00 PM
    Message      : Successfully got the modules from pull server using
Download Manager WebDownloadManager.
    EventType    : OPERATIONAL
    TimeCreated  : 8/01/2015 4:18:00 PM
    Message      : The content validation for module xWebAdministration
completed with status code 0.
    EventType    : OPERATIONAL
    TimeCreated  : 8/01/2015 4:18:00 PM
    Message      : The modules xWebAdministration were installed at the
location C:\Program
                   Files\WindowsPowerShell\Modules\xWebAdministration.
    EventType    : OPERATIONAL
```

DSC successfully downloaded any DSC resources that were needed and verified that the downloaded files matched the checksum stored in the DSC pull server, all without any action on our part. This is much easier than pushing DSC configurations around.

Now that DSC has the correct DSC resources residing on the target node, it asks for the next step to perform. We'll look at the first record for the logs from that execution:

```
[PS]> (get-xdscoperation)[0].AllEvents | fl
    TimeCreated  : 8/01/2015 4:27:59 PM
    Message      : WebDownloadManager for configuration 07f528b9-0f22-4029-
a3a7-b836f8843d3d Do-DscAction command with
                   server url: http://192.168.0.12:8080/PSDSCPullServer.svc.
    EventType    : OPERATIONAL
    TimeCreated  : 8/01/2015 4:27:59 PM
    Message      : Attempting to get the action from pull server using
Download Manager WebDownloadManager. Configuration
                   Id is 07f528b9-0f22-4029-a3a7-b836f8843d3d. Checksum is
0A6066B1398ABBEBA442775512E60E5392C3873F3F13C9E5B1E80B3C3FC681A4.
Compliance status is true.
    EventType    : OPERATIONAL
```

DSC checks to see whether the MOF file resident on the target node is the same as the one on the DSC pull server before it continues to make sure things have not changed since the last time. It then issues a call to see what the next action is, which is to apply the MOF file to the target node:

```
        TimeCreated : 8/01/2015 4:27:59 PM
        Message     : Configuration is sent from computer NULL by user sid
S-1-5-18.
        EventType   : OPERATIONAL
        TimeCreated : 8/01/2015 4:27:59 PM
        Message     : WebDownloadManager for configuration 07f528b9-0f22-4029-
a3a7-b836f8843d3d Do-DscAction command, GET Url:
PSDSCPullServer.svc/Action(ConfigurationId='07f528b9-0f22-4029-a3a7-
b836f8843d3d')/GetAction.
        EventType   : OPERATIONAL
        TimeCreated : 8/01/2015 4:27:59 PM
        Message     : WebDownloadManager for configuration 07f528b9-0f22-4029-
a3a7-b836f8843d3d Do-DscAction command, GET call
                      result: Ok.
        EventType   : OPERATIONAL
        TimeCreated : 8/01/2015 4:27:59 PM
        Message     : Running consistency engine.
        EventType   : OPERATIONAL
        TimeCreated : 8/01/2015 4:27:59 PM
        Message     : Successfully got the action Ok from pull server using
Download Manager WebDownloadManager.
        EventType   : OPERATIONAL
        TimeCreated : 8/01/2015 4:28:04 PM
        Message     : Consistency engine was run successfully.
        EventType   : OPERATIONAL
```

The last several events show that DSC applies the MOF file to the target node and reports success as a result. If we wait until the next DSC consistency check, we can see DSC determine whether the system is still in the desired state. We use the first record because this is now the most recent event in the system:

```
    [PS]> (get-xdscoperation)[0].AllEvents | fl
        TimeCreated : 8/01/2015 4:42:11 PM
        Message     : Configuration is sent from computer NULL by user sid
S-1-5-18.
        EventType   : OPERATIONAL
        TimeCreated : 8/01/2015 4:42:11 PM
        Message     : Attempting to get the action from pull server using
Download Manager WebDownloadManager. Configuration
                      Id is 07f528b9-0f22-4029-a3a7-b836f8843d3d. Checksum is
0A6066B1398ABBEBA442775512E60E5392C3873F3F13C9E5B1E80B3C3FC681A4.
Compliance status is true.
```

```
EventType     : OPERATIONAL
```

Reporting on the target node status

If you're interested in a quick view of the status of a target node in WMF 5, there is a built-in cmdlet to report on a target node's status, called Get-DscConfigurationStatus. This runs a PSJob that interrogates the state of the DSC runs on the target node and returns the status information:

```
PS C:\Windows\system32> Get-DscConfigurationStatus | fl *
DurationInSeconds      : 4
Error                  :
HostName               : DSC-BOX2
IPV4Addresses          : {10.0.2.15, 169.254.35.43, 192.168.50.2,
192.168.50.4...}
IPV6Addresses          : {fe80::c524:57eb:b077:5419%7, ::2000:0:0:0,
fe80::d80e:a48b:f347:232b%2, ::4000:0:0:0...}
JobID                  : {E5104F0B-7BD6-11E7-9662-080027928F7F}
LCMVersion             : 2.0
Locale                 : en-US
MACAddresses           : {08-00-27-5B-B7-7B, 08-00-27-E1-B2-24,
08-00-27-92-8F-7F, 00-00-00-00-00-00-00-E0...}
MetaConfiguration      : MSFT_DSCMetaConfiguration
MetaData               : Author: vagrant; Name: SetupTheSite; Version:
2.0.0; GenerationDate: 08/08/2017 00:59:30;GenerationHost: DSC-BOX1;
Mode : Pull
NumberOfResources      : 6
RebootRequested        : False
ResourcesInDesiredState  : {[WindowsFeature]IIS, [WindowsFeature]AspNet45,
[xWebsite]DefaultSite,[File]WebContentDir...}
ResourcesNotInDesiredState :
StartDate              : 8/8/2017 1:14:16 AM
Status                 : Success
Type                   : Consistency
PSComputerName         :
CimClass :
root/microsoft/windows/desiredstateconfiguration:MSFT_DSCConfigurationStatu
s
CimInstanceProperties      : {DurationInSeconds, Error, HostName,
IPV4Addresses...}
CimSystemProperties        :
Microsoft.Management.Infrastructure.CimSystemProperties
```

Notable information to see here is the listing of `ResourcesInDesiredState` and `ResourcesNotInDesiredState`. This is immediately useful information to determine what was successful and what was not successful in the last run, and it can be used along with the DSC logging already covered to pinpoint and diagnose failures.

Reporting on the target node status with the DSC pull server

The information we have seen so far is great if you have access to PowerShell and you can run these commands either locally or through PowerShell remoting sessions. It's great for developing and troubleshooting DSC configurations on DSC pull servers, but what if you want something more, such as a dashboard that displays the state of all systems attached to your DSC pull server?

Even with two releases over the last several years, DSC is still very much a new product, and it is still lacking features that products such as Puppet and Chef have. Reporting on the target node status is still a major feature that DSC does not have in parity, the main example being that DSC doesn't have a dashboard-like report that shows the status of all our target nodes and our DSC pull servers across our environment.

WMF 5 pull server reporting

We can approximate something similar using the reporting capabilities that come in the WMF 5 release using PowerShell and the web API endpoints in the DSC pull server. The data we can see is the data that the LCM on each target node sends back to the DSC pull server each time they perform a DSC execution. We set this up earlier in the chapter when we configured the DSC target node. We can see this data by issuing a PowerShell command that interrogates the REST API endpoint, which is wrapped up in a PowerShell function, as follows:

```
function Get-DscLCMStatusReport
{
 [cmdletBinding()]
 param(
 [Parameter()]
 [string]$AgentId,
 [Parameter()]
 [string]$serviceURL = "https://localhost:8080/PSDSCPullServer.svc"
 )
 $requestUri = "$serviceURL/Nodes(AgentId= '$AgentId')/Reports"
 $params = @{
```

```
'Uri' = $requestUri
'ContentType' =
"application/json;odata=minimalmetadata;streaming=true;charset=utf-8"
'UseBasicParsing' = $true
'Headers' = @{Accept = "application/json";ProtocolVersion = "2.0"}
}
$request = Invoke-WebRequest @params
$object = ConvertFrom-Json $request.content
return $object.value
}
```

When we run the preceding function, we get the following data:

```
Get-DscLCMStatusReport -AgentId 'CC7F944E-7BD4-11E7-9662-080027928F7F'
JobId                  : e5fe95bb-7b83-11e7-9662-0800279dfc74
OperationType          : LocalConfigurationManager
RefreshMode            : Pull
Status                 : Success
ReportFormatVersion    : 2.0
ConfigurationVersion   :
StartTime              : 2017-08-07T15:20:09.783
EndTime                : 2017-08-07T15:20:12.783
RebootRequested        : False
Errors                 : {}
StatusData :
{{"StartDate":"2017-08-07T15:20:09.7830000+00:00","IPV6Addresses":
<#..
#>{"CLRVersion":"4.0.30319.42000","PSVersion":"5.1.14393.206","BuildVersion
":"10.0.14393.206"}}}
```

If we use `ConvertTo-Json` cmdlet, we can see the `StatusData` for the last job in greater detail:

```
StartDate            : 2017-08-07T15:20:09.7830000+00:00
IPV6Addresses        : {fe80::a524:d07a:954f:8284%8, ::2000:0:0:0,
fe80::b071:249b:c850:f9ef%5, ::4000:0:0:0...}
DurationInSeconds    : 3
JobID                : {E5FE95BB-7B83-11E7-9662-0800279DFC74}
MetaData             : Author: vagrant; Name: HTTPSTargetNodeLCM; Version:
2.0.0;GenerationDate: 08/07/2017 15:20:08; GenerationHost: DSC-BOX1;
Status               : Success
IPV4Addresses        : {10.0.2.15, 169.254.249.239, 192.168.50.2,
192.168.50.4...}
LCMVersion           : 2.0
NumberOfResources    : 0
Type                 : LocalConfigurationManager
HostName             : DSC-BOX2
RebootRequested      : False
```

```
MACAddresses        : {08-00-27-5B-B7-7B, 08-00-27-89-F0-97, 08-00-27-9D-
FC-74, 00-00-00-00-00-00-00-E0...}
MetaConfiguration : @{AgentId=E5286536-7B81-11E7-9662-0800279DFC74; <#..#>
}
Locale              : en-US
Mode                : Pull
```

Other products, such as Puppet and Chef, provide this type of reporting out of the box and without extra effort; however, with a little extra work, you can have something similar. While this is still raw data, it could be put into a data warehouse system that queries could be run against and reports generated about for the rate of change in your environment.

WMF 4 pull server reporting

While earlier in the chapter we said that WMF 4 DSC Pull servers have been deprecated, if you are still using one, we have the ability to cobble together something with less information than WMF 5 that is still useful.

We can get a simple status from the DSC pull server using the `ComplianceServer` endpoint we set up at the beginning of this chapter. While most of its functionality is not documented and not really exposed to the user for use, there are some public features of the DSC `ComplianceServer` we can take advantage of. We can interrogate the HTTP endpoint for information about our target nodes by issuing an HTTP request at `http://localhost:9080/PSDSCComplianceServer.svc/Status`. It returns JSON, and there are some credentials we need to use, so let's wrap this into a function we can use more than once:

```
Function Get-DscPullServerInformation
{
  [cmdletBinding()]
  Param (
    [string] $Uri =
"http://localhost:9080/PSDSCComplianceServer.svc/Status"
  )
  Write-Verbose "Querying node information from pull server URI  = $Uri"
  $invokeParams = @{
    Uri                 = $Uri
    Method              = "Get"
    ContentType         = 'application/json'
    UseDefaultCredentials = $true
    Headers             = @{Accept = 'application/json'}
  }
  $response = Invoke-WebRequest @invokeParams
  if($response.StatusCode -ne 200){
```

```
        throw "Could not access $uri"
    }
    ConvertFrom-Json $response.Content
}
```

This example function assumes a lot about your setup, but it is a nice place to start. It is adapted from a blog post on the PowerShell blog here: `http://blogs.msdn.com/b/powershell/archive/2014/05/29/how-to-retrieve-node-information-from-pull-server.aspx`. If we run this against our DSC pull server, we get the following output:

```
PS C:\vagrant> Get-DscPullServerInformation | select -expand value
TargetName         : 192.168.0.13
ConfigurationId    : 981c0096-a241-48ea-bbe7-15781c229459
ServerCheckSum     :
07E474F06E89FEC570647C85375FEEE1A3A61C854995AA3044E549C3A3EE70A8
TargetCheckSum     :
07E474F06E89FEC570647C85375FEEE1A3A61C854995AA3044E549C3A3EE70A8
NodeCompliant      : True
LastComplianceTime : 2015-08-01T21:06:16.5232617Z
LastHeartbeatTime  : 2015-08-01T21:06:16.5232617Z
Dirty              : True
StatusCode         : 0
```

The important properties to note here are `NodeCompliant` and `StatusCode`. `NodeCompliant` tells us whether the state of the target node is in compliance with what the DSC pull server thinks it should be. `StatusCode` is a number that represents the result of the last pull operation performed by the DSC agent on the target node. `StatusCode` of 0 means that the last operation was successful; anything else most likely means an error. A list of the numbers and what they mean is provided in the blog post, but it comes with a warning that it reserves the right to change in future releases. This has held true, as we have seen with the additional output WMF 5 brings us.

Summary

In this chapter, we covered end to end all the steps required to install, configure, and use a DSC pull server. We also covered some example ways of using diagnostic tools to check on the status of DSC pull servers. In the course of the chapter, we saw several different approaches to handling how to make DSC configuration scripts for both deploying DSC pull servers and also target nodes. Along the way, we covered the differences between WMF 4 and WMF 5 features and the possible ways to use them in your environment.

In the next chapter, we will look at some exciting new things for DSC: cross-platform support!

7
DSC Cross Platform Support

"Around here we don't look backward for very long. We keep moving forward, opening up new doors and doing new things, because we're curious... and curiosity keeps leading us down new paths."
- Walt Disney

In Chapter 6, *Pulling DSC Configurations*, we covered how DSC pulls DSC configurations from a DSC Pull Server and how to report and check its status. In this chapter, we are going to take a short sidestep and talk about an exciting new development in the DSC world: cross-platform support for DSC and PowerShell!

In this chapter, we will cover the following topics:

- DSC cross-platform support
- Using DSC on Linux
- PowerShell Core

DSC cross-platform support

One of the earliest concepts we covered in this book was that DSC is a *platform* that enables the management of target nodes. It's a platform because it provides the low-level tools that higher-level abstractions can take advantage of. An example of this is Puppet or Chef integrating with DSC by directly invoking DSC resources inside their own manifests. A better example is DSC managing more than just Windows operating systems.

Up until now, DSC only installed and managed Windows OS desktop and server platforms. As we covered in the first chapters of this book, DSC comes bundled in the WMF installation for the OS you are using, the latest of which is WMF 5.1. The WMF 5.1 release includes Windows PowerShell 5.1, which is the last major version of Windows PowerShell that will be released. Implied in the name, Windows PowerShell is only installable on Windows OS, so when Microsoft decided to extend DSC to work on other platforms, they had to use something other than Windows PowerShell, since PowerShell Core was a long way off. Enter `DSC for Linux`.

Using DSC on Linux

DSC for Linux is the bucket term for the set of software that allows Linux and Linux-derived OSes to be managed by DSC. DSC on Linux is comprised of a server implementation of OMI (`https://collaboration.opengroup.org/omi`) and a set of scripts that are analogous to the DSC cmdlets available in WMF. The OMI server acts as the LCM and executes DSC resources specifically written for the Linux OS. It largely operates the same as DSC on Windows, with a few differences we will cover in a bit. First, let's cover how to install the prerequisites and the initial setup.

Installing DSC on Linux

Installing DSC on Windows is as simple as using Windows Update or installing the MSU for your architecture and OS. Installing DSC on Linux requires more work and effort and will vary with the Linux distro you choose. In this book, we will pick CentOS 7 as our target platform; if you choose another distro, you might have to change a few commands with regard to package installation.

Our first step is to install the dependencies required in order to compile and install OMI and DSC on our Linux server. We can do this using `yum`, the RPM package manager. This will take some time, as `yum` initializes the repositories and downloads the packages before it installs them onto your server:

```
sudo yum -y groupinstall 'Development Tools'
sudo yum -y install pam-devel openssl-devel python python-devel libcurl-
devel wget
```

 The name of the preceding packages will vary with your Linux distro. If you use something other than CentOS, then you will have to search for the correctly named package using tools from that distro.

The next step is to download and install the RPM packages for OMI and DSC:

```
wget
https://github.com/Microsoft/omi/releases/download/v1.1.0-0/omi-1.1.0.ssl_1
00.x64.rpm
wget
https://github.com/Microsoft/PowerShell-DSC-for-Linux/releases/download/v1.
1.1-294/dsc-1.1.1-294.ssl_100.x64.rpm

sudo rpm -Uvh omi-1.1.0.ssl_100.x64.rpm
sudo rpm -Uvh dsc-1.1.1-294.ssl_100.x64.rpm
```

The RPM packages will install and set up the OMI server for you with the default configuration set. It will also install the built-in set of DSC resources that work on Linux systems:

- nxGroupResource
- nxFileResource
- nxUserResource
- nxArchiveResource
- nxServiceResource
- nxScriptResource
- nxFileLineResource
- nxPackageResource
- nxSshAuthorizedKeysResource
- nxEnvironmentResource

You'll notice that these mirror the built-in DSC resources in the WMF installation almost exactly. This is entirely on purpose, and it allows you to manage your Linux systems with some extra code needed.

Pushing a DSC configuration to a Linux node

Once DSC for Linux is fully installed and set up, we can begin to use DSC configurations on the Linux node. The following is an example DSC Configuration for a Linux node that ensures a very important file is present:

```
Configuration LinuxDemoSetup
{
 Import-DSCResource -Module nx

 Node 'localhost'
```

```
  {
    nxFile myTestFile
    {
      Ensure = "Present"
      Type = "File"
      DestinationPath = "/tmp/dsctest"
      Contents = "This is my DSC Test!"
    }
  }
}
```

Note how it looks exactly like the DSC configurations we've been using in the entire book. The promises we read about in the first chapter of using a DSL for multiple platforms without learning new syntax or systems has finally come true.

In order to push this DSC Configuration to our Linux target node, we'll put it in a `.ps1` file and use the knowledge we gained in the previous chapter to extract the configuration data to a manifest file. Then, we'll compile the DSC Configuration into an MOF for deployment. Since DSC uses the same transmission protocols regardless of whether it's on Windows or Linux, we can author and compile the DSC Configuration scripts on our Windows desktop. This is the code to do that, and in the downloadable source code for this book is the full source for the DSC Configuration and attendant files:

```
$outputPath = ([IO.Path]::Combine($PSScriptRoot, 'LinuxDemoSetup'))
$dataScript = ([IO.Path]::Combine($PSScriptRoot, 'linux_config_data.ps1'))
$configData = &$dataScript

.\linux_configuration.ps1 -OutputPath $outputPath -ConfigData $configData
```

This approach should look familiar; we used the same approach in the previous chapter to install DSC Pull Servers.

We can use the built-in remoting capabilities of the DSC cmdlets to push our compiled DSC Configuration to our Linux server. This should look familiar to the approaches we covered in Chapter 6, *Pushing DSC Configurations*, with the exception of using specific settings and options to control the remoting session:

```
$password = "password" | ConvertTo-SecureString -asPlainText -Force
$credential = New-Object
System.Management.Automation.PSCredential('root',$password)
$CIOpt = New-CimSessionOption -SkipCACheck -SkipCNCheck `
                           -SkipRevocationCheck -Encoding Utf8 -UseSsl
$CimSession = New-CimSession -Authentication Basic -Credential $credential `

                           -ComputerName 'dsc-box2' -port 5986 `
                           -SessionOption $CIOpt
```

With the remoting session set up and connected, we can now interrogate the remote target node to ensure we can manage it with DSC:

```
[PS]> Get-CimInstance -CimSession $CimSession -namespace root/omi -
ClassName omi_identify

InstanceID : 2FDB5542-5896-45D5-9BE9-DC04430AAABE
SystemName : dsc-box2
ProductName : OMI
ProductVendor : Microsoft
ProductVersionMajor : 1
ProductVersionMinor : 1
ProductVersionRevision : 0
ProductVersionString : 1.1.0-0
Platform : LINUX_X86_64_GNU
OperatingSystem : LINUX
Architecture : X86_64
Compiler : GNU
ConfigPrefix : GNU
ConfigLibDir : /opt/omi/lib
ConfigBinDir : /opt/omi/bin
ConfigIncludeDir : /opt/omi/include
ConfigDataDir : /opt/omi/share
ConfigLocalStateDir : /var/opt/omi
ConfigSysConfDir : /etc/opt/omi/conf
ConfigProviderDir : /etc/opt/omi/conf
ConfigLogFile : /var/opt/omi/log/omiserver.log
ConfigPIDFile : /var/opt/omi/run/omiserver.pid
ConfigRegisterDir : /etc/opt/omi/conf/omiregister
ConfigSchemaDir : /opt/omi/share/omischema
ConfigNameSpaces : {root-omi, root-Microsoft-DesiredStateConfiguration,
 root-Microsoft-Windows-DesiredStateConfiguration}
PSComputerName : dsc-box2
```

Satisfied that we can connect and interrogate the target node, we can now push our DSC Configuration out to the Linux node:

```
[PS]> Start-DSCConfiguration -CimSession $CimSession -wait -Verbose -Path
$outputPath
VERBOSE: Perform operation 'Invoke CimMethod' with following parameters,
''methodName' =
 SendConfigurationApply,'className' =
MSFT_DSCLocalConfigurationManager,'namespaceName' =
 root/Microsoft/Windows/DesiredStateConfiguration'.
 VERBOSE: Operation 'Invoke CimMethod' complete.
 VERBOSE: Time taken for configuration job to complete is 0.225 seconds
```

We can verify that the DSC Configuration we pushed was applied by running `Get-DSCConfiguration` and `Test-DSCConfiguration`:

```
[PS]> Get-DSCConfiguration -CimSession $CimSession

DestinationPath : /tmp/dsctest
SourcePath :
Ensure : present
Type : file
Force : False
Contents : This is my DSC Test!
Checksum :
Recurse : False
Links : follow
Group : root
Mode : 644
Owner : root
ModifiedDate : 8/10/2017 2:51:11 AM
PSComputerName : dsc-box2
CimClassName : MSFT_nxFileResource

[PS]> Test-DscConfiguration -CimSession:$CimSession
True
```

We can verify this manually by logging onto the Linux server and checking the file contents:

```
[vagrant@dsc-box2 ~]$ cat /tmp/dsctest
This is my DSC Test![vagrant@dsc-box2 ~]$
```

With a little extra effort, you are now able to manage the Linux nodes in your environment from your desktop, just like any other Windows node.

PowerShell Core

As you have worked through the examples throughout this chapter, you may have noticed that DSC for Linux provides DSC functionality on the target nodes you're managing, but there is something that's still missing. Even though it's DSC, it's not PowerShell.

Up until now, Windows PowerShell was available only on, well, the Windows OS. With the advent of .NET Core, Windows PowerShell is now PowerShell Core: a multi-platform shell and scripting language. This means PowerShell Core can be installed on Windows, macOS, and Linux. Now, there isn't a platform you can't use PowerShell on!

PowerShell Core is in late beta stages, so some of the information in this chapter may change. While Microsoft have finished a lot of work, there is still some more to go. Some functionality may be limited until they get to that area of implementation.

The goal for PowerShell Core is to behave just as Windows PowerShell did, just having greater reach. The PowerShell team has been working for a long time to make PowerShell portable and use the platform libraries on each target OS. Your experience on a macOS or Linux PC will be the same as your Windows PC!

 Replace the versions here with the most current release available when you begin to install PowerShell Core. These versions are what was current at the time of writing this.

Installing PowerShell Core on Windows

Installing on Windows is much as you'd expect. You install from the MSI provided at `https://github.com/PowerShell/PowerShell/releases`. You can either follow the GUI MSI wizard, or you can invoke the installation from the command line:

```
msiexec /i PowerShell-6.0.0-beta.5-win10-win2016-x64.msi /q /l*xv
C:\log.txt
```

Installing PowerShell Core on macOS

Installing PowerShell Core on a macOS can be accomplished in a few different ways. If you are familiar with macOS package managers, you might be familiar with *Homebrew*, which installs macOS software from the Terminal, or you could install it manually yourself.

Homebrew

Installing with *Homebrew* is a matter of a few simple commands. More information on *Homebrew* links and how to install it is available on the `https://github.com/PowerShell/PowerShell/readme.md` page.

First, ensure that the `cask` plugin is installed and ready, then install PowerShell:

```
brew tap caskroom/cask
brew cask install powershell
```

Updating the version of PowerShell takes another few simple commands:

```
brew update
brew reinstall powershell
```

Manual

Download `powershell-6.0.0-beta.5-osx.10.12-x64.pkg` from `https://github.com/PowerShell/PowerShell/releases/latest`:

```
sudo installer -pkg powershell-6.0.0-beta.5-osx.10.12-x64.pkg -target /
```

Installing PowerShell Core on Linux

Installing PowerShell Core takes a bit more work than the other platforms, but that is mostly because of the flexibility of Linux and the many different ways in which you can install. There are many different Linux distros out there. Enumerating how to install PowerShell on each of those would be difficult to accomplish in this book, so take a look at `https://github.com/PowerShell/PowerShell/blob/master/docs/installation/linux.md` for individual distro instructions. Here, we have chosen Ubuntu as a common distro for an example.

Ubuntu

On our example Ubuntu system, we run the following commands in order to setup the apt-get repository to point to Microsoft's repo, then run `apt-get` to install PowerShell.

```
# Import the public repository GPG keys
curl https://packages.microsoft.com/keys/microsoft.asc | sudo apt-key add -

# Register the Microsoft Ubuntu repository
curl https://packages.microsoft.com/config/ubuntu/14.04/prod.list | sudo
tee /etc/apt/sources.list.d/microsoft.list

# Update apt-get
sudo apt-get update

# Install PowerShell
sudo apt-get install -y powershell
```

Summary

This chapter has been an exciting tour of the new roads PowerShell is taking in the coming years. It has moved from managing just one platform to managing many different platforms and has evolved from just another Windows Shell to something that can handle any OS you throw at it.

In the next chapter, we will apply everything you have learned so far in this book in a real-world example using DSC to deploy internal applications and respond to the changing requirements in production systems.

8
Example Scenarios

"Now this is not the end. It is not even the beginning of the end. But it is, perhaps, the end of the beginning."
- Winston Churchill

Here we are at the end of our story, and you might be wondering what there is left to cover. We've gone over all there is to go over in an introductory book, except how to handle certain situations in the real world. In our testing environments, we've had known quantities and clear requirements. We were able to use the latest software and, therefore, had an easy time using DSC. However, the real world is messy and filled with complex and conflicting requirements, old legacy software, and inflexible deployment processes. How does DSC fit into situations like this?

In this chapter, we will cover the following topics:

- Real-life DSC usage
- Setting up a common installation base
- Installing the software
- Configuration management refresher
- Selective software upgrades
- Reporting status

Real-life DSC usage

After coming this far, you're on the bandwagon and are ready to implement DSC in your production environment. You're the admin for numerous servers and you want to start getting things in order right away. You've talked it over with your boss and you both know there isn't enough room on the VM server for a dedicated instance just to stand up to the DSC pull server when it hasn't proven itself yet. You've agreed to start out with pushing DSC configurations to show progress and, in a month, re-evaluate what the progress is.

When you open the list of servers you manage, you notice that there is a mix of Windows 2008 R2 and Windows 2012 R2. A sigh of relief escapes your mouth when you remember the last of the old Windows 2003 servers were migrated off a couple months ago in preparation for the end of life cutoff that happens this year. With the list of different OS and IP addresses handy, you decide to use PowerShell to investigate how many of them have **PowerShell Remoting (PSR)** up and running:

```
[PS]> New-PSSession –ComputerName (gc ./servers.txt) –ErrorAction  0 –
ErrorVariable "+sessionErrors"
```

 The preceding example uses the error capturing functionality PowerShell provides in order to allow `New-PSSession` to continue running regardless of any errors connecting to any of the servers in the list provided. Any errors are collected in the variable name provided for the user to look at after the execution run completes.

It's a crude but effective test, as any server with a running and configured PSR endpoint will respond, and those that don't will not respond. You know that installing PowerShell and enabling PSR is part of the initial manual build process to install the OS in your environment, but even so, there are a few machines that don't respond.

 As covered earlier in the book, you know you do not have to have PowerShell Remoting enabled in order for DSC to function; the only requirement is to have WinRM configured.
In your environment, enabling PowerShell Remoting handles setting up WinRM but also enables your ad hoc remote administration, so it's a no-brainer to use this as your opportunity to ensure it's enabled on every machine in your environment.

Invoking `Enable-PSRemoting -Force` on the remaining servers wouldn't be too much trouble manually, but doing that with Sysinternals `psexec` works quicker because you have administrator access to the target machines:

```
[PS]> Get-Content ./non_compliant_servers.txt | % { psexec $_ -s -h -d
powershell Enable-PSRemoting -Force }
```

It may feel like cheating to drop down to `psexec` in order to get PSR running, but you know it won't be required much longer as all Windows 2012 R2 installations come with PSR enabled and are securely configured by default.

Setting up a common installation base

With all your target machines up and configured for remote access, you move on to looking at what your common base installation should look like. Since you've been doing this stuff manually by yourself for a long while, you know by heart what needs to be installed on every server and configured.

Looking back at this book as you go, you jump right into making a DSC configuration for your base setup. Since the custom software your company develops uses *Roman* names for code names for releases, you decide to name your configuration `Pantheon` and author the following DSC configuration script:

```
Configuration PantheonDeployment
{
  Import-DscResource -Module xRemoteDesktopAdmin
  Import-DscResource -Module xTimeZone
  Import-DscResource -Module xComputerManagement
  Import-DscResource -Module xSystemSecurity
  Node ($AllNodes).NodeName
  {
    LocalConfigurationManager
    {
      ConfigurationId      = $Node.ConfigurationId
      RefreshMode          = $Node.RefreshMode
      ConfigurationMode    = $Node.ConfigurationMode
      AllowModuleOverwrite = $Node.AllowModuleOverwrite
      RebootNodeIfNeeded   = $Node.RebootNodeIfNeeded
    }
    xComputer NewName
    {
      Name = $Node.MachineName
    }
    xTimeZone UtcTimeZone
```

```
    {
      TimeZone          = 'UTC'
      IsSingleInstance = 'Yes'
    }
    xRemoteDesktopAdmin RemoteDesktopSettings
    {
      Ensure              = 'Present'
      UserAuthentication = 'NonSecure'
    }
    xIEEsc DisableIEEscAdmin
    {
      UserRole  = 'Administrators'
      IsEnabled = $false
    }
    xIEEsc EnableIEEscUser
    {
      UserRole  = 'Users'
      IsEnabled = $true
    }
    xUac SetDefaultUAC
    {
      Setting = 'NotifyChanges'
    }
    WindowsFeature TelnetClient
    {
      Ensure = "Present"
      Name   = "Telnet-Client"
    }
  }
}
$data   = Join-Path $PSScriptRoot 'data_example_01.psd1'
$output = Join-Path $PSScriptRoot 'PantheonDeployment'
PantheonDeployment -ConfigurationData $data -OutputPath $output
```

The previous code is nothing too fancy and mostly in line with what you have learned throughout this book. The only thing out of the ordinary is that we are changing the name of the target node. After testing this, you find that renaming the target node requires a reboot, which DSC does not do by default. To handle this, you add the RebootNodeIfNeeded property to your ConfigurationData hash so that DSC will reboot the host and continue working after it has come up.

You know there are more things you can add here, but this is a good start, so you stick with it. Using snippets from this book, you can wrap it up in a PowerShell script that accepts a `ConfigurationData` hashtable like this one:

```
@{
    AllNodes = @(
        @{
            NodeName        = 'app01'
            ConfigurationId = 'ab2c2cb2-67a3-444c-bc55-cc2ee70e3d0c'
        },
        @{
            NodeName        = 'app02'
            ConfigurationId = '8e8f44e6-aaac-4060-b072-c9ae780ee5f7'
        },
        @{
            NodeName            = '*'
            RefreshMode         = 'Push'
            ConfigurationMode   = 'ApplyAndAutoCorrect'
            AllowModuleOverwrite = $true
            RebootNodeIfNeeded  = $true
        }
    )
}
```

You can use the approaches outlined in Chapter 5, *Pushing DSC Configurations*, to compile and push your DSC configurations to your target nodes. You occasionally check whether DSC has kept the servers in the state they should be in, but you know you don't have to, thanks to the `ApplyAndAutoCorrect` configuration mode you set the LCM to. With this setting, the LCM constantly monitors the state of your servers for drift and keeps them in compliance even if you're not looking, whether you are using push deployments or pull servers.

Installing software

Time goes on, and your boss is impressed with the speed at which you are able to provision new servers on demand and replace faulty ones as they break. He/she notices, however, that the response time drops off severely after you hand off the servers to the application team to install the company's custom software. After discussing it with the application team, you are cleared to codify the installation requirements and configuration for the company's application called *Apollo* and add it to your DSC configuration. Since you've already added the base installation requirements to the DSC configuration script, it's a simple matter to add the MSI installation steps for the Apollo application.

The Apollo application is only supposed to be installed on the app servers, so you need a way to tell DSC not to install it on any other target node. You can create a new `Node` statement and use the filtering capability of PowerShell, where the statement to select only the target nodes that have the `appserver` role defined is located:

```
Configuration PantheonDeployment
{
  Import-DscResource -Module xPSDesiredStateConfiguration
  Import-DscResource -Module xRemoteDesktopAdmin
  Import-DscResource -Module xTimeZone
  Import-DscResource -Module xComputerManagement
  Import-DscResource -Module xSystemSecurity
  Node ($AllNodes).NodeName{ <# ... #> }
  Node ($AllNodes.Where({$_.Roles -contains 'appserver'})).NodeName
  {
    xPackage ApolloPackage
    {
      Ensure    = 'Present'
      Name      = $Node.Apollo.Name
      ProductId = $Node.Apollo.ProductId
      Path      = $Node.Apollo.Source
      Arguments = $Node.Apollo.Arguments
    }
    Service ApolloService
    {
      Name      = 'apollo'
      State     = 'Running'
      DependsOn = @("[xPackage]ApolloPackage")
    }
  }
}
$data   = Join-Path $PSScriptRoot 'data_example_02.psd1'
$output = Join-Path $PSScriptRoot 'PantheonDeployment'
PantheonDeployment -ConfigurationData $data -OutputPath $output
```

You chose to use the newer `xPackage` DSC resource from `PSGallery` because it has a couple of newer bug fixes and parameters compared to the PowerShell V4 release. So now, you have to add the `xPSDesiredStateConfiguration` module to your `Import-DSCResource` statement. This choice means that you now have to copy the `xPSDesiredStateConfiguration` module to all your target nodes before you push the new version of your DSC configuration script. You make a mental note to ask your boss about a DSC pull server again.

Your updated `ConfigurationData` hash looks like this:

```
@{
  AllNodes = @(
    @{
      NodeName         = 'app01'
      ConfigurationId = 'ab2c2cb2-67a3-444c-bc55-cc2ee70e3d0c'
      Roles           = @('appserver')
    },
    @{
      NodeName         = 'app02'
      ConfigurationId = '8e8f44e6-aaac-4060-b072-c9ae780ee5f7'
      Roles           = @('appserver')
    },
    @{
      NodeName            = '*'
      RefreshMode         = 'Push'
      ConfigurationMode   = 'ApplyAndAutoCorrect'
      AllowModuleOverwrite = $true
      RebootNodeIfNeeded  = $true
      Apollo   = @{
        Name              = 'Apollo'
        ProductId         = '{e70c4829-91dc-4f0e-a404-4eba81f6feb9}'
        SourcePath        =
'http://build.pantheon.net/apollo/packages/releases/apollo.1.1.0.msi'
        Arguments         = 'CONFIG='
        ConfigFilePath    =
"$env:ProgramFiles\Apollo\config\app.config"
        ConfigFileContents = "importantsetting=`$true"
      }
    }
  )
}
```

Another choice you made was to extract the MSI package information to your `ConfigurationData` block. You remembered the section of this book that explained how this allows you to increment the version number or change the package location without editing your DSC configuration. You used the `$Node` keyword to access the hash table for each target node and access all the special MSI information the `xPackage` DSC resource needs to operate.

Testing this out in your dev setup works out nicely, so you push your new DSC configuration to your target nodes. DSC automatically tests each target node for compliance and only installs the Apollo application on the new target nodes that need it, or the target nodes that have an outdated version. Upgrades of existing installations work because the Apollo developers followed MSI conventions for point releases and did not change anything that required a full uninstallation of the previous version.

Configuration management refresher

A few weeks pass and you get an escalation call from the application team that your **DSC stuff** broke their application. A few minutes of investigation using the `xDSCResourceDiagnostics` module shows successful DSC executions that detected configuration drift and corrected it. After showing this to the application team, they eventually admit that they updated the configuration file used by the Apollo application with different values without telling you since they were used to deploying the application themselves.

Since you had set the LCM to `ApplyAndAutoCorrect`, DSC had detected the content difference in the file specified in `$Node.Apollo.ConfigFilePath` and changed it back to the value you specified in `$Node.Apollo.ConfigFileContents` in the DSC configuration data file, just like it was designed to do. The application team didn't think that DSC would change the file; they thought it was a one-time-only installation tool. You explain that DSC is a configuration management tool that works for the life of the server and is not just for the initial installations. In the after action reports, it was decided that all the engineering teams would learn enough about configuration management and DevOps practices to avoid mix-ups like this in the future.

This decision marks a turning point in the company. The applications and systems teams start moving toward declarative configuration files that are kept up to date as things change instead of having to keep the information in their heads all the time. They become less concerned with golden images and special servers and instead focus on how to automate the steps outlined in the MS Word document for a release. This reduces the time spent on deploying the applications on new or existing servers and the time spent on figuring out why one server has a different setting than another one. Less time fighting fires and more time doing valuable work for the company starts to pay off in new features being deployed quicker and bug fixes being patched sooner.

The continued success of using DSC in your environment has finally convinced your boss to allocate an instance for a dedicated DSC pull server. Refer to Chapter 6, *Pulling DSC Configurations,* and use it to create a DSC configuration script to set up a DSC pull server. You can even use the functions there to add a new step to your DSC configuration script that will handle copying the versioned DSC resource module archive files for you to the new pull server.

Next on your list is renaming the MOF files for all the target nodes to ConfigurationId and creating the new checksum files for each one. Make a note to wrap that in a simple PowerShell function to be invoked after compiling the MOFs when you have some free time.

Now that you have your MOFs named with their ConfigurationId, you have to point them to your new DSC pull server. We can do this by adding the DSC pull server URL to the existing ConfigurationData hash. In total, only two files are touched: the DSC configuration script and the DSC configuration data file:

```
Configuration PantheonDeployment
{
  <#
  Import-DscResource -Module...
  #>
  Node ($AllNodes).NodeName
  {
    LocalConfigurationManager
    {
      ConfigurationId          = $Node.ConfigurationId
      RefreshMode              = $Node.RefreshMode
      ConfigurationMode        = $Node.ConfigurationMode
      AllowModuleOverwrite     = $Node.AllowModuleOverwrite
      RebootNodeIfNeeded       = $Node.RebootNodeIfNeeded
      CertificateId            = $Node.CertificateId
      DownloadManagerCustomData = @{
        ServerUrl = $Node.PSDSCCPullServer;
      }
    }
    <#
    ...
    #>
  }
}
```

We could have split this into another DSC configuration script, but keeping these parts together means it's kept up to date along with any new target nodes or changes to the ConfigurationData hash automatically.

Our updated ConfigurationData hash looks like this:

```
@{
    AllNodes = @(
        @{
            NodeName        = 'app01'
            ConfigurationId = 'ab2c2cb2-67a3-444c-bc55-cc2ee70e3d0c'
            Roles           = @('appserver')
        },
        @{
            NodeName        = 'app02'
            ConfigurationId = '8e8f44e6-aaac-4060-b072-c9ae780ee5f7'
            Roles           = @('appserver')
        },
        @{
            NodeName            = '*'
            RefreshMode         = 'Push'
            ConfigurationMode   = 'ApplyAndAutoCorrect'
            AllowModuleOverwrite = $true
            RebootNodeIfNeeded  = $true
            Apollo    = @{
                Name            = 'Apollo'
                ProductId       = '{e70c4829-91dc-4f0e-a404-4eba81f6feb9}'
                SourcePath      =
'http://build.pantheon.net/apollo/packages/releases/apollo.1.1.0.msi'
                Arguments       = ''
                ConfigFilePath  =
"$env:ProgramFiles\Apollo\config\app.config"
                ConfigFileContents = "importantsetting=`$true"
            }
        }
    )
}
```

After compilation, we can run Set-DscLocalConfigurationManager against the resulting metadata generated and update all our target nodes at once.

Now that you have the target nodes set up and talking to the DSC pull server, sit back and relax until you remember your boss wanted a report to show that all your target nodes are in compliance. Refer to Chapter 6, *Pulling DSC Configurations*, and use the PowerShell functions there to set up a PowerShell script that queries the DSC pull server and outputs the status to a .csv file, and then email it to your boss every week. He/she can then open it in a spreadsheet program and check how things are working out.

Complicated deployments

The time saved from the automated deployment of both DSC resources and DSC configuration scripts, along with configuration status reporting, was of enough value to allow you to finally start working on those things you would do if only you had the time. You're leaving on time nowadays and coworkers are lining up to take advantage of being added to your list of managed servers.

The target node count has increased significantly. Since you started this project, the company has grown and the Apollo application is handling more requests than ever. The application team decides that the available time for new features is being compromised by having to deploy the company website code named Aurora by themselves. After talking with your boss, both your teams decide to hand off deploying Aurora to you. A couple of knowledge transfer sessions happen later and you have a list of software requirements and configuration steps for Aurora.

Adding the software requirements to your DSC configuration is a piece of cake. All the IIS features required to build a web server on Windows 2012 R2 are already built-in; they just need to be enabled. For security and access restriction reasons, the company has decided that any web server software cannot just be installed on any server that has the application database on it, so you add a new Node statement to your DSC configuration script and a new role to your ConfigurationData hash for web servers.

Getting the website to the target nodes is slightly more difficult. The application team doesn't use MSIs to install the Aurora website and, instead, uses ZIP files that they used xcopy with to transfer to the web server as well as a simple bat script to extract them and overwrite the existing files. They know this is a fragile and error-prone approach and are working to get a better installer made for the site, but it's not high on the priority list. Realizing you can't wait for that to happen, you decide to move forward with what you have right now. After attempting to use the File DSC resource to download the ZIP file, you realize it can't handle remote files over HTTP.

Fortunately, there is a xRemoteFile DSC resource that does exactly what you need. You chain xRemoteFile to an xArchive DSC resource to download and extract the file to a temporary location. Now, you can use the File DSC resource to check whether the destination contents match your extracted folder. All that is left is creating a web application pool and site:

```
Configuration PantheonDeployment
{
  <#
  Import-DscResource -Module..
  #>
  Node ($AllNodes).NodeName{ <#..#> }
  Node ($AllNodes.Where({$_.Roles -contains 'appserver'})).NodeName{
<#..#> }
  Node ($AllNodes.Where({$_.Roles -contains 'WebServer'})).NodeName
  {
    WindowsFeature IIS
    {
      Ensure = 'Present'
      Name   = 'Web-Server'
    }
    WindowsFeature IISConsole
    {
      Ensure   = 'Present'
      Name     = 'Web-Mgmt-Console'
      DependsOn = '[WindowsFeature]IIS'
    }
    WindowsFeature IISScriptingTools
    {
      Ensure   = 'Present'
      Name     = 'Web-Scripting-Tools'
      DependsOn = '[WindowsFeature]IIS'
    }
    WindowsFeature AspNet
    {
      Ensure   = 'Present'
      Name     = 'Web-Asp-Net45'
      DependsOn = @('[WindowsFeature]IIS')
    }
    xWebsite DefaultSite
    {
      Ensure       = 'Present'
      Name         = 'Default Web Site'
      State        = 'Stopped'
      PhysicalPath = 'C:\inetpub\wwwroot'
      DependsOn    = @('[WindowsFeature]IIS','[WindowsFeature]AspNet')
    }
```

```
    xRemoteFile DownloadAuroraZip
    {
      Uri              = $Node.Aurora.Sourcepath
      DestinationPath = (Join-Path 'C:\Windows\Temp' (Split-Path -Path
$Node.Aurora.Sourcepath -Leaf))
      DependsOn        = @('[xWebsite]DefaultSite')
    }
    xArchive AuroraZip
    {
      Path             = (Join-Path 'C:\Windows\Temp' (Split-Path -Path
$Node.Aurora.Sourcepath -Leaf))
      Destination     = 'C:\Windows\Temp'
      DestinationType = 'Directory'
      MatchSource     = $true
      DependsOn        = @('[xRemoteFile]DownloadAuroraZip')
    }
    File AuroraContent
    {
      Ensure           = 'Present'
      Type             = 'Directory'
      SourcePath       = Join-Path 'C:\Windows\Temp'
([IO.Path]::GetFileNameWithoutExtension($Node.Aurora.Sourcepath))
      DestinationPath = $Node.Aurora.DestinationPath
      Recurse          = $true
      DependsOn        = '[xArchive]AuroraZip'
    }
    xWebAppPool AuroraWebAppPool
    {
      Ensure = "Present"
      State  = "Started"
      Name   = $Node.WebAppPoolName
    }
    xWebsite AuroraWebSite
    {
      Ensure       = 'Present'
      State        = 'Started'
      Name         = $Node.Aurora.WebsiteName
      PhysicalPath = $Node.Aurora.DestinationPath
      DependsOn    = '[File]AuroraContent'
    }
    xWebApplication AuroraWebApplication
    {
      Name         = $Node.Aurora.WebApplicationName
      Website      = $Node.Aurora.WebSiteName
      WebAppPool   = $Node.Aurora.WebAppPoolName
      PhysicalPath = $Node.Aurora.DestinationPath
      Ensure       = 'Present'
      DependsOn    = @('[xWebSite]AuroraWebSite')
```

```
            }
         }
      }
   $data    = Join-Path $PSScriptRoot 'data_example_04.psd1'
   $output = Join-Path $PSScriptRoot 'PantheonDeployment'
   PantheonDeployment -ConfigurationData $data -OutputPath $output
```

With all this new configuration data to track, it's no wonder you need to update your `ConfigurationData` hash:

```
@{
   AllNodes = @(
      @{
         NodeName        = 'app01'
         ConfigurationId = 'ab2c2cb2-67a3-444c-bc55-cc2ee70e3d0c'
         Roles           = @('appserver')
      },
      @{
         NodeName        = 'app02'
         ConfigurationId = '8e8f44e6-aaac-4060-b072-c9ae780ee5f7'
         Roles           = @('appserver')
      },
      @{
         NodeName        = 'web01'
         ConfigurationId = 'b808fb65-5b16-4f83-84c6-aa398a6abdd5'
         Roles           = @('webserver')
      },
      @{
         NodeName             = '*'
         RefreshMode          = 'Pull'
         ConfigurationMode    = 'ApplyAndAutoCorrect'
         PSDSCCPullServer     = 'https://dsc01:8080/PSDSCPullServer.svc'
         AllowModuleOverwrite = $true
         RebootNodeIfNeeded   = $true
         Apollo    = @{
            Name            = 'Apollo'
            ProductId       = '{e70c4829-91dc-4f0e-a404-4eba81f6feb9}'
            SourcePath      =
'http://build.pantheon.net/apollo/packages/releases/apollo.1.1.0.msi'
            Arguments       = ''
            ConfigFilePath  =
"$env:ProgramFiles\Apollo\config\app.config"
            ConfigFileContents = "importantsetting=`$true"
         }
         Aurora = @{
            SourcePath      =
'http://build.pantheon.net/aurora/releases/aurora.zip'
            DestinationPath      = "$env:SystemDrive\inetpub\www\aurora"
```

```
        WebApplicationName  = 'Aurora'
        WebSiteName         = 'Aurora'
        WebAppPoolName      = 'AuroraAppPool'
      }
    }
  )
}
```

You already have a hash for Apollo, so all you have to do is add a new hash for Aurora with the appropriate details.

Handling change

After successfully running DSC in production for all this time, you sit back amazed that all the work you have been doing is addictive. You haven't had to undo work you've previously done to get something new automated, and you can handle the most insane list of requirements life can dish out with ease.

Of course, it wasn't always easy and might have required some extra thought or preparation. It might have required changing how you approached things to something more aligned with the configuration management processes you read in the beginning of the book. DSC didn't have a DSC resource built in for every piece of software in your environment or every task you needed to accomplish, but we can say that for any CM product on the market. The point of any CM is not to provide a way to do everything but to provide a way to do most things, along with a way for you to do the rest that's unique to your environment. From reading this book, you know how to create DSC resources to handle your special cases.

Things are, in fact, going so well that something was bound to come up and ruin your parade. The application team has come to you to tell you that they have finished working on the next major version of the Apollo application. This is great news as it will mean a faster application that can handle more load with fewer nodes than before. You start thinking of the one line you need to update in order to change the version installed in your environment but are interrupted by the application team. They admit that you can't update the environment all at once; you will have to do it in batches and some servers will need to remain on the old version for customers that have not upgraded their systems yet.

This is a quandary at first; how are you going to install software only on some of the target nodes and not others? You start thinking about making a custom DSC resource that detects software versions on a target node and then checks a file for a list of servers that need to be updated. Then, you start planning to manually remove servers from your beautiful DSC setup while secretly crying inside. Happily, you remember the first chapters of this book explaining and praising the benefit of splitting the configuration data from the execution script and have an epiphany when you realize you've already done half the work when you made your `ConfigurationData` hash. Each individual `Node` hash overrides the information provided in the wildcard `Node` block (the one with *). All you have to do is specify the older version number on the servers for them to keep the older version:

```
@{
    AllNodes = @(
        @{
            NodeName        = 'app01'
            ConfigurationId = 'ab2c2cb2-67a3-444c-bc55-cc2ee70e3d0c'
            Roles           = @('appserver')
            Apollo = @{
                Name            = 'Apollo'
                ProductId       = '{e70c4829-91dc-4f0e-a404-4eba81f6feb9}'
                SourcePath      =
'http://build.pantheon.net/apollo/packages/releases/apollo.1.1.0.msi'
                Arguments       = ''
                ConfigFilePath  =
"$env:ProgramFiles\Apollo\config\app.config"
                ConfigFileContents = "importantsetting=`$true"
            }
        },
        @{
            NodeName        = 'app02'
            ConfigurationId = '8e8f44e6-aaac-4060-b072-c9ae780ee5f7'
            Roles           = @('appserver')
        },
        @{
            NodeName        = 'app03'
            ConfigurationId = 'c880da2b-1438-4554-8c96-0e89d2f009c4'
            Roles           = @('appserver')
        },
        @{
            NodeName        = 'web01'
            ConfigurationId = 'b808fb65-5b16-4f83-84c6-aa398a6abdd5'
            Roles           = @('webserver')
        },
        @{
            NodeName        = 'web02'
            ConfigurationId = '2173f5d7-7343-4a16-a8a8-5188f2d1cdb0'
```

```
        Roles              = @('webserver')
    },
    @{
       NodeName            = '*'
       RefreshMode         = 'Pull'
       ConfigurationMode   = 'ApplyAndAutoCorrect'
       PSDSCCPullServer    = 'https://dsc01:8080/PSDSCPullServer.svc'
       AllowModuleOverwrite = $true
       RebootNodeIfNeeded  = $true
       Apollo    = @{
          Name             = 'Apollo'
          ProductId        = '{e70c4829-91dc-4f0e-a404-4eba81f6feb9}'
          SourcePath       =
'http://build.pantheon.net/apollo/packages/releases/apollo.2.0.0.msi'
          Arguments        = ''
          ConfigFilePath   =
"$env:ProgramFiles\Apollo\config\app.config"
          ConfigFileContents = "importantsetting=`$true"
       }
       Aurora = @{
          SourcePath       =
'http://build.pantheon.net/aurora/releases/aurora.zip'
          DestinationPath  = "$env:SystemDrive\inetpub\www\aurora"
          WebApplicationName = 'Aurora'
          WebSiteName      = 'Aurora'
          WebAppPoolName   = 'AuroraAppPool'
       }
    }
 )
}
```

Things have gotten quite cozy among the engineering teams as the concepts and practices of DevOps and continuous integration have started to really become ingrained in the company. Teams have started moving to more agile processes, adopting sprints, and producing more frequent releases. You're still in charge of systems, but the day-to-day information entry is now done by the teams initiating the changes. Bringing them down to the system configuration level has opened their eyes to the pain points of the configuration and maintenance of their applications, and they have fast-tracked updating the installation process of the Aurora website in order to enable a simpler and faster deployment process.

The increased releases didn't add any extra workload for you, as the `ConfigurationData` hash you have kept up to date all by yourself has now been added to the version control system all the teams use. Updating versions and configuration data has become part of the release process, which is now auditable from development to deployment. Teams can see how the products have changed over time and how different releases have either increased or decreased in configuration complexity.

Summary

We have come a long way from where we started. We covered what configuration management is and what desired state really means. We heard a thing or two about DevOps and what it takes to utilize its practices in your day-to-day roles. You learned the ins and outs of how CM products approach configuration management and then how PowerShell DSC does it.

We dove right into the deep end of the DSC pool by covering its feature set across the two different versions that have been released so far, and then we went further down the rabbit hole in discovering what push and pull modes mean. We used the push model to deploy software and set the configuration of target nodes on demand. We set up DSC pull servers to automate DSC resource and DSC configuration script distribution, centralize the management of our target nodes, and create a central reporting system for the configuration status.

We ended our journey with some real-world use cases for DSC and you learned how to respond to changing requirements using DSC. We also showed how versatile DSC is, given that can to be used by other configuration management software to accomplish a common goal.

I hope you have enjoyed this book and will continue to use configuration management tools and DevOps practices in your environments.

Index

Made in United States
Orlando, FL
15 March 2022

15830484R00150